THE SHADOW
OF A NATION

Also by Nick Clarke

Alistair Cooke: The Biography

THE SHADOW
OF A NATION

The Changing Face of Britain

Nick Clarke

Weidenfeld & Nicolson

LONDON

First published in Great Britain in 2003
by Weidenfeld & Nicolson

A CIP catalogue record for this book
is available from the British Library.

ISBN 0 297 60770 7

Typeset by Selwood Systems, Midsomer Norton

Printed in Great Britain by
Butler & Tanner Ltd, Frome and London

Weidenfeld & Nicolson

The Orion Publishing Group Ltd
Orion House
5 Upper Saint Martin's Lane
London WC2H 9EA

For Ali, Tom, Pete, Benedict and Joel
who have made me very happy

CONTENTS

The author with his parents in the early 1950s

CAST OF CHARACTERS

Margaret – The Fairy Princess
Born to inherit the unqualified love and respect of her people, she is finally brought down by the plague of celebrity and the death of deference. Her story ends in tears when the gap between the real and the imagined in her life becomes too great for the heroine to bear.

Charles Saatchi – A Merchant of Dreams
Who is this dark figure, often in disguise, lurking on the boundaries of the real world, tempting us with unwanted wares and turning base art into gold? Is he the alchemist of the Elizabethan age?

Elizabeth David and Delia Smith – Imaginary Cooks
The first offered recipes with ingredients that no one could find in post-war Britain, the second – in an age of plenty – decreed that we should be told which spoon and dish to buy.

Arthur Scargill – A Working Man
He rises from humble beginnings to bestride the land as a colossus of industrial might, before being cast down by his own ambition. He ends his days in a strange half-world of meaningless titles and empty honours.

David Frost – Television Man
The scourge of the Establishment who became, effortlessly, one of its leading figures: does that slight smile playing across his lips denote ironic detachment or simple self-satisfaction?

John Clarke – Father of the Author

PROLOGUE

All the World's a (Television) Stage

Everyone knew where they were, and who they were, back in the 1950s. The solid reality of everyday existence provided a bedrock to people's lives. Then, over the intervening half-century, something happened to those reassuring certainties: we allowed them to crumble away, or watched them being dismantled by the media in general and television in particular.

In every material sense we are far better off than we were when Elizabeth II inherited the throne, but for all the gains in health, wealth and wisdom, something has been mislaid. There seems no other way to explain our reluctance to relinquish the past. The sense of regret expresses itself in different ways, not least in a class system which has proved stubbornly resistant both to the assaults of its enemies and to the passage of time. As late as 1989, when the *Sunday Times* published its first 'Rich List', 55 of the top 200 plutocrats were educated at Eton. If Britain had ever wanted a genuinely meritocratic society, those Etonians would surely have faced more competition. At the other end of the scale, a MORI poll in 2002 found that 68 per cent of the population were happy to identify themselves as working class, a figure which astonished the pollsters. One noted that a Labour government had brought 'a remarkable renaissance in working-class solidarity', during a period in which, by all conventional measurements, the size of this group had continued to decline. It was almost as if those questioned were seeking the comfort of a familiar place in the social structure, regardless of their personal circumstances.

Plenty more anecdotal evidence can be found of this country's inability to shake off the past, from our obsession with pastoral detective stories set in chocolate box villages, to a taste for steamed puddings and an affection for old red telephone boxes. Our foreign friends find these traits endearing, if eccentric. Most countries celebrate aspects of their history, or look back wistfully to some supposedly happier period in their collective experience. Yet nothing quite matches the (often unconscious) nostalgia which imbues our national psyche. What is it about this folk memory that still haunts us? And whatever it was, where did it go? *How did our lives become less real?*

I set out to identify a group of people whose own lives might shed light on these puzzles. Any resemblance to Lytton Strachey's *Eminent Victorians* is intentional but superficial, limited to the fact that Strachey produced four short biographies to paint a picture of a period, and that each of my subjects achieved eminence in the second Elizabethan era. In his introduction, Strachey describes how the historian might choose to 'row out over that great ocean of material, and lower down into it, here and there, a little bucket, which will bring up to the light of day some characteristic specimen from those far depths, to be examined with careful curiosity'. I prefer a different metaphor: the biographer drilling back through the last half-century looking for slivers of history, like the cores of earth and rock extracted by the geologist. The lives of my subjects, and the way they have been regarded over the years, are intended to illustrate how the nation has become less substantial – more shadowy – since the war.

Readers may have their own ideas of people whose stories might have served just as well. I toyed with characters as diverse as Glenda Jackson and Robert Runcie, Richard Branson and the Amis family, Germaine Greer and Harold Pinter, or even my old headmaster Anthony Chenevix-Trench (to echo Strachey's choice of Thomas Arnold). Sporting heroes, like Ted Dexter, were tempting, too. After a great deal of heart-searching, I pared away the shortlist and ended up with six names: two agents of the changes that have taken place – David Frost and Charles Saatchi; two victims of those changes – Princess Margaret and Arthur Scargill; and two specialist writers, Elizabeth David and Delia Smith, whose careers provide an unexpected insight into the cultural shifts of the past half-century.

As a point of principle I decided not to approach any of the living subjects in person. It is a natural human instinct to explain, justify and embellish one's own story, and I was searching for something less varnished, less well-disguised by powder and eyeshadow. Consequently I turned to those who know or knew the cast members well, some friendly, some less well-disposed. Many of my informants were happy to be quoted, though a few preferred to remain anonymous. Above all, I sought to look at my chosen lives through the prism of the mass media – the dominant influence in moulding all our perceptions of the world around us and those who inhabit it.

The final player in this book is my father, John Clarke, who would certainly have had something trenchant to say about these matters if he had lived long enough. Like a minor figure in a Shakespearean play, it is his, and his family's, story that provides the backdrop to the tragedy (or comedy) that follows. As a keen experimenter with new gadgets, from the hand-cranked movie camera to the mini reel-to-reel tape recorder, he would have embraced new technology with enthusiasm. But he would certainly have been taken aback by the draining away of social, cultural and family certainty and cohesion, and the consequent need for the individual to find new ways of defining who he or she is supposed to be.

1   Cold but Happy

My father was born on the eve of the First World War and never quite shed the mind cast of that long-forgotten age. But he was also an open-minded man, who died in 1966, just as the momentous changes in British post-war life were beginning to unfold. (It was the year in which the credit card first appeared, substituting the illusion of wealth for the pound in your pocket.) I would love to have read his assessment of those changes, in the books and articles he planned to write when he had the time, and the autobiography on which he had been working sporadically for years.

Many aspects of day-to-day life in my boyhood were comparatively inconvenient and uncomfortable, but whenever I reflect on that period (1952–60) I am also struck by how solid and substantial it seems. The postal service is a prime example. My father was a tireless correspondent who regarded letter-writing as part of his daily routine. Family letters were handwritten in a small, neat script, but otherwise he preferred to use his portable typewriter, with carbon copies filed as a diary substitute when he was too busy to keep a diary. One of my earliest chores was to take his letters to the box at the end of the road and my recollection is that the last post went at 6 p.m. on the dot. Twice-daily deliveries were just as reliable and when my father was away (which was often) I would sometimes sit on the stairs waiting for the postman's footsteps on the path, hoping for a missive smothered in exotic foreign stamps.

My father regarded even domestic phone calls as extravagant, and calls from overseas were confined to emergencies, birthdays and Christmas. The need to book overseas calls ahead of time gave them an added significance. You couldn't contact someone abroad on a whim and certainly not with any real prospect of getting through. Forethought and planning were required, especially at busy holiday periods, and, for a child, this imbued the process with a special kind of magic. Anticipation grew as the appointed hour approached and I remember coaching myself with the salient things my father might like to hear. There was no danger of getting carried away. Far too soon, the operator's stern voice would break into the conversation: 'Your three minutes are up. Do you wish to pay for a further time?' Usually my father declined.

He was much happier with the written word. Many of his papers, diaries and carbon-copy letters were destroyed in a flood after his death, but those that remain provide tantalising glimpses of the comparative stability of our lives. In the early 1950s we were a middle-class family, living in a quiet avenue (not street) in Bishops Stortford, 30 miles north-east of London. I discover that in 1953 my father's annual salary as a journalist had reached £1488, somewhat above the average, but distressingly below our expenditure. Every few weeks my father would make a determined effort to balance the books, which usually involved an anguished (and in my mother's case, futile) attempt to cut back on cigarettes. In January 1953, for instance, my father decided to track household spending for 90 days:

January 1 – Sausage rolls 1/8, Stamps 2/1, Fat 1/6, Xmas Box 2/6, Choc 5/8: John Papers 1/9, Cigs 1/9: Ruth cigs 3/7. Total 21/1 [total, just over £1, or £15 today].

January 2 – Lux 1/6, Prunes 8d, Biscuits 1/4, spagh 2/-, 3 eggs and sprouts 3/4, Church play 4/6, programme 6d, Ruth cigs 3/7, John cigs 1/9, Church Times 4d. [And then, in an echo of a long-gone credit facility], *Additional cigs on a/c at The George 3/7. Total 19/6.*

When was the last time a pub offered goods on tick? This assiduous budgeting lasted until the 17th, resumed for three days on the 24th, then petered out until 21 February. At which point the record ceases. Maybe the paperwork was claimed by the flood, but more likely he got bored with the chore and depressed by the evidence. One contemporaneous diary entry reads,

To early church. Mood filthy, partly thanks to lack of tobacco for a day, which made me find it difficult to go to sleep last night. Dubious about church-going in such a mood but thought I might thereby be cured, which, presently, I was.

St Michael's Church was real to him, so much so that he became its churchwarden. In time it became real to me, too, especially when I was old enough to go round with the collecting plate and to present the proceeds with a theatrical genuflection at the altar steps.

In the approved fashion, my father treated Sunday as being quite different from other days of the week. As children, we often found it a dull day, enlivened only by Sunday lunch. Prep school magnified the problem: with no lessons and no sport to break up the daylight hours, the day was interminable and the church services, letter-writing and walks did little to dispel the gloom. My impression is that, in the 1950s at least, the country ground to a halt, but there must have been more pressure than I realised to brighten up the Sabbath. I have in front of me a leaflet from the Lord's Day Observance Society, dated as early as 1934 and headed: 'The Hosts of Darkness are Advancing! The Enemy is at the Gate! Alas, Traitors in some of our Churches are opening the gates to let the Sunday Destroyers in!!' It invited donations to continue the fight against Sunday Shops, Theatres, Cinemas, Sports, Dog Races, Prize Fights ... Not much of any of that was going on in Bishops Stortford.

My father's job on the *Evening Standard* required regular commuting to Fleet Street, as well as journeys further afield by train and bus. In 1954 we invested in our first car – an innovative, timber-framed Morris 1000 station wagon – but it was purely for domestic use. At this stage private motoring expenditure in Britain had still not regained 1938 levels and we always thought twice about getting the car out of the garage. When we did, it sometimes needed a turn of the cranking handle to get the engine going. And to celebrate each outing there was always the friendly AA man on his motorbike, saluting the little yellow badge on the radiator grille.[1]

In the circumstances, it was just as well that my father was fascinated by all forms of transport – boat, plane, bicycle or train. Sometimes he recorded his progress – in this case, on a train trip to Guildford, a distance of some 60 miles.

---

1 The original AA badge in the shape of a crest had been redesigned to a trendy yellow square by the time I acquired my first car. By then, I'm sure the reassuring mechanic on his motorcycle (with sidecar) had retreated into a van. Astonishingly, the familiar AA roadside telephones survived until 2002, when a selection of boxes were designated historic structures to be saved for posterity. Obviously, the phones were removed first. Anyway, I don't ever remember any car I was in breaking down near enough to a box to be able to make use of the service.

*I started by the 6.53 train from BS [Bishops Stortford], I was in G by
9.20, but coming back my times were more spectacular; I caught
the 1.18 from Guildford and was at Stortford by 3.16.*

One hour and 58 minutes. I've just called the ticket line and the best
time available on today's twenty-first-century railway, and then only
with a following wind, is two and a quarter hours. My father trusted
the trains, just as he believed in the importance of the Church (if only
to dispel his ill humour) and the social status of the medical
profession. On one occasion, in January 1952, he developed a sore foot
during an afternoon walk with his son and, since it was a Sunday, he
decided to appeal to a friendly doctor. An appointment was only agreed
'after a great deal of persuasion'. The treatment did the trick, but as he
reflected later,

*'H' received me with tolerable good grace, but the attitude of the
doctor-caucus here is such as to make you as chary of asking for
attention as of gate-crashing a levee; you appear to be acting in the
worst of taste if you consult them.*

General practitioners, then, were figures of high social standing, pillars
of the community, to whom respect was due, even if it was sometimes
grudging. Or undeserved.

As with medicine, so with the law. By 1952 my father had a well-
established column in the *Standard* called 'John Clarke's Casebook',
which chronicled the human stories told each day in lowly courts, far
from the glamour of the Old Bailey. It was perhaps the first time anyone had bothered to sit through so many humdrum cases and to
wonder about the pimps, tarts, vagrants and petty thieves who paraded
past the bench each day.[2] The Casebook lasted eight years, on and off,
and in the course of this patient prospecting for journalistic gold, its
writer displayed a proper, if critical, respect for those who administered

---

2 Offences like vandalism, criminal damage and the daubing of graffiti are conspicuous
by their absence in these articles. Of the first 30 stories I selected at random from my
father's 1954 Casebook file the charges were: theft 12, shoplifting 6; begging 3; insulting
behaviour 2; 'walking abroad and lodging in the open air' 2; and 1 each for drunk in charge
of a bicycle, fine arrears, loitering for the purpose of betting, stopping an escalator, and
(this is my favourite) swimming beyond the official limits in the Serpentine. The
swimmer compounded his felony by refusing to give his name and address. I have a
theory that popular modern activities like smashing up a bus shelter, or daubing a wall
with a favourite motif are products of the perpetrator's desperate need to leave his mark
– literally – on an outside world that, in every other way, declines to recognise him.

the justice system – like the Bow Street Magistrate, Mr Bertram Reece, or Mr Paul Bennett VC at Great Marlborough Street.[3] Mr Bennett, in particular, dispensed justice like a benign monarch. On 26 January 1951, 'Larry' was brought before him, having pleaded guilty to stealing money from a friend. It emerged that he had been brought up by his uncle, Jem, a coalman, who was summoned to speak up for the boy.

> Jem said, 'For two years, sir, the boy's not had a chance ...'
> 'How have you managed?' Mr Bennett asked. 'Who has done the cooking?'
> 'I have, sir.'
> 'What about the cleaning?'
> 'We've done it between us, sir ...'
> Jem twirled his cloth cap uncomfortably in his hands. 'Thank you,' Mr Bennett said.

A probation officer was asked to look for a new home and a job for Larry. He succeeded and the boy was returned to Great Marlborough Street.

> Mr Bennett said to Larry, 'There must be no more dishonesty, ever. I'm sure you'll make a success of your life – you look as though you would. You're intelligent and hard-working.

My father concluded his piece,

> They showed Larry out. I hoped that somehow the magistrate's last words would reach Jem; he would have been proud like a father.

The Dickensian ring of these exchanges is typical of the atmosphere conjured up by the Casebook. There was no guarantee that Larry

---

3 Paul Bennett won his honour at le Transloy, during the Battle of the Somme in 1916. The citation reads: *Lieutenant Bennett was in command of the second wave of the attack, and finding that the first wave had suffered heavy casualties, its commander killed and the line wavering, he advanced at the head of the second wave and reached his objective with only 60 men.* This record did not protect him from media intrusion: my father noted in his diary that a divorce case covered in the paper 'mentioned the wife's "unhealthy relationship" with Mrs Paul Bennett'. As the victim of a messy divorce himself, my father added, 'Very hard for him to have to sit in court tomorrow knowing that so many will have read that unsympathetically.'

would not abuse the indulgence of the court, but at least the redemptive process was understood and acknowledged by all sides. It was real.

My father had married my mother in 1947 at the Chelsea Register Office in London. (He was divorced and she was a war widow). He cycled from his home to the station at Haslemere in Surrey, and she from a hotel nearby where she had been decorously lodging. They stored their bicycles in the left-luggage office, and took tea and hot-buttered toast on the train to Waterloo. (They were not travelling first class.) After a stroll down the King's Road, they made use of the public lavatories in Sydney Street before indulging in a morale-boosting pink gin at the Six Bells with their friends.

The ceremony, in my father's words, was 'short and unattractive', the superintendent-registrar wished them well and they posed for a photograph, before repairing to the Black Lion. 'The total drinks bill for six people and about an hour and a half', he wrote to my grand-mother afterwards, 'came to just under £1.15.0 [£1.75], which wasn't bad; happily, after an initial large gin, everyone drank beer quite contentedly.' By some oversight the lunch was taken at an unlicensed restaurant, the Chantilly, but the Greek proprietor rustled up some cider for a toast. When the couple got back to Haslemere they played billiards, then dined at the George Hotel, where they were fêted by the management and treated to a glass of Drambuie after the meal. And that was that.

Their honeymoon treat was an afternoon watching Haslemere Cricket Club in a match against 'Miss Molly Hide's Women's XI':[4] otherwise, 'we've lived more or less normal lives and Ruth, in the first week of marriage, has sewed, darned and laundered my things like a mad thing'. (My mother's enthusiasm for darning did not last long.) Oh yes, he added as an afterthought. The day before the ceremony they had realised they couldn't afford the train fare to town and had to borrow the wherewithal from the landlord of the White Horse. The same letter offers grateful thanks to two local tradesmen: the grocer, who offered an extra half-pound of butter as a wedding gift, and the butcher, who provided 'an extra large lump of lamb'. It also mentions new government cutbacks in supplies of newsprint, which were likely to pose a threat to journalists' jobs.

---

4 Molly Hide was the England women's cricket captain before and after the war. She was awarded an MBE for her services to the game and had a taste for good cigars.

For a time my parents lived in the Surrey village of Wormley, where my mother looked after an elderly couple in return for board and lodging. Unfortunately, while my father was away on freelance journalistic business in Bournemouth, my mother had a spectacular falling-out over the Wormley breakfast table with the paterfamilias, Mr Stratton. Later, my father transcribed the conversation:

> *Stratton: I really must ask you not to take more salt than you need on your plate.*
> *Mother (rather light-heartedly): Oh, I always like to have plenty of salt.*
> *Stratton: Well, you must not do so. It is an absolute waste.*
> *Mother: Perhaps I'd better buy some salt for myself.*
> *Stratton (going a little purple): You shall have no salt at all. There's one Master in this house and that's me. If you don't like it you can get out.*
> *Mother: Very well then, we'll get out.*

The threat may have sounded histrionic, but it was real, and the next day they were off. None of this boded particularly well for my arrival. As my father wrote to my grandmother,

> *If I take myself aside for a second I can see all sorts of squalid things ahead: we ain't got a home, nor a stick of furniture, nor a stitch of clothing. We shall be like two people tied to an infant in a squalid screaming flat with clothes-lines of nappies and shredded shirts hung diagonally across – hating the world, the infant and each other. Deo Gratia, I don't often take myself aside for a second.*

It wasn't as bad as all that, fortunately. Our first home was in a picturesque, if tiny, cottage in Haslemere, before the family followed my father's star to a much larger Edwardian house in Bishops Stortford.[5] The story of how he came across it is charming. On 13 March 1950, as a diversion from his usual Casebook, he wrote about his difficulty in finding a house in the country at a price he could afford. One estate agent forgot to mention a reform school next door,

---

5 The purchase price was £3900 – or £70,000 in turn-of-the-century money: but house prices have long ceased to operate according to solid economic logic. A local estate agent confirmed that the same house would cost around £500,000 today.

he complained, while another missed out the fact that 'not having to spend a penny on renovations' could not make up for the fact that the property was underneath a railway viaduct in full-time use for shunting practice. My father ended with a prediction that from 1 April he would be on the street, joining the vagrants charged with being 'of no fixed abode'. The next day a resourceful vendor, whose elderly uncle had just died, read the piece and wrote to him at the paper, 'The x pounds you have to spend would have to equal nearly £4,000. Does this appeal to you? Or do you prefer to give yourself up on April 1st, or is your article just hooey?' Two weeks later contracts were exchanged.

The location turned out to be close to the country seats of the upper-class friends he'd made during the surreal years of the war, when he had forgotten his place in the order of things.[6] This forgetfulness was forgivable because of the company he kept during the war. His secretive business was disinformation, a polite way of describing propaganda, and he was posted, variously, to Canada, South America, Egypt and India, before witnessing the Japanese retreat from Burma and Singapore. He had acquired this glamorous job by virtue of winning a journalism prize in 1938, which set him apart from most of those who gravitated to this rather agreeable line of work through establishment contacts and connections. It is hard to know for sure, because they were bound by oaths of secrecy long after the war, and my father never got round to telling me the full story before he surprised us all by dying at the age of 53.

Any child trawling back through a parent's past can fall prey to sentimentality. But this is not, or not intentionally, an exercise in nostalgia. Apart from anything else, much of what has dematerialised in the intervening half-century is no loss to anyone. Starting handles were a wretched nuisance. Doctors were no doubt getting away with

---

6 Naturally, this made it inevitable that money would have to be found to send me away to boarding school – the 1956 fees for the first term were £116, including laundry. Heaven knows how my parents afforded it, though I don't think that was the only reason why mother cried all the way to the south coast. My father, with his freelance instincts finely tuned, sold the story of my banishment to the *Evening Standard*. Under the heading, 'The Day Nicholas Went to School', it told a fearsome story: 'The drive to school was 100 miles. The boy was so pale, so was his mother, so, possibly, was I. We played every game, every permutation of those games you can play with children in cars. But the tang had gone out of them, the competitive spirit sub-zero. By the time we reached Sussex, the fatal county, there was nothing much to pick between the blood-curdling long silences, and the flashes of brittle-bright, wholly false conversation that we lobbed in like hand grenades to break them up. Mouths became unaccountably dry, and eyes just about managed to remain so.' They remained so only until the half-timbered Morris had disappeared from sight.

murder and priests with sexual abuse of small children. Vicars (according to Alan Bennett) had a penchant for stroking the legs of small boys. Magistrates with First World War medals were just as likely to be rabid reactionaries as their modern counterparts – would Paul Bennett VC have known who 'Gazza' was? Smog killed 4000 people and an unspecified number of cattle at Smithfield Market in the December of 1952. And no one mourned the passing of food coupons. At the time of the coronation, bacon, meat, butter, cooking fats, cheese and sugar were still rationed, while eggs, tea and sweets had only recently been removed from the list.[7] My mother would have wanted me to add to this 'good riddance' list (to name but a few): a stone sink and decaying wooden draining board; a filthy 'coal-hole' adjoining the kitchen; and the bitter cold which gripped the house from November to March, coal fires notwithstanding.

Soon after my fiftieth birthday I had the chance to revisit the Bishops Stortford house: it was warm, comfortable and convenient. But I could still hear the echoes of that earlier age, whose passing has caused so many people such a surprising degree of regret.

---

7 In November 1952 the Minister of Food was authorised to tell the Commons, 'Any shortage of sweets that still remains $7^1/_2$ years after the war is not enough to warrant our retaining a cumbrous and extravagant system for such a commodity.' But it was enough to make them an irregular treat in our house. A quarter of lemon sherbets, tipped from a jar into a paper bag, had to last for some days. At least in coronation month, everyone was allowed an extra 1 lb of sugar and 4 oz of margarine.

2   A Talisman for Friendship

If there is one prime suspect as the villain of this piece, it is the box in the corner of the living room. Television was the butterfly that emerged from its chrysalis towards the end of the 1950s, flitting from subject to subject, delighting everyone with its increasingly bright colours and its restless search for new sources of sustenance. But as time went on, it grew into a ravening beast. Instead of simply reflecting what it observed in the real world, television and its handmaidens (the newspapers, radio, cinema, and – in due course – the computer and the Internet) began to consume their subject matter. They were voracious. They swallowed everything they could capture with camera or microphone, until there was nothing real left in the land – except they themselves and the things they chose to portray.

One institution after another has tottered beneath the subsequent onslaught: the family, royalty, the Church, the law, the professions, politics – nothing has been immune. Teachers are among those who feel aggrieved at what television has done to them: delegates at a conference of the Professional Association of Teachers in 2001 wondered how they were supposed to act as role models for children who'd been brought up on soaps and TV dramas portraying them as heavy-drinking, lazy, dishonest, irresponsible and promiscuous. Their profession, they claimed, had been brought into disrepute. In other words the television version of their working lives had become more real than anything that happened in the classroom: as far as pupils and parents were concerned it was the reality.

This has not been an even or measured process, because for several years after the end of the war, even though everything had changed, nothing much changed at all. In Jonathan Miller's words, 'England was stuck in the Thirties until the Sixties.'

The tone for the decade was set with the Festival of Britain in 1951, which attracted 8¹/₂ million people to London in a spirit of celebration, and was as much a salute to the way things had been as a promise of better times to come. Who says so? The Archbishop of Canterbury, writing in the Festival guide: 'The chief and governing purpose of the

Festival is to declare our belief and trust in the British way of life, not with any boastful self-confidence nor with any aggressive self-aggrandisement, but with sober and humble trust that, by holding fast to that which is good and rejecting from our midst that which is evil, we may continue to be a nation at unity in itself and of service to the world.'

The Labour Foreign Secretary of the moment, Herbert Morrison (Peter Mandelson's grandfather), added, 'The Festival is the British showing themselves to themselves – and to the world.' The Festival, in other words, was self-referential – it was about the British and for the British, with the rest of the world treated peremptorily. Even the Commonwealth (the continuation of Empire by other means) played only a bit part, reflected in a small programme of exhibitions at the Imperial Institute in South Kensington, well away from the main Festival site. The description of this event (on the Museum of London website) has a condescending feel: a display of life in various colonies, a show of traditional craft and sculpture and a Colonial Office exhibition 'Focus on Colonial Progress'. Well done, Africa.

Soon after the débâcle of our very own Millennium Dome (that high altar of unreality) *The Times* looked back at the 1951 Festival: 'Nobody looking through its catalogue of exhibits today can fail to be startled by its lavish eulogies to the British coal, steel, ship-building and motor industries – complacent plaudits apparently devised in astounding ignorance of the problems that would overwhelm each of them within twenty years.' The 1951 Festival cheered many people up, but it was also an exercise in self-delusion.

This was not uniquely a British experience, but for a number of reasons it was felt more keenly in Britain than elsewhere. Unlike many other European nations we had no need, after the war, to tear up the narrative of our past and reinvent ourselves and our institutions. After all, it was our way of doing things that had triumphed: why change a winning formula? Yet despite appearances, and unlike the United States, Great Britain had been profoundly shaken by the events of 1939–45 and it wasn't just the physical environment that had been damaged. The pre-war social structures had taken more of a pounding than most people realised. Foundations had been undermined. Unseen cracks and fissures had developed. In due course many aspects of life, which seemed to have escaped unscathed, would be threatened by collapse.

Matters were not helped by the fact that the British were so busy trying to keep themselves fed and watered that they were rarely tempted to raise their eyes above the horizon. The first years of peace saw conditions for most people failing to improve or even deteriorating. An energy shortage meant that the vicious winter of 1946/7 – freeze followed by flood – closed down the country from January to March. Bomb sites continued to scar cities and towns, while overseas the British Empire began to crumble and the Cold War gripped Europe. None of this felt like the deserts of victory or the dawning of a new age.

It took five years of austerity before the British economy began to extricate itself from its wartime black hole, and a further five to do away with rationing and price controls altogether. The introduction of National Service in 1947 – and the Korean War of 1950 – perpetuated the sense that peace was provisional and that nothing had happened to alter Britain's need to sustain its self-appointed place in the world, whatever the cost. Keeping an army of occupation in Germany, for instance, helped prolong bread rationing back home. 'Such were the spoils of victory,' according to the historian, Peter Clarke. 'Britain behaved like a great power and offered a broad back for such burdens.'

In my researches for this book I came across a slim volume published in 1940 by the ex-Prime Minister, Stanley Baldwin. *The Englishman* was written in a spirit of thoughtful patriotism and doubtless intended to offer comfort at a time of uncertainty.

> *So long as the sea was an inviolable boundary, so long the Englishman felt secure, and human nature is such that it does not take long for a man to attribute that desirable state of things to his own ability and foresight rather than to Providence. Hence it is not difficult to imagine the growth of a certain appearance of complacency and a pleasing sense of superiority over those countries which have failed to take similar precautions for their own safety.*

This spirit of solidity, blind to signs of decay, was alive and well at the time of Suez and still in pretty good shape during Harold Macmillan's 'you've never had it so good' election of 1959.

Public policy, even when the economy had been resuscitated, reflected how deeply ingrained was our skewed vision of the world around these islands. What else could explain the fervour with which we determined to have our own nuclear deterrent, or the disdain with which we spurned the early flowering of European unity? As Peter Clarke says of the early negotiations leading to the signing of the Treaty of Rome in 1957, 'The Foreign Office succeeded in catching the mood of the British public in watching with sceptical condescension while the six European countries set about pooling their inferior resources in a common market. [Prime Minister, Anthony] Eden had other fish to fry.' These included the Suez adventure, which seemed like a solid idea at the time, but turned out to be a distinctly flaky fish.

As for television, a shortage of timber, and of glass for cathode-ray tubes, severely limited the number of sets being produced. It remained a minority distraction. In his *History of Broadcasting*, Asa Briggs discusses the laggardly progress here compared with the United States, where 3 million sets were in use by the end of 1948 and where, to quote Alistair Cooke's *Letter from America* – television was already 'as humble as a hot dog'. Briggs contrasts that with a report from the north-east of England, where television had still failed to penetrate at all. 'Although television tends to keep you at home,' it reads, 'it is also a talisman for friendship. Put an H-aerial up over your house, and you will be astonished to find how many friends you have in the street.'

The absence of mass communication helped to ensure that, in the early fifties, it was still Britain and the rest, us and them. The country's class system, too, headed by a royal family held in high esteem, carried on as if nothing had happened. Half a million people had turned out for the wedding of Princess Elizabeth to Philip, her childhood sweetheart, in 1947.[8] It was an authentic moment of national unity and a breathtakingly colourful performance for a populace starved of spectacle.

The Archbishop of York, Dr Garbett, stressed the point in his address: 'Never before has a wedding been followed with such intense interest by so many, and this has not been merely passive; it has been accompanied by the heartfelt prayer and good wishes of millions.' He went on, 'One of you, the daughter of our much loved King and Queen,

---

8 My father got caught up in the crowds later that week, when the royal couple were on their way to Waterloo for the start of their honeymoon. He was held up on his way back from a job interview, trying to cross the road to the public library, and he saw them at close range. He thought her 'young and slim and quite attractive, though she looked to have a great deal too much make-up on'. Philip came across as 'rather grey-faced and already long-suffering'. I don't know how much of an expert my father was on make-up, but the *Daily Mirror* claimed to have discovered the Princess's secret formula, the result of eight months of work by experts. It consisted of 'a peach tint liquid foundation, a film of rouge, light pink powder, eye mascara and eyeshadow and a red-blue toning lipstick'.

has gained already by charm and simple grace the affection of us all; and the other, as a sailor, has a sure place in the hearts of a people who know how much they owe to the strong shield of the Royal Navy.'

These were simple statements of fact, but he didn't know when to stop: '... notwithstanding the splendour and national significance of the service in this Abbey, it is in all essentials the same as it would be for any cottager who might be married this afternoon in some small country church in a remote village in the Dales.'

Dr Garbett can be forgiven his rhetorical excesses on such a day, and most of those who heard and read his words will have accepted the sentiments at face value: that the heir to the throne and her consort were subject to the same scriptural strictures as the rest of the population. But that was as far as the parallels went. In no other sense was there any comparison between the fate of the young bride on her throne and that of the King's subjects, rich or poor. She alone was destined to be the monarch of all she surveyed.

3   What the Bishops Saw

Like many others of that post-war generation, my first memory belongs to the young Queen: in my recollection her coronation in June 1953 heralded the arrival of a television in the corner of the living room and consequently the start of the dissipation of my juvenile sense of reality.[9]

That grainy picture was a miracle. We had the cinema, of course, but it was a palace of unreality, with a ticket seller, an usherette and an ice-cream girl to create a sense of excursion, as well as a curtain, ritualistically drawn in front of the screen to prove that everything we saw was part of the show – even the newsreels. Our television had none of the mechanics of separation. It sat on the faded blue carpet and invited us to believe that we were inside the Abbey alongside all those fine people.

In truth, we children quickly lost interest in the novelty that day. There were long periods where nothing much seemed to be happening. We fidgeted and chattered at the most solemn moments, and after much parental tutting we were dispatched to a neighbouring garden, supervised by an au pair who was unengaged in the proceedings by virtue of being Swiss. Nonetheless, we were probably still counted among the 27 million people who watched the show. (This figure was reached by taking the estimated number of televisions in the land – it leapt to 2.75 million ahead of the big day – and multiplying by the ten people judged to be watching each set.)

---

9 Childish memories are notoriously insubstantial, even dreamlike. It dawned on me after I started work on this book that the box must have arrived long before June 1953. First I noticed one of my father's diary entries – 'watched cup final, Blackpool 4 – Bolton 3': the match, the Matthews final, took place on 2 May, a month before Elizabeth's big day. Soon afterwards I started finding TV criticisms in my father's name dating back more than a year. But television really was in its awkward adolescence before the coronation. A diary entry revealed that, in early 1952, a friend called round to watch a football match between British and French army teams playing for the Kentish Cup, in which the cup had been donated by the friend's uncle. It was cancelled, but they watched the boat race instead:

> This was a ludicrous performance, television-wise. The cameras died in an explosive series of blinding flashes; for sound we were transferred to the Light Programme commentary; their launch ran out of petrol. TV did produce a blurred and bad picture of the finish, but that was about all.

So – in those early days at least – television could still be much less real that 'real life'.

The coronation coverage intensified public fascination with the royal family: no titbit was too trivial. My father kept a cutting from the *Evening Standard*'s 'London Last Night' column (23 December 1953) reporting that Princess Margaret had been spotted at a performance of *The Boy Friend* at the Embassy, Swiss Cottage.

It was an informal evening. The men wore lounge suits. The Princess was in a blue velvet cocktail dress. After the show the Princess and her friends had a quiet supper at a side table in a Greek restaurant off Tottenham Court Road.

The point of this account is that anything Margaret did was worthy of notice, even if it was something utterly ordinary – something that readers of the paper could do equally well for themselves. The innate significance of the report was fully understood and accepted by most people. It was real.

Even on the Queen's big day the BBC did not broadcast uninterruptedly: there was a four-minute interval at 5.22 in the afternoon, between the end of the coronation coverage and the start of children's programmes (younger viewers were offered a 'youth tattoo' staged in the studio). And then, at 6.30, the screens went blank for 90 minutes before the resumption of services.

One late change to the evening schedule was caused by news, which had broken less than 24 hours earlier, of the conquest of Everest. This was not an easy story for television to deal with. The producers opted for a brief statement by the announcer, Mary Malcolm: 'Now before we take you to the Embankment to watch the display of coronation fireworks, here is a picture of the highest mountain in the world.' This led into a five-minute talk by Dr Raymond Greene, 'a member of one of the previous eight expeditions that led the way for this latest triumph'. It was reassuring to know that this astonishing feat, although carried out by a New Zealander and a Sherpa, was 'a British expedition led by Colonel Hunt'.

Radio was still the dominant medium. On 3 June 1953, the day after the coronation, listings in the *Daily Express* show full details of programmes on the Home Service, which opened up at 6.30 a.m. with some rousing music from the Manchester CWS (Co-operative Wholesale Society) Band; the Light Programme, which went on the air at 9 a.m. for ten minutes of news followed by *Forces Choice*; and the

Third Programme, although classical music lovers had to wait until 6 p.m. for their first fix of Mozart. All three networks continued to broadcast until the late evening. By contrast the TV schedule is fitted into a small separate box with minimal information: programmes ran from 3.15 to 5.55 p.m., and from 8 p.m. until midnight, and then only because it was a special occasion. The usual close-down was 10.30 or 11 p.m.

The *Radio Times* for that week carried 29 pages of programme information; television's output covered no more than three. The magazine boasted that it hoped for sales of 9 million for its coronation issue, adding an apology: 'Printing capacity has precluded us from producing more than a fifty-two-page paper – and will do so for many months to come.'

Yet straws were there to be spotted in the unseasonal wind (and rain) of that week in June. The Express carried a piece by its television reporter, Robert Cannell. It bore the headline: 'TV millions saw more than Abbey peers'. He explained that the placing of the cameras – one of them 'peering down over the Archbishop of Canterbury's shoulder' – gave spectators at home a clear advantage over the congregation. 'Thirty million viewers', he wrote (with perhaps a hint of journalistic exaggeration), 'will recall how, in the Abbey hush, the Archbishop placed St Edward's Crown on the young Queen's head, how she lifted her eyes and how, gently and shyly, she smiled. But inside the Abbey, it was a secret smile. Only the Archbishop saw it. For the great chair of St Edward hid the Queen from the congregation.'

It was the same with a second smile from four-year-old Prince Charles, 'with his neatly brushed hair like any little boy at a party'. Cannell was captivated by the thought that this touching moment was something 'the privileged, the well-born and the influential in the Abbey could not see. Their gilded invitations took them into the Abbey, but almost all of them had to wait for last night's television film to see a connected version of what happened, and the incidents which lit the solemn ritual.' The choice of words was interesting: he believed that television, using its artificial techniques of recording, editing and 'connecting', had produced a more authentic version of the event than was available to those present. Reality had begun to shift its ground. 'Those who sat before the TV sets with their families', Cannell went on, 'virtually rode with the Queen through London and stood near to her in the ancient Abbey itself.'

Out in the real world people got wet and tired, and the best they could hope for was a fleeting glimpse of the carriages trundling by. The number of people who fainted during the day was 6873 and 313 were taken to hospital. The worst casualty was a man whose foot was crushed by a horse.

Below Cannell's article appears an advertisement for Decca televisions: the cheapest standard set, with a 17-inch tube, cost 83 guineas. At today's values that represents an outlay of around £1400. On the same basis my father's pre-tax salary would have been around £22,600 and I assume the newspaper must have subsidised his set, or perhaps it was rented: Radio Rentals, in coronation week, were offering televisions at the rather attractive price of 40 shillings a month (£30 today), though an (undisclosed) down payment was always required. Little wonder that radio was still the broadcasting medium of choice for most people, though good radios weren't cheap either: a small Roberts portable, complete with batteries and 'waterproof zip carrying cover', was being advertised for 14 guineas, the equivalent of £220 (40 per cent of the cost was represented by the dreaded Purchase Tax).[10] In our Bishops Stortford kitchen we had a large and impressive-looking Pye 28, described in the brochure as 'superheterodyne table receiver for A.C. mains' – hardly a Saatchi & Saatchi sort of slogan.

In addition television coverage of the country was still not complete: the BBC was in the middle of a five-year plan to establish new transmitters for those parts of the country – particularly in Scotland, Wales and the West Country – without access to a signal. By the end of 1951 only 209 television licences had been issued in Scotland and 7348 in Wales. Even at the end of the development period, in 1955, 8 per cent of the population remained without a service.

The new medium was bound by Reithian rules, too: no entertainment programmes were permitted on Sunday afternoons which might distract the audience from contemplation of higher things. The general ethos was summed up by the Director-General Sir William Haley in his introduction to the 1952 BBC Year Book: 'Television is an integral part of Broadcasting,' he wrote. 'The essence of Broadcasting is that it is a means of communication capable of conveying intelligence into every

---

10 The official list of everyday items used to compile the monthly Retail Price Index shows that in 1952 the electrical goods most people were likely to own were vacuum cleaner, electric fire and electric iron. In 2002 this category included cooker, washing machine, fridge-freezer, microwave, dishwasher, vacuum cleaner, smoke alarm and selected small appliances such as telephone, iron, food processor and kettle.

home simultaneously. In British Broadcasting it has been consistently
sought to ensure that intelligence shall be made up of information,
entertainment and education.' Fine words.

Yet in these hesitant and worthy beginnings can be seen the first
faint outline of a process which could not have been guessed at the
time: television has not itself been the cause of all the trouble, all the
disintegration, deterioration and dismantling of the solid structures of
the nation over the intervening fifty years. But it has played its part. It
has also proved a perfect medium for the development of an alternative
universe, vivid, easy to understand and presented in a beautifully
designed box – a Legoland society.

In his biography of the Queen, Ben Pimlott noted that from 2 June
1953, 'television became the means by which the public would
perceive the Royal Family and – with ever more fascinated intimacy –
relate to it'. In many ways that promised intimacy has turned out to
be an illusion. As we – and more acutely, they – now realise, public
fascination with royalty has been a destructive force. The very process
of learning what they were like sapped royalty (and the institution of
the monarchy) of its vitality – robbing it of its stature as a significant
feature of most people's lives. We transformed princesses into frogs
with our kisses. But that was only one of the many ways in which the
Queen and her subjects would find their perceptions altered as the
solid realities of post-war Britain began to crumble.

4   You Can Do Radio in the Dark

The last week of July 2001 was a period of intense national excitement. No royals were getting married, there had been no great sporting triumph. The weather was quite pleasant. Railtrack were in trouble for giving away shares to employees, but that was one of few stories from the real world that interested tabloid editors that day.[11]

No, the intense national excitement was generated by the imminent conclusion of two television shows – *Big Brother* and *Survivor*. The former in particular had become a matter of obsessive interest to the popular press, with rival papers vying for the votes of readers on behalf of the two final contenders. Both programmes fell into the general category of 'Reality TV', one of the great misnomers of our age. With their carefully constructed scenarios and performing stars, it was hard to decide whether the *Big Brother* house in east London or the *Survivors'* tropical island in the South Seas was a less authentic representation of real life. Which makes it even more startling that, in the 2002 National Television Awards, *Big Brother* should have been named 'Best Factual Programme' of the year.

On 25 July, in the same vein, the five tabloid newspapers carried between them some 15 pages of stories about the heroes and villains of these programmes – for those who've forgotten, their names were Brian and Helen and Charlotte and Jackie and Dean – not just in the television or showbiz sections, but in the main body of the newspapers. In itself, that statistic might be understandable, in a quiet news week close to the start of the summer holiday. But it didn't end there.

The news pages also featured seven items from the world of television soaps,

---

11 The shares must, briefly, have seemed real to the recipients. Three months later the gift turned to dust when the government declared that the company was bankrupt. This probably seemed like natural justice to those who originally described the shares as 'blood money' because of Railtrack's crash record. But this episode – indeed the stock market collapse of 2000–3 as a whole – underlines the ethereal nature of monetary assets in the modern age. The expansion of share ownership has made this eternal truth available to all. And then, to compound the Alice in Wonderland atmosphere, the government capitulated to pressure and funded a scheme to recompense Railtrack shareholders handsomely while the rest of the stock market losers looked on in disbelief.

Martine from Eastenders *appearing in a West End show; an incestuous kiss in* Eastenders *(x2, including an editorial page feature, 'A Kiss Too Far'); an* Eastenders *star meeting a girl in a bikini on a beach; a raunchy new advertisement for the Australian series,* Home and Away; Coronation Street *bringing back a popular hunk;* Sex and the City *stars not speaking to each other: [5 stories based on other TV shows,] an 'exclusive' profile of the actor, Steve Coogan; Jeremy Clarkson's wife talking about life with the TV presenter; the possible prosecution of Michael Barrymore; a* Thunderbirds *fan thanking the programme for helping him out of a coma; a topless Channel 5 'babe'; [3 previews of the feature film* Planet of the Apes; *5 pieces on the non-sporting activities of sporting celebrities,] Boris Becker's love-child; David Beckham 'milking' Victoria's breasts; cartoon depictions of 'Posh and Becks' in their virtual mansion (x2); Andre Agassi and Steffi Graf expecting a baby; [and an impressive 16 reports on the non-performing activities of star performers,] the young singer, Charlotte Church, gets a new sophisticated look (x3); the girl band Atomic Kitten celebrate a Number One hit (x3); Liam Gallagher and Nicole Appleton go on tour and leave their baby behind; Tom Cruise's divorce plans (x2); Gwyneth Paltrow in a swimming costume; Jason Donovan's baby; the actress Christina Ricci sporting a see-through dress; a fan of Jennifer Lopez wants her to autograph his buttocks; and Britney Spears in a tasselled top (x3).*

One further item deserves a mention – a series of closed-circuit TV pictures of a policeman apparently assaulting a man in the street. This has the feel of something 'real', although the story only earns its place in the papers because of the CCTV images – images which represent a blurring of the real and imagined world, like crimes acted out in television reconstructions.

The total number of pages devoted to all this material, drawn from the worlds of television, entertainment and celebrity, on that single summer's day, was 56. For millions of readers there is nothing exceptional about such a news diet. Editors judge that the activities of the stars are simply of more interest than the activities of anyone else in society and they must be right. There are no prizes for ignoring Britney Spears. The fascination with screen celebrities is a phenomenon dating back to the earliest, yearning days of the movies. Yet there is a difference, and not just a difference of scale and taste.

It is only comparatively recently that every man, woman and child in the country could realistically aspire to be on television, thereby gaining recognition and, in a minority of cases (usually temporary), fame and fortune. The director Paul Watson is often identified as the originator of the genre, in Britain at least, with his 1974 series, *The Family*, which thrust the Wilkins family of Reading – a bus-driver husband, his wife a greengrocer's assistant – into the spotlight. Watson had become infuriated with programmes in which the people discussed 'the poor' in the abstract and thought they should be allowed to speak for themselves. The first episodes left many viewers, and BBC managers, bewildered about why anyone should be interested in these workaday lives, but the human dramas, including a baby born out of wedlock, became as compulsive as any soap.

Watson says his documentary was one of the inspirations for the much later comedy drama series, the *Royle Family*, proving that art does still imitate nature, but these days the equation is more often reversed. Chris Rojek, in his book on celebrity, describes how ordinary people '… are vaulted into public consciousness as noteworthy figures, primarily at the behest of mass-media executives pursuing circulation or ratings wars.'[12] Achieving this sort of celebrity is now the focal point of popular culture and the opportunities are legion:

The *'reality' contests* – Big Brother, Survivor, Castaway
The *'fly-on-the-wall' documentaries* – Hotel, Airport, Driving School
The *ersatz 'fly-on-the-wall'* – Club 18–30, Holiday Rep
The *lowbrow game shows* – Wheel of Fortune, Family Fortunes
The *higher-brow game shows* – Millionaire, Countdown, Weakest Link
The *True Life stories* – 999, Police Camera Action
The *public discussion shows* – Kilroy, Question Time
The *home video-clip shows* – You've Been Framed!
The *talent competitions* – Popstars, Stars in Their Eyes, Fame Academy
The *untalent competitions* – Blind Date
The *lifestyle programmes* – *Home and garden make-overs, fashion, cookery, antiques*
The *best CCTV clip shows* …

---

12 Rojek's book, *Celebrity*, distinguishes between three types: celebrity which is achieved (by sports or entertainment stars), ascribed (to royalty, for example), or attributed. The producers of *Big Brother*, by choosing the contestants, broadcasting the details of their daily lives and arranging for personal publicity stories to be distributed to the rest of the media, attribute celebrity to Brian, Helen and the rest.

The 'stripped reality shows' – Pet Rescue
The confessionals – Jerry Springer, Oprah, Trisha

The categories are fluid and the list is far from exhaustive, but it is certainly enough to encourage the would-be celebrity. (I don't know what a 'stripped reality show' is, except that this is a phrase used by Bazal, one of the premier companies in the reality TV business.) The American website Talk Show News Tracker lists no fewer than 133 TV and radio talk shows in the United States and Britain.[13] The *Guardian*, in September 2001, listed 26 different titles for lifestyle programmes featured on BBC1 during the previous year: *Can't Cook, Won't Cook, Ready Steady Cook, Celebrity Ready Steady Cook, Charlie's Garden Army, Charlie's Wildlife Gardens, Changing Rooms, Chelsea Flower Show, Classic Rhodes, Curious Gardeners, Delia Smith's Summer Collection, DIY TV, DIY SOS, DIY SOS LIVE, Flying Gardener, Planet Patio, Garden Arguments, Ground Force, Garden Invaders, Big Garden, Hampton Court Flower Show, House Invaders, Home Front in the Garden, Real Rooms, House Call, Master Chef, Trading Up.* Apart from anything else, an immense strain is being placed on those responsible for dreaming up new titles.

As for CCTV, a few random and staccato images – Princess Diana and Dodi Fayed slipping out of the Ritz in Paris on the way to their death, Jill Dando shopping, James Bulger hand in hand with his killers, the last moments of Holly Wells and Jessica Chapman – these have helped to elevate a simple security device into yet another facet of celebrity culture. So much so that people perform for the cameras in shop windows for the pleasure of seeing their grainy image on the screen and – if they're really lucky – performing so extravagantly that the image ends up on television.

Rojek's 'mass-media executives' are the agents of this process, but the real driving force comes from the aspiring participants themselves. And the urgency of their desire is a potent force at the start of the second half-century of Queen Elizabeth's reign. If so many people – directly or indirectly (by phoning their *Big Brother* votes) – feel the need to express themselves through the medium of television, it suggests that the rest of life has become seriously flimsy and insubstantial.

---

13 The Tracker gives you the chance to keep up to date with what your favourites have been up to – from David Frost to Johnny Carson, Michael Parkinson to Barbara Walters, Ruby Wax to Joan Rivers, Oprah Winfrey to Monica Lewinsky and Sarah Ferguson.

Rojek invites us to see celebrities as part of the 'culture of distraction'. In a world characterised by 'structured inequality and the meaningless-ness of existence following the death of God and the decline of the Church … Celebrity and spectacle fill the vacuum'. Or to put it another way, television provides full validation for human individuality and endeavour, and participating, even as a viewer, brings a sense of belonging to a virtual community. 'Reality television is not the end of civilisation as we know it,' Germaine Greer has written. 'It is civilisation as we know it.'

It is also at one remove from reality. Almost anyone invited to appear in a television studio, man or woman, is offered a splash of make-up: the professionals, of course, make sure that all the cracks are papered over, all the blemishes camouflaged. This attention to physiognomical detail is no different from what happens in the theatre.

Some of the normal features of the human body do not look good under lights. In the late 1980s I was appearing as one of the junior presenters on *Newsnight* and I happened to catch sight of a monitor on which I saw myself perched at the back of the set. There was an angelic radiance around my head, which emitted a beam not dissimilar to that of a small lightship. My bald pate and I had learned to live at peace together long before, but this fleeting glimpse on a television screen was a shock: what hit me was the terrible realisation that – for the audience at home at this particular moment – this was the real me. A chap with a big, shiny forehead and an incipient double chin. As soon as the camera was on me I would thrust the chin forward, studious, youthful and lean. And sideways on I could look positively hirsute. But that chance encounter with a stray image told a higher truth. The rest of my television career would be spent dodging those rogue rays of artificial light.

You can do radio in the dark.

5 No Good Will Come of It

The artificiality of a performing art: what better symbol could there be than the powder puff, with which all of us strove – and strive – to keep nature at bay? The film and theatre people who staffed the studios in post-war years were under no illusion: even factual television was simply an extension of the entertainment business. What made it so exciting for the audience was the way it conveyed immediacy (unlike a cinema newsreel) by reducing the layers of separation between the viewer and the subject. And the make-up? The official explanation is that it merely undoes the damage done by fierce studio lights, but the truth is that it reimposes a further subtle barrier between performer and audience. (Even poor old Richard Nixon, in the first make-up catastrophe of the television age, didn't ignore the stuff altogether. He was just given some very bad advice about what sort of disguise he needed.)[14]

The separation has always been there, but in the early days of television in this (or any other) country, nobody was in much of a mood to notice. Practically everything that was seen on television was new and exciting, and as a minority activity it had an extra savour. This novelty value lasted a surprisingly long time, certainly when it came to television news. Even in 1973, when I joined the BBC, the arrival of a local television crew could still cause a stir in small towns and villages in the north-west of England. We were not a very glamorous bunch, me in my shabby Morris 1100, with Arthur and Harold unloading their bedraggled equipment from the back of an ancient Volvo. Yet people were excited at the idea of being on the box, and treated my colleagues and me with uncommon respect. We were

14 Daniel J. Boorstin wrote his celebrated book *The Image* soon after the Nixon–Kennedy debates in 1960, in which Nixon suffered the indignity of looking like a man who'd been up all night carousing. Boorstin offers the inside story. 'A television camera projects electronically, by an "image-orthicon" tube which has an X-ray effect. [The image-orthicon was the second generation of camera used in the US.] This camera penetrates Nixon's transparent skin and brings out (even just after a shave) the tiniest hair growing in the follicles beneath the surface. For the first decisive program, Nixon wore a make-up called "Lazy Shave" which was ineffective under these conditions. He therefore looked haggard and heavy-bearded by contrast to Kennedy, who looked pert and clean-cut.'

1973
X

the butterflies and we brightened their lives. The connection between us and our regional audience was solid, and fully understood by both sides.

The sense of occasion was always heightened if we were filming somebody, or something, that had never been filmed before. And in 1973 that still happened frequently. When I posed my first question on camera, on a bitter January afternoon of that year, one in fourteen households still had no television set.[15] Without undue effort or imagination, broadcasters could discover virgin territory, where events in the real world could be captured as they happened and shown to a fascinated wider audience that had never seen them before. An appearance on our regional television station, Look North, was a notable occurrence, quite likely to warrant front-page coverage in the local newspaper, and this – in an age of comparative innocence – was a bonus, not the purpose of the exercise for those who were featured.

Gradually, however, as television ownership edged towards saturation point, an insidious familiarity started to creep into the process. Fewer and fewer local stories were genuinely fresh. We'd done them before and our audience had seen them before. We were running out of material. Television had eaten all the stories. Before I left Look North we had started doing gardening and cookery spots to fill in the gaps, little realising that we were at the forefront of 'lifestyle' television.

What was true locally became true nationally and internationally, too. Television, however, couldn't just stop. It had to go on and on, always seeking new ways to present the same stories – standing up, sitting down, on film, on tape, with or without graphics or commentary or music. Only when covering matters of life and death does news recapture the blinding simplicity of its early days, and with it our full attention, because of the realisation that we could have been in that tower or on that train. And the blood, and smoke, and pain, and grief are real.

In 2001 the *Times* critic, Joe Joseph, was watching the 24-hour TV news channels covering the start of the trial of Lockerbie suspects at a special court in Holland. After less than an hour of the historic, but undramatic, proceedings, he could sense the producers in London beginning to panic. Viewers knew what a TV trial was supposed to

---

15 I was sent to cover a display by the Sealed Knot, whose re-created Civil War battles – I confess – hardly qualified as 'real life'.

look like and this wasn't it. By the end of the first day, coverage of the case had been reduced to the best soundbite, with the dull bits summed up by a reporter outside the court.

The fact that television news began to lose its allure might have worried nobody but television people: but over the past fifty years television has not turned out to be just another passive source of entertainment like a kaleidoscope or a 'What the Butler Saw' machine. It has been highly active, changing the way people think about themselves and most other aspects of the world around them. It has done so by building solid stereotypes (like the feckless teacher or the plucky, under-paid angel of mercy in our overcrowded hospital wards) to replace the old, broken certainties outside the studio walls. 'We have grown so used to believing that television drama is a version of reality', Joe Joseph remarked, 'that we are jolted when we visit a hospital and find that it is not like *ER*.'

In the pre-broadcasting age, books and newspapers disseminated knowledge and information and were quite capable of influencing public opinion or driving through social change: television carried that process to its logical conclusion, especially when it achieved universal coverage of the population. As the basis of viewers' lives has become less and less secure (unemployment, job mobility, family breakdown, fall in church-going, collapse of trade union power, disillusion with political parties, consumer choice, increased leisure, decline in group social activities[16]), one thing has remained constant – the television in the corner: creating order out of chaos, giving significance to what would otherwise be humdrum and, above all, promoting celebrity. An appearance on television has gone from being a minority opportunity to a commonplace, to an almost universal ambition – and all in the space of a couple of decades. In January 2002, the *Observer* advertised for would-be entertainment stars as a way of investigating what motivated celebrity seekers. All those who responded 'mentioned extreme effort and sacrifice. It became clear that celebrity ... was very much a full-time job.'

---

16 This is a very short indicative list which relates to the extraordinary research done by Robert D. Putnam in *Bowling Alone*. (He was studying the United States. I suppose the equivalent in Britain would be *Darts Alone*, or *Snooker Alone* – as a way of summing up social breakdown.) Some of his graphs are magical. At one point he produces polling evidence to distil the nature of avid TV-watchers: those for whom 'Television was the Primary Form of Entertainment' were twice as likely as occasional viewers to gesticulate obscenely at other drivers – and half as likely to have worked on a community project.

There is a generational element in all of this, admittedly, but for that reason it seems even more likely to influence the future development of society. In his autobiography, *Somebody, Someday*, Robbie Williams muses on this phenomenon. 'If I wasn't Robbie Williams right now, I'd probably be auditioning for the *Big Brother* household. I would. Some people's dreams are different. I think a huge majority of people's dreams are the same. They want to be bigger, better, they want the glamour, the fame, the celebrity.' Such honesty is rather rare and mainly heard from those whose celebrity is secure. An intending celebrity was quoted – just before the final of the *Pop Stars* talent show – as saying, 'The idea of being nobody tomorrow doesn't affect us and it doesn't mean you are a nobody if you are suddenly not receiving exposure in the tabloid newspapers.' That may be easier to say than to prove.

Television is the key to fulfilling such dreams, not least because it unlocks the interest of the rest of the media, as the newspaper review of 25 July 2001 proves. Six months after the first edition of *Big Brother*, nine of the ten contestants had jobs of some kind on television or radio (commercial radio DJ, reporter on Channel 5 or Sky) and the tenth had become a professional musician.

Fame can also bring fortune on its coat-tails, but even some of the most ardent suitors of celebrity know in their hearts that they are unlikely to get rich. It doesn't necessarily matter, because fame has an inherent value of its own: it demonstrates the solidity of one's own existence. The person who has appeared on the screen, even fleetingly, may well be recognised in the street the next day – or, if they're lucky, befriended by the monster that created them. In a society which has lost the knack of recognising people, visibility is a considerable asset. To be 'Helen off *Big Brother*', or 'that guy Anne Robinson humiliated on *The Weakest Link*', bestows a sense of identity and meaning. To be a successful teacher, or a bank manager, or a skilled engineer does not.

This sense of loss also helps to explain the current obsession with personal genealogical research, which offers unsuspected links and connections across the country, or even the world. A family tree is one of the strongest manifestations of identity, a token of mutual recognition. And these days, of course, the research can be carried out in front of a computer screen – without the tiresome business of ploughing through dusty parish records or rubbing the moss from headstones. The Friends Reunited website fulfils a similar function. Your old school was a community in which everyone knew his or her place.

The desire to appear on television is certainly as old as television itself. To start with, though, it was more likely to be driven by a wish to perform – the same extrovert instinct that might lead someone to take part in amateur drama, or to do card tricks at a children's party. The box provided another outlet for the talents of a would-be entertainer. By contrast, when it came to news or factual programmes, people generally responded as themselves – confident or shy, forthright or reserved. Chance had thrust them in front of a camera, in the street perhaps, and they did not have the guile to put on an act: television was too much respected as an arbiter of reality.

In the modern era it has become practically impossible to get anything approaching a natural response from anyone in any circumstances. Everyone knows what is expected, how it will look, what the programme-makers are up to. To be confronted by a camera, inside or outside a studio, is an opportunity to perform and to make a mark.

Consequently, nothing can now detract from the misery of the worst job in television: the vox pop. We reporters pretend that we genuinely wish to listen to 'the voice of the people' (vox populi), as we lurk on street corners, preying on the unwary. In truth, we have a predetermined idea of what we want to hear and are compelled to pester passers-by until somebody 'performs' satisfactorily by delivering a witty, succinct soundbite. The reason why some victims flee our extended microphones is because they fear they will not be able to perform satisfactorily. Despite its pretensions, the vox pop is one of the most artificial kinds of broadcasting ever devised.

In extreme cases no attempt is made to conceal the diabolical compact between programme-maker and subject. I once watched what purported to be a fly-on-the-wall story about the day-to-day workings of the travel company, Club 18–30. It was as natural and unaffected as a French farce. Everyone was acting, the company reps, the holiday-makers, the bar staff. The implicit deal was straightforward: 'The more outrageous the behaviour, the more likely we are to use the material.' Nobody needed a second invitation and, before long, Rebecca from Dartford was recounting in considerable detail a highly enjoyable threesome with two boys she'd met earlier in the evening. It was one of the most explicit descriptions of sexual activity I'd heard on a mainstream channel: all available orifices, she said, had come into play. Although the cameras remained outside the bedroom door for the few crucial minutes, nothing much was left to the imagination. And in subsequent programmes we saw plenty more of Rebecca, in every sense.

It may well be that Rebecca and her friends would have behaved in much the same way without a camera crew in attendance. But no one can doubt that she was performing. What's more, if this had been a drama, rather than a slice of 'real' life, her scenes – and a sub-plot involving an improbable virgin soldier seeking sexual solace – might well have been cut in the interests of taste and verisimilitude. On this sort of programme, however, anything goes, because it's really happening. In a manner of speaking, anyway.

For Rebecca, her Greek island holiday must have been intensely pleasurable and who can blame her for co-operating so enthusiastically with the makers of her myths? With minimum effort on her part, they turned her into a celebrity, something that she would have been hard pressed to achieve in Dartford. She will have returned home a heroine.

Not all the opportunities for television exhibitionism are quite so exotic (or erotic), but the possibilities are plentiful, so plentiful that nobody need feel excluded. Hardly anybody does. Nor is the desire for easy fame and pseudo-existence confined to the young.[17] As a closer acquaintance with this book's cast of characters will reveal, the substitution of a spurious reality for 'the real thing' has permeated every corner of society – a society in which service industries (media, leisure, money) have swept aside the dull business of making things and 'politics' has become a synonym for management.

Those seeking celebrity, or recognition, or validation, know what they expect from television. Their ardour is crucial to filling the long hours of airtime, whether it's by trading family secrets with Jerry Springer, or by allowing their garden to be provided with a formicarium and their house to be painted puce. And they're not the only ones anxious to give the programme-makers a helping hand.

As long ago as 1961 Daniel J. Boorstin (in *The Image*) identified what he called the 'pseudo-event', something that is staged with the express purpose of attracting media attention. This proves how quickly people

---

17 This fact was brilliantly caricatured in a recent series of *Absolutely Fabulous* which, as Bryan Appleyard noted in the *Sunday Times*, was an anthem to unreality: 'Work is still a curse, but persistent idleness does not seem to have had any adverse consequences. Debauched as they are, Edina and Patsy have risen effortlessly – the former's PR business has now expanded to include a television production company, and the latter has risen even higher in the world of fashion magazines. The implication is that neither PR, fashion nor television are real jobs. They are, rather, performances in which to appear to be doing is all that counts.'

involved in politics, advertising, public relations – and, indeed, celebrities themselves (once established as such) – latched on to the idea of how to exploit the media by manufacturing news: 'With the mushroom-fertility of all pseudo-events, celebrities tend to breed more celebrities. They help make and celebrate and publicise one another. Being known primarily for their well-knownness, celebrities intensify their celebrity images simply by becoming widely known for relations among them-selves. By a kind of symbiosis, celebrities live off each other.' He was writing about America, but Britain soon caught up. Forty years on, you can flick through any edition of *OK* or *Hello!* and you'll see what Boorstin means.

Politicians (or their functionaries) are past and present masters of these surreal arts. Take the simple case of the political speech. In the early 1970s we young journalists were still compelled to learn short-hand, partly so that we could take an accurate note of what was said on public platforms. Teeline (a cheap and cheerful successor to Pitmans and other 'real' shorthand systems) was specifically designed to deal with frequently repeated speech formulations: 'as I said earlier', 'taken year on year', 'the final point I'd like to make' and so on.

These days political reporters rarely need those skills. Any significant speech will first be trailed in a Sunday newspaper: 'X is expected to say in a speech next week …'; this will lead to discussions on radio and television giving rise, in turn, to further newspaper coverage. Sometimes the speech will then be tweaked to take account of any adverse or quizzical reaction. On the eve of the 'event', a text will be released to the press in the hope of grabbing some more media space the following morning: 'X announces policy U-turn'; as a con-sequence, the politician may then pop up in a studio to debate the contents (as made available to the newspapers), *even though the words of the speech have still not been uttered*. Finally, in front of a captive audience of business people or schoolchildren, the politician will rise to his feet and recite the well-rehearsed and predigested words. Journalists are supposed to 'check against delivery' by following closely the press release they've been handed; when the speaker deviates from this pre-published text – perhaps adding an aside, which could possibly be interpreted as a veiled jibe against a colleague – a whole new set of stories may be generated. (A residual need for short-hand here.) In this way the same 'speech' or 'event' can get six or seven outings.

Which parts of this process (if any) are real? Especially if we've all gone through the same process, with the same basic facts, a few months before?

Members of the public are not usually fooled. In fact, they're so well attuned to the system of pseudo-events that they are perfectly capable of staging their own. One of the most memorable moments of the 2001 general election campaign came when Tony Blair visited a hospital in Birmingham. The visit was a picture opportunity (a pseudo-event) which went horribly wrong when it was hijacked by a woman with a grievance: Sharon Storer put on a bravura performance of rage and dismay about the way her partner was being treated, and was rewarded with star media billing for several days. The real facts of the case were irrelevant, subsumed in the drama of confrontation and the stumbling demeanour of the Prime Minister. She was a celebrity.

It is hard to find any corner of life immune to the decay of old realities. The lack of self-confidence about our national identity produced what Stephen Haseler (in his book *The English Tribe*) calls 'theme-park Englishness', in which we tried to match up to the – mainly American – TV image that people had of us:

> As the culture of Englishness came under threat, it reacted militantly, yet in a manner needed by the growing world-wide leisure and tourist industry – by becoming more and more rural, more and more nostalgic, more and more contrived and artificial. The British broadcasters programmed even more re-runs of Brideshead Revisited and The Jewel in the Crown.

Teachers, whose complaints have already been registered, used to be respected members of the community: now we spend our time resenting them for giving up extra-curricular activities, complaining that they're making exams easier, accusing them of laziness because of their long holidays and wondering whether it's really healthy for a grown man to be in charge of a class of adolescent girls. Endless media discussion of the charges against them has undermined the foundations of the profession.

The law has not fared much better: our faith in the legal system has been worn down by miscarriages of justice (which prove that so many judgements were unreal in the first place), police corruption, irrational sentencing and the fear of being a victim of crime. None of these is new, but the constant repetition of stories and images has magnified the nature of the problem and exaggerated the shortcomings of those we used to trust.

The medical profession has taken a terrible beating, too. The reality of the way patients experience health care, the highly publicised cases of incompetence and abuse, the arrogance of some practitioners, the constant political exchange of high-flown promises, management theories and meaningless jargon (leave aside cases of casual mass murder and the theft of babies' organs): these are the media's meat and drink, and they have left doctors, nurses and the rest diminished in our estimation.[18]

The Church of England has lost our respect and most of its congregation, the Catholic Church is blighted by lurid tales of priestly abuse, the Muslim faith labours under a huge burden of public suspicion and apprehension and Judaism suffers from public weariness over its perpetual sense of grievance. Vicars and priests and imams and rabbis have a peripheral role in this aggressively secular society.

Sport may be as popular as ever, but it has also changed out of all recognition over the past half-century: performance (and recreational) drugs, obscene wealth, yobbishness and a tendency to despise authority figures (referees, umpires, line judges) have tarnished the reputation of many sportsmen and women, with the eager participation of the media. Young people with some sporting talent are just as likely to be seduced by the prospect of celebrity as by the chance of gaining the respect of their fans. And as Stephen Moss reported in a special edition of the *Guardian* in November 2000, the solid community links with sports clubs have gone completely.[19] A local football team, with a

---

18 Dr Jonathan Miller reflected (in a BBC interview with Sue MacGregor on Radio 4, part of a series called *50 Years On*) on a paradoxical aspect of our growing scepticism about the professional classes. 'In the days when people were so deferential towards doctors, the doctors themselves were almost impotent.' He conjured up the image of the bearded figure by the bedside of a dying child, with grieving parents weeping in the background. 'He gave clients the idea that his words had the power of law,' Miller reckoned, 'but his authority was invested in his class, not his competence.' Miller pointed out that public respect for doctors has declined in inverse proportion to the likelihood that they might make us better.

19 Fifty years ago sports coverage tended to be both brief and restrained. Moss quoted from the *Manchester Guardian* of 2 January 1950: the lead report, by an anonymous writer calling himself 'Old International' covered Manchester United's victory away to local rivals Manchester City. The match must surely have attracted a passionate capacity crowd, yet the headline was austere, even for the serious-minded *Guardian*: 'Manchester City Effort'. Moss reminds us that sport never occupied more than two-thirds of a page, rugby union got as much space as association football and schools sports were covered in detail. And there was never anything resembling a profile of a star player.

preponderance of local players, was a source of civic pride. Now Chelsea can field a team with only one Englishman (though admittedly sometimes a Londoner) and be cheered to the echo by the home crowd.

Cricket has gone the same way: it's hard to recall now the stringent residence rules, which meant that you had to have been born in a county, or to have lived there for more than a year, to qualify to play for its cricket team. My father worried a great deal about this and used to reassure me, as a young resident of the lowly minor county of Hertfordshire, that I could play for high-flying Surrey, the county of my birth, when I was old enough. (I have just looked up the details of Surrey's 2001 squad: of the 27 players registered at the start of the season, five were Surrey-born, the same as the number coming from overseas.)

Generalisations given credence by the media go on and on: politicians are hypocritical, prison officers are bullies, librarians are grey, farmers are pessimists, journalists are liars, builders are crooks, the City is crass, business executives are greedy and railway workers are just plain hopeless.

As for language ...

Television and its cohorts have had the direst effect on adjectives. One of my first news editors informed me in 1973 that if I used the word 'massive' in one of my scripts I wouldn't last long. I was so moved by this warning that I have abstained to this day, even when an object or event manifestly deserves the description, like a star system or a mountain of cast-off fridges.

The adjectival degradation in matters of size, scale and degree, which began all those years ago, has now reached ... what word should I use? 'Serious' proportions would sound pathetic these days. 'Appalling', 'alarming', 'shocking', 'terrible', 'disastrous', 'astonishing', 'incredible', not to mention 'massive', of course: all could now serve in that otherwise unemotive sentence. Every faintly critical report is 'damning' or 'scathing' (as are all indictments), reactions are likely to be 'hostile', behaviour is 'unacceptable', ships in trouble are invariably 'stricken', warnings are 'stark', redundancies are always 'devastating' (to the local community), while sports setbacks can be anything from 'horrific' to 'calamitous' and 'catastrophic'. Lies invariably come in 'tissues' and errors in 'catalogues'. And we all know where the devil resides. Many of these words have been robbed of their power and stripped of their meaning. When something happens that honestly deserves the description 'devastating' or 'catastrophic', writers now feel the need to add an adverb, like an RSJ in a crumbling ceiling, to prop up their sentiments: the flood was 'absolutely devastating', 'utterly disastrous', 'completely catastrophic'.

Laziness is partly to blame for this damage to the language, but it also reflects the need to sell a story in a competitive market. The correspondent who told his editor that an official report was merely 'critical' would be unlikely to fight his way into a news bulletin. Whereas a 'shocking' report containing 'ferocious' criticism – how could any editor resist? (Naturally, those responsible for reports, inquiries, investigations, surveys and other pseudo-events are well aware of the need to compete for airtime and publish the most enticing adjectives in a helpful one-page summary near the front, where even the idlest journalist can't miss them.)

The need to revive the power of words was felt keenly on September 11 2001. Broadcasters and journalists, like all television viewers, were confronted by a series of images that defied description. In their hesitant, bewildered commentaries you could hear professional wordsmiths groping for the tools of their trade. Often they found none. It was the same, or worse, for those who witnessed the scenes, or were touched directly by what was happening. Many displayed a shocked inarticulacy that was more powerful than any predictable phrase from the vocabulary of horror, debased by overuse.

The terrorist attacks also laid bare the nature of the difficulties we have created for ourselves. Somehow, none of it looked real. It could not be happening in the world we inhabited. Surely, in some obscure way, it must be a pseudo-event? Significantly, the television pictures reminded many people of action movies, with their sublimated and harmless violence. The best fiction requires a suspension of disbelief, much aided by the sophistication of special effects. Now the process had to be put into reverse: the disbelief on which we are all weaned had to be suspended *in order to believe that these unbelievable things had really happened*.

The attackers, and certainly those who planned the exercise, exploited the world's loss of grip on reality: we didn't imagine that such a thing could happen; we couldn't believe it when it did happen; and afterwards we found it impossible to work out why it had happened. Our responses were inchoate and probably unrealistic, because we had no real idea what might come next. Outside the BBC in west London, for instance, there was a proliferation of men with clipboards, as if by listing lots of names and car numbers we could somehow codify and neutralise the threat. Elsewhere, a war was launched to pursue the perpetrator and was declared a victory long before anyone knew what had really become of him – a pseudo-victory at best.

As for the pictures themselves, a self-denying ordinance has limited the number of times they can be shown: they are simply too real to be palatable.

Is this a purely British experience?

Many other countries shared our perplexity over September 11. Almost all have had to learn to live with television. (The last television-free sanctuary – the island of St Helena – received its first CNN pictures in March 1995.) Foreign viewers have the same tastes as we do: the *Big Brother* format has been a huge international success, taken up by more than 40 nations. We are not alone, either, in experiencing growing doubts about the purpose of politics, or disenchantment about revered institutions. And we are co-beneficiaries of the wonders of the Internet, which enables 'solid' activities like shopping or banking to be carried out in a parallel world. Yet there are some factors that tend to exaggerate the nature of the 'reality problem' in Britain, as it has developed during Elizabeth's reign.

Among these I would count: a vibrant and powerful national newspaper market to impose and reinforce media stereotypes; the burden of an island history, with its outdated emphasis on strength and separateness; the entrenched position of our institutions, even after two world wars; the centralised nature of English (and until recently, British) society; the dogged persistence of a class system built on such hazy concepts as accent, taste and attitudes to money; and above all, the dominance of a small number of universally available television stations.

Back in the 1920s the *Guardian* editor, C. P. Scott, feared the worst as soon as he heard the name chosen for the new invention. 'Television? No good will come of this device. The word is half Greek and half Latin.' While Bertrand Russell reportedly warned Grace

Wyndham Goldie, a radio pioneer who was preparing to move to television, 'It will be of no importance in your lifetime or mine.' She survived until 1986, but long before that Russell should have been eating his words.

ONE

Margaret –
The Fairy Princess

Halfway through the writing of this chapter Buckingham Palace announced that Princess Margaret had died, during the night of Friday, 8 February 2002, at the age of seventy-one. It was two days after the fiftieth anniversary of her father's demise: perhaps, consciously or not, she'd been hanging on to a life which she had begun to find tiresome, so that she could mark the date and then go.

The nation, which had greeted her arrival in the world with jubilation, dealt calmly with her passing. After the initial announcement the BBC, which had long since downgraded the Princess's death to a 'Category 2' royal event, continued more or less as if nothing had happened. Within half an hour BBC 1 had reverted to its regular schedules and BBC 2 followed suit an hour later. There was no point in pretending to cater for some shared national grief, though the rapid abandonment of any such pretence was not rapid enough for many viewers, who resented even the brief interruption of their regular programmes. It meant that the bulk of the coverage was on continuous news channels on radio and television – and then only until it was time for a Saturday afternoon of sport. Newspapers were ready with obituary material, led by the *Daily Mail*, which devoted 36 pages to its Monday morning coverage. But two Sunday papers did not even think it was the most important story of the weekend, preferring another twist in the row over a controversial vaccine (*Independent on Sunday*) and the involvement of a British politician in the Enron Collapse (*Observer*).

More poignantly, the areas set aside for 'floral tributes' were ignored by the public and the pages of the books of condolence told a story of their own.[20] A mere 21 MPs signed an Early Day Motion in the House of Commons expressing their sympathy: Hickey in the *Daily Express* pointed out that three times as many queued up to condemn the way the Spanish treat their quail chicks. A Cabinet minister, who went to Kensington Palace to sign his name, told me he was shocked by the contrast between the careful preparations for a rush of mourners and the empty room. He was not the only one to think back to the floral effusion following the death of Princess Diana. This time the victim was the antithesis of a 'People's Princess' and when Tony Blair said that the whole nation would be deeply saddened by her death, even he can hardly have believed what he was saying. His words conveyed all the passion of a ditty on a 'condolences' greetings card.

In 2002 the Metropolitan Police did not need to deploy officers for crowd control at Kensington Palace. Nobody stayed up all night. No candles were lit. Elton John did not sit down to pen a new elegy 'Farewell, Margaret Rose'.

The surviving royal family were judged to have performed rather better than when Diana died: the flag flown at half-mast over the Palace, for example, and Charles's off-the-cuff tribute to his 'darling Aunt' in a television statement before 24 hours had passed. But for them Margaret was the genuine article – a member of 'the firm' from birth. It was for the rest of us that she had become almost invisible – a shadowy figure at the periphery of public life. Her last, brief appearance on her mother's 101st birthday was a shocking reminder of her physical decline and – for those who remembered – a horrible

---

20 The laying of flowers near the place of a person's death is a modern secular ceremonial: somehow the roadside memorial sanctifies the spot and gives reality to their existence – like a cross in the graveyard. By the same token, bright yellow police crime signs bring home a harsh unpleasantness: 'MURDER', 'RAPE', 'VIOLENT ATTACK' – in your street, or mine. The Metropolitan Police have recently responded to complaints from local people who find that much reality unappealing: a new, nicer sign in pastel shades is to be introduced.

contrast with the beautiful young woman who used to inhabit that body. A film director would have been accused of exaggeration. The hunched figure in the wheelchair was bad enough; was it necessary to add the dark glasses and the sling? And surely there was no need to enforce upon her the final indignity – instructing her how to wave – she who had imbibed with her mother's milk the lesson of how to acknowledge her sister's subjects? The message came back that Margaret had not been coerced into this show of family unity, she had insisted on one last performance before slipping off the stage for good.

The beginning of Margaret's story was suitably theatrical: she was born at her mother's ancestral home, Glamis Castle, during a melodramatic summer storm. 'Act 3, Scene 5, Thunder ... Enter the three witches' – the Globe's stage manager would have been proud of the sound effects on that August night in 1930. Reasonably enough, the bard himself took a flexible attitude to historical reality and the real Macbeth was nothing like the weak-willed psychopath that Shakespeare cracked him up to be. He wasn't even Thane of Glamis, since the title didn't exist until long after the death of the historical figure. As far as anyone knows, Macbeth ruled much of Scotland benignly (by the standards of the Dark Ages) for 17 years and is most unlikely to have murdered Duncan.

The infant Margaret Rose would have similar difficulties with purveyors of royal stories as she grew up. In fact, the stories started almost immediately. One of them concerned the notification of her birth. It was discovered that her name would be number 13 in the register: but a local couple somewhat reluctantly agreed to put their son, George, ahead of Margaret Rose – so that she could be number 14. The story goes that the Duchess of York did not want her daughter to grow up with the superstition clinging to her, so that any trivial mishap would cause people to purse their lips and say, 'It all happened because of the spell.' If you were superstitious, you might feel that fate couldn't be tricked so easily. What happened to young George is not recorded.

It was required (by the sort of dusty precedent on which Gormenghast thrived) that the birth should be verified by the civil authorities. This was more than a mere formality: one Home Office official was worried how it would look – a royal arrival in such a remote location. Might people not feel that this important constitutional event was being handled in 'an irregular, hole-in-the-corner way'? Consequently, the Home Secretary, John Clynes, was despatched to Scotland in good time – very good time, as it turned out. Having set out from London on 5 August, he had to kick his heels in eastern Scotland for 16 days before receiving the summons to Glamis.

He did not witness the delivery itself, of course, so it would have been quite possible for the family, with the connivance of doctors, to substitute a different baby.[21] However, when Home Secretary Clynes was shown the infant, he estimated that she was the real thing, reporting her to be a 'fine chubby-faced little girl lying wide awake'. Thus reassured, the nation was able to celebrate, with 41-gun salutes at the Tower of London and in Hyde Park, and the ringing of church bells across the land. A huge beacon above Glamis village attracted thousands of tourists and ten kilted pipers. There was some disappointment in Scotland that the Duchess of York had not produced a son – a modern Bonnie Prince Charlie: even her father, according to unsubstantiated accounts, was briefly disconcerted. But a shortage of young royals meant that Margaret immediately joined her sister as a focus of national and international attention. Not many babies have a commemorative tea service created to mark their birth and public interest was magnified when the girls' father was crowned King George VI. Margaret was just six years old, but her 'ascribed' celebrity, to use Rojek's phrase, was never in question.

The lives of the royal children, whatever the level of public interest, were lived almost completely in private, so much so that a rumour developed that the younger princess might be deaf, dumb or deranged. The public was drip-fed occasional images and titbits of information, leaving the media to fill in the gaps as best they could, using their imagination. That job fell to the newly vibrant popular press.

The *Daily Mail*, launched in 1896, was the first mass-circulation daily, but by the time of Margaret's birth it had given ground first to

---

21 That was how the tradition of vetting royal arrivals had begun, in 1688, when Mary of Modena, wife of James II, produced a much-needed son at a crucial moment. The King's enemies, faced with the unwelcome reality of a Catholic heir to the throne, protested that the child was an impostor, perhaps fathered by Sir Theophilus Oglethorpe and smuggled into the bed chamber in a warming-pan. Whether they were right or not, public opinion moved against James and by the end of the year he had been deposed.

the *Daily Mirror*, then to the *Daily Express*. There was no real competition from broadcasters. BBC Radio was eight years old, but still behaved with the sort of solemnity towards news that befitted a self-appointed pillar of the Establishment. Things went very differently in the United States, where the heyday of the tabloids had come and gone in the 1920s. Radio, commercial from the start, had stolen their thunder, their readers and most of their advertising revenue by concentrating on variety, music, sport, gossip and celebrity interviews: this had been the meat and drink of the tabloids, and without it they were doomed.[22]

In Britain, meanwhile, a single public service broadcaster made no serious attempt to challenge a popular press, which expanded steadily for more than two decades, gaining a total circulation of 9 million in 1930 and 12 million by the start of World War II. Nonetheless, it was a brutally competitive market and the tabloids knew what sold papers: from the moment the infant *Daily Mirror* printed front-page photographs of Edward VII and his family in April 1904, the public appetite for royal stories had proved inexhaustible.

When it came to offering royal insights, however, newspapers had to try to satisfy their customers within the very severe limits imposed by the spirit of the age – the same spirit that kept the Wallis Simpson affair under wraps until it exploded into the open across the Atlantic. And the children were definitely off limits.

Crawfie (the children's governess, Marion Crawford), in her groundbreaking 1950 account of life behind the Palace railings, *The Little Princesses*, offers a telling anecdote of one encounter. She had taken to conducting walks with the children, incognito, in Hyde Park. 'Only once were we beleaguered by the press,' she writes. 'A persuasive young man recognised the children and wanted to take a picture. I

---

22 By the end of World War II the 'tabloidisation' of American radio was rampant. *Time* magazine of 11 March 1946 carries a feature entitled 'Zany Radio – Stunts grow wilder and wilder in audience-participation shows'. The writer observed that 'people submit to embarrassment, ridicule and indignity to take part in programs. They ride on ice-cakes, fight with pillows, do stripteases, make cross-country trips, go into lions' cages.' Ice-cake rides must have made great radio. One game in the programme *Truth and Consequences* had the contestants trying to find the matching half of a thousand-dollar bill by travelling across the country shouting 'Heathcliff!'. The lions' cage game involved a box containing 12 pairs of nylons which had to be extracted without provoking the lion. The piece concludes, 'The end seems nowhere in sight.' He was right. And, with foresight, he added, 'Ominously, even television has taken up the idea.' The magazine shows a picture of a wife trying to extinguish her husband's cigar with a soda syphon. The prize – a set of *Porgy and Bess* records. British Broadcasting had a long way to go.

knew that if this happened it would be the end of our unofficial outings, so I drove him off mercilessly.' Elizabeth (Lilibet) was delighted: 'Crawfie, you were savage!' No one else dared intrude on the princesses' private world and it took a rash of IRA letterbox bombs and 'other nuisances' to put an end to these anonymous excursions.

Margaret's permitted exposure to the world's media began in earnest on the day of her grandfather's Silver Jubilee, in 1935, when the diarist Chips Channon described the young princesses, identically dressed, as 'two tiny pink children' driving past in a large landau. Then came her father's coronation in 1937. For days, according to Crawfie, there had been crowds outside the Palace waiting for something to happen, 'though we could not imagine what'. Gazing back through the lace curtains 'was a grand new amusement for the children on wet winter afternoons'. On the day itself, after a minor tiff over the length of her train, the six-year-old Margaret behaved well enough. She was dressed in a lace frock with silver bows, a cloak edged with ermine and a specially designed lightweight coronet, identical to her sister's, but scaled down ('silver-gilt with jewel-like chasing mounted with fleur-de-lis'). For the journey to the Abbey, Margaret's seat in the carriage was built up so that she could see and be seen. She waved with much enthusiasm.

One magazine, boasting the 'first photographs' of coronation day, carried a report from the royal route signed Periscope: 'Gleaming glass coaches from fairyland have surely come to life! "Three cheers for Queen Mary!" bursts spontaneously from one of the older children and, as Princess Elizabeth smiles happily out of her glass coach, up jumps a small boy near me and cries, milk and crisps forgotten, "Look, she likes me as much as I like her ..."' Periscope is almost overcome with emotion. 'Sometimes we British are told we are an undemonstrative people – even unromantic, matter-of-fact, casual! But are we, when there is something fine and grand and worthwhile to be demonstrative about? Here we are as a nation today, celebrating something that is most precious – the priceless heritage of Kingship.' This he describes as 'a deep-down force, an inspiration that has coloured the world all down the centuries with beauty and love, with loyalty and valour'.

An illustrated booklet, published by the National Sunday School Union during the war, contains an article by the author Frances Tower on the impact of the coronation: 'It was the kind of transporting event that leaves one in a semi-ecstatic state from which descent to every-day level is difficult. The carriage processions drove back through seas of cheers to the Palace, and the crowds stayed outside the gates all day, with more thunderous cheers when the King and Queen came onto the balcony with their crowns, and the princesses nodded heads and coronets gaily.'

It would be an unusual six-year-old who was not infected by such sentiments, especially one given to poring over photographs of her mother and father in magazines and, as her reading skills improved, absorbing the sentiments of Periscope and his like. When the King and Queen travelled to North America in 1939, Frances Tower wrote of the girls, 'They read all the Press eulogies and were thrilled by photographs of their mother looking both beautiful and majestic in gracious crinolines ...'

Their parents wished the children to keep their feet on the ground, but the system was against them, as Crawfie understood.

Just how difficult this is to achieve, if you live in a palace, is hard to explain. A glass curtain seems to come down between you and the outer world, between the hard realities of life and life at court, and however hard a struggle is made to avoid it, escape is not entirely possible. This strange atmosphere is not engendered by royalty itself. I myself had never done striving to keep this miasma of unreality from the children, and thanks to their parents' open-mindedness in these matters, I often succeeded.

But royalty has to engender that 'strange atmosphere', or how would anyone know that its members were different from the rest of us? It would have been difficult, anyway, to dispel the miasma of unreality and more so for Margaret than her sister. Margaret was P2, the number two Princess. When her uncle abdicated, making her father King and her sister the heir apparent, she squeezed Lilibet's hand and said, 'Poor you.' But she felt sorry for her own plight, too, having recently learned to write out her name in full. 'I used to be Margaret of York,' she complained, 'and now I am nothing.' Her whole life would be spent seeking to answer the question: who am I?

When war broke out, any possible process of change in relations between the royal family and its loyal subjects was frozen. Although some newsreel footage of Princess Elizabeth, and less frequently of her sister, was released, this was always on the Palace's terms. And after the war the King acquired a Press Secretary, Commander Richard Colville, who regarded it as his solemn duty to keep journalists at bay. The Commander was described by Ben Pimlott as 'an unbending ex-naval officer with no knowledge of the press, which he treated with a combination of distrust and lordly contempt'. This approach helped to create a pent-up demand for stories about the fairy-tale princesses.[23]

For the majority of people the royal family was a real and important part of the backdrop to their lives, and a symbol of the strength of national character that had seen the country through another desperate struggle for survival. It was natural for the VE-Day crowds to gravitate to Buckingham Palace: throughout the day of Tuesday, 8 May 1945 the royal family returned to the balcony again and again to acknowledge the connection between themselves and the people who cheered, sang and waved their flags in the streets below. Late in the evening the two princesses slipped out to join the throng and experienced this powerful sense of community at first hand.

Yet when the cheering had died down, nobody could tell the 14-year-old Margaret what she was for, beyond being a figure of adulation to whom commoners curtsied and bowed. Elizabeth was the heir to the throne, a role that not only defined who she was, but also ensured that she would be protected from the explosion of media activity in the post-war years. Margaret emerged into young adulthood carrying a burden of frustrated public affection and an easy prey for ill-informed press attention.

From the day of her first solo public engagement – opening a play centre in north London in 1946 at the age of sixteen – she became the property of the press, acting on behalf of a willing readership. A dearth of glamorous figures in the royal houses of Europe gave her added value, and she slipped effortlessly into the role of celebrity.

When Marion Crawford's book was published (Margaret was just nineteen) it caused a sensation. The world rights were bought in the United States by the *Ladies Home Journal* which, in turn, sold on the British rights to *Woman's Own* for a huge fee. This magazine

---

23 Over the next two decades Colville would routinely refuse all requests for access by newspapers, radio and television. But at least he always replied by return of post.

promoted its serialisation heavily to recoup its costs and delayed publication so that the expected increase in sales would not be constrained by the rationing of newsprint. The tactics worked and the circulation of *Woman's Own* jumped by half a million. What's more, rivals felt they had to respond: *Woman* came up with 'The Real Princess Elizabeth', while *Woman's Weekly* countered with a series of more or less paltry revelations of its own: 'When the Royal Family Travels by Air', 'Nanny to a Baby Prince' and 'The Story of Clarence House'. According to one history of the magazine business, these events 'turned the British royal family into show business'. From now on they would be 'just another promotional device'.

The Little Princesses, though, had unassailable authenticity and the Palace's chagrin only reinforced the point. The Queen, having received proofs of the book, wrote that the whole thing had been 'a great shock' and she could only imagine that the governess had 'gone off her head'. As punishment, Crawfie lost her grace and favour home, and was ostracised by the whole family in perpetuity. But as stable doors slammed shut all around the unfortunate governess, the horse was long gone.

No wonder the family was so upset – not least by the evidence of the kind of young woman Margaret was and might become. According to Crawfie, the child was 'often naughty, but had a gay bouncing way with her that was hard to deal with'. In the eyes of her father she could do no wrong; she was 'a plaything'; from the age of ten onwards, she was positively encouraged to enjoy 'a good deal of social life'. One elderly visitor confessed that he was frightened by Margaret, because she had 'too witty a tongue and too sharp a way with her'.

The younger sister was often jealous of Lilibet's special treatment, but soon slipped into the habit of discounting the disagreeable facts of her life. So, after first resenting that she was not allowed to dress up like her sister in the uniform of the ATS (the Auxiliary Territorial Service), she felt better when she saw 'how unbecoming khaki was'. And when it became clear that Lilibet would always be a much better shot than she was, Margaret decided that shooting was an unfeminine activity – nor could she ever be found up to her thighs in icy water, casting for salmon. She preferred distractions in the warm – canasta, charades or the piano. This last skill was always said to be remarkably well developed, though crueller critics felt she should confine herself to singing.

But she was stunning, everyone agreed about that. In the autumn of 1946 a young woman with a fiancé in the Queen Mother's household was invited to join a royal theatre outing to see *Annie Get Your Gun*. Half a century later, she still remembered her first impression of the two princesses – Margaret at 16 and Elizabeth, four years older – stepping out of the lift from their apartments at the Palace. 'They were enchanting,' she remembered, 'both so tiny and thin, with perfect skin and lovely blue eyes. I couldn't get over how beautiful Margaret was, with her long pink chiffon dress, and a pearl and diamond cross around her neck.'

Three months later the family left for the first great post-war tour, to South Africa. A disgruntled Crawfie thought that the moment might have come to retire, but the Queen wouldn't hear of it. 'Her Majesty did not relish the thought of having to deal alone with what might prove to be a spoiled and disorganised girl. Margaret had always had so much of her own way, and so much more freedom than her sister. In my own mind I had come to the conclusion that this very grown-up trip would be the last straw. She was always wilful and headstrong. "When she comes back after all this," I thought, "she will not settle down."'

Crawfie went on to claim that Margaret had proved her wrong: on her return, she was as good as gold and, surprisingly demurely, turned up in the classroom with her box of pencils and dressed in a plain wool frock. 'Her character is like a well-cut diamond,' she cooed. 'It has facets in every direction which reflect all kinds of light.' It was a remarkable description – a small, sparkling jewel for the delectation of all, beautiful, dazzling but unyielding. By the time of Elizabeth's wedding in May 1947, Crawfie really had become redundant to Margaret's needs and she looked forward to the future with foreboding.

The public lapped all this up, of course. They read the conclusions of the woman who knew the Princess better than anyone – perhaps even better than her mother and father – that Margaret was 'no more frivolous or flirtatious than any other high-spirited and pretty girl of her age, who has been a little spoiled'. But, if they happened to have access to an American copy of *The Little Princesses*, they could also read the second half of the same paragraph – excised in the British edition. 'In every family there arrives from time to time the clever child who refuses to conform. It is Princess Margaret's tragedy that the talents and individuality that would in any other walk of life be such an asset to her are a drawback in a palace, where brilliance and originality and superabundant vitality incline to be a nuisance, and where those who say what they think, present a problem among others who are discreet to the point of never saying anything at all!'[24]

And Crawfie showed that she was well aware of the risks posed by this dysfunctional individuality. 'It was her misfortune', she wrote, 'that the ordinary exploits of adolescence, the natural life of a healthy and vivacious girl, in her case made newspaper paragraphs, instead of being dismissed with a laugh.'

For the press, Margaret was a godsend. Soon after her seventeenth birthday she started to gulp in London's nightlife like a prisoner released after a long sentence; the *Sunday Pictorial*, after one particularly energetic period, gave publicity to 'Princess Margaret's Week of Late Nights'.[25] The last few pages of *The Little Princesses* disclose the concern felt by courtiers and the blind indulgence shown by her parents. 'More and more parties, more and more friends, and less and less work,' cried Crawfie in muted despair. When she plucked up courage to mention her worries to the Queen, warning her that Margaret was wearing herself out, she was told, 'We are only young once, Crawfie. We want her to have a good time. With Lilibet gone, it is lonely for her here.' In rare gaps between social distractions she mooned about, sulking – 'one little girl alone in the palace, with no sister to go about with and nothing much to do, and no one of her age to play with.' Finding people to play with was never Margaret's problem.

---

24 The American publishers, Harcourt, Brace and Co., published the book in 1950 a few months ahead of Cassell in Britain, and included a number of additional passages which, in a spirit of self-censorship, were kept from the domestic audience: these included 18 personal letters from the royal family or senior staff; five detailed references to Mrs Simpson and the Abdication; a dozen stories about the family which cast them in a less than lovely light; and half a dozen potentially controversial comments by Crawfie on sensitive subjects, including one about the Queen commandeering excess handkerchiefs from Lilibet's trousseau for sale in charity bazaars. Another, in this last category, pointed up one of the early (metaphorical) cracks in the royal edifice – staff troubles. 'The pay and conditions were no longer attractive,' Crawfie complained, 'and there were no longer so many young people whose greatest ambition was to serve the King and Queen.'

25 In his book, *Margaret, Princess without a Cause*, Willi Frischauer listed the activities from a fortnight in 1949: 'She attended a military concert followed by supper with the officers; visited the theatre and went on to dance at a club until the early hours; danced at a ball and again at a night-club the next night; went to a reception at the Danish Embassy where she was seen drinking "hard liquor") (gin) with Prince George of Denmark who was, quite wrongly, counted among her suitors. Night-club again, the Ballet, next to see a revue in Oxford while staying at Blenheim Palace with "Sonny" Blandford, son of the house and heir to the Duke of Marlborough.'

In vain did Crawfie point out that other girls, in these modern times, couldn't lie in bed all day after a late night. They had to cook their own breakfast, catch a bus and go out to work. Shouldn't a royal princess be setting them an example? Margaret joked, 'Even if I wanted to cook my own breakfast, I couldn't, because there's nothing here to cook on.' Crawfie thought she was joking. It sounds to me like the literal truth.

For the first time in British royal history a senior member of the family was exposed – and was exposing herself – to the regular glare of public scrutiny beyond the gilded safety of the Palace. But Margaret was still a child of a different age, brought up to believe in the absolute rights bestowed by her position. Unquestioningly, she expected to enjoy the real world and yet to remain shielded from its excesses. Her parents and protectors failed to detect the changes that were taking place – in particular, the difference the post-war media might make.

No precise moment marks the end of the age of deference and restraint, but it was in a fragile condition, more fragile than the royal Establishment realised. For the time being an acceptance of the hierarchical gap between royalty and the rest of the population remained real for both parties, and allowed Margaret to become a figure of international renown and romance. Perhaps the family even hoped to win some advantage from the worldly activities of a glamorous young woman. But celebrity was a siren voice and the rocks were lying in wait.[26]

In the absence of any official guidance – bright but undereducated – the Princess decided that she would work out her own destiny: she would enjoy herself, as a princess was surely entitled to do. And if it happened that people chose to copy her clothes, her make-up, her choice of restaurant or club, so be it. She didn't set out to be a cultural icon; in fact, she denied being a leader of fashion, but she became one anyway.[27] It isn't often that a character from a fairy tale becomes quite so tangible – and the clock striking 12 never interrupted the revels.

---

26 Chips Channon wrote in his diary that he had met Margaret at Ascot, and detected 'a Marie Antoinette aroma about her'. My encyclopaedia contains these phrases about the unhappy Marie: 'Young and inexperienced ... aroused criticism for her extravagance and disregard for conventions ... possessed the power of inspiring enthusiasm ... failed to understand the troubled times.'

27 She latched on to designers from an early age, starting with Norman Hartnell who had created her bridesmaid's dress for the wedding of the Duke of Gloucester in 1935, and who held sway at the Palace through to the coronation in 1953. Margaret was voted one of the 14 best-dressed women in the world in 1951. After her death, Vogue published a tribute describing her as 'the first member of the House of Windsor to understand how positive an injection of glamour and style can be to those who look on – and, more importantly and crucially to her life – how those qualities could marry with a sense of duty, responsibility and tradition.'

Even at a distance of half a century her authorised biographer, Christopher Warwick, was entranced by the spell she cast – when the world was seduced by the 'young, sensual and stunningly beautiful' creature on display in countless newspapers and magazines. 'Scarcely a day passed without her photograph making the front page,' he wrote, 'if for no other reason than whatever she did appealed to the public and was good for sales.' Others have found the same images less appealing. Willi Frischauer, whose 1977 biography was unauthorised, cast a jaundiced eye over the landscape of late-night watering holes favoured by the Princess and her friends. 'Outstanding ... was the 400 Club in Leicester Square, the darkish, comparatively sedate haunt of prosperous young men and society girls emerging from the chrysalis stage – and international roués casting their nets to catch attractive butterflies for their private collections.'

At the time, however, the Princess did not have to fear such sniping. Most of the publicity was respectful and some of it nothing short of fawning. Between 1948 and 1954 the Pitkin publishing house produced an annual record of Margaret's achievements, each bristling with glamorous pictures of her public appearances and details of her official engagements. The text sighs with pleasure at its task. In the 19th birthday book, it describes the 'informal, home-loving tastes of this girl born to grandeur and exalted rank'; 'Princess Margaret, dignified, lovely in a sweeping gown of pink silk brocade and soft feather headdress, captured the hearts of the citizens of Amsterdam';[28] 'Even on holiday, Princess Margaret, like other members of the royal family, never turns a deaf ear to a deserving call on her time or presence'; 'She is a serious, responsible girl, whose eagerness to serve is as strong as her enjoyment of the social life in which she likes to take part'. And this is my personal favourite: 'Naturally Princess Margaret has a generous share of social life but often the Ball or West End party comes at the end of a tiring day of correspondence and arduous official duties.' Most readers nodded indulgently and smiled with pleasure at the energy of youth.

For the tabloids, this was base metal which could be turned into journalistic gold.

The leering eyes of the cameras pursued her at home and abroad. On a trip to Capri, a carefully staged viewing of the royal limbs was

---

28 And of Group-Captain Peter Townsend – as we shall see.

organised as a way of placating the hordes. The result was stunning. A combination of the bright sunlight and a carelessly (?) chosen swimsuit caused one Fleet Street picture editor to cry, 'My God, she's naked!' The *Daily Express* did the decent thing and touched up the photo to darken the costume. It became known that the King considered the photos very undignified, while *The Times* said sternly that Margaret should not be treated as a peep-show. But that's exactly what she was, and usually by her own choice – performing for an adoring public.[29]

Many stereotypes about the Princess were established at this time and never lost their potency. In the autumn of 1949 she attended a Hallowe'en Ball at the Dorchester Hotel and during the evening produced a cigarette holder in public for the first time. Or rather, that is just one of dozens of versions of the story. An Internet celebrity smoking site lists 61 separate anecdotes: one moves the scene from the Dorchester to a Chelsea dinner party where Margaret 'produced a large ivory cigarette-holder into which she placed an untipped cigarette, then waited for a light'. 'Waited for a light' has a convincing ring. The holder became her trademark, anyway, helping to fix in people's minds that she was the royal who smoked, and who eventually developed a 60-a-day habit.[30] The sight of her puffing away, with her rather effete accessory raised at a coquettish angle, would, in due course, become the defining image of a hedonistic Princess. Famous Grouse whisky became one of her props, too.

Yet those running the primitive systems of public relations at work at the time clearly hoped and expected that the Princess's life would send out a different message. The Pitkin books were one result. Another was the hagiographic picture book *The Younger Sister* by the journalist Godfrey Winn, published in 1951. So great was the appetite for information that Winn's associated articles for the *Sunday Despatch* increased that paper's circulation by a quarter of a million. The book itself sold 100,000 copies. He was 'privileged to meet the

---

29 Pitkin produced a special brochure for the Italian trip. In none of the many pictures is the Princess anything other than fully dressed. In Capri, according to the text, the Princess 'sometimes put on a swim suit and was taken out by rowing boat, her boatman being the six-foot, bronzed Carmine Natale ... The stalwart Carmine, dressed in striped sailor's jumper, blue slacks, and blue rope-soled shoes was the proudest man on Capri.' I bet.

30 I am told that when, in later years, she stayed with the poet Sir Harold Acton in Tuscany, she aroused the ire of the old aesthete by throwing her cigarette ends into the loo. As the visit progressed, the plumbing in his villa (La Pietra) began to seize up, but servants refused to dig into the bowl to retrieve the debris.

Princess personally', and was 'mesmerised by the unusual colour and brilliance of her violet-blue eyes'. They reminded him of Elizabeth Taylor.

Margaret, he told his readers, knew that after her sister's wedding she herself would take up a new place 'in the dedicated pattern that had made her own family so infinitely beloved'. His description of her passion for party-going (which could hardly be ignored) was a work of benign imagination. Her love of dancing, Winn said, sprang from her bubbling-over vitality; her love of going out for the evening was 'part of her eagerness to meet new people, to see new faces and listen to new points of view, and wherever possible, without loss of royal dignity, to make new friends from other worlds than her own'. He compared this with 'the same kind of eagerness that will take other girls of her age to the local *palais de danse* on a Saturday night, or to stay a week in a Butlin camp. The impulse is perfectly natural and reasonable.' In case anyone should be misled by newspaper photographs, the public should know that her social contacts were severely constrained and she would never invite a man friend to her apartments unless she was certain there would be 'a dozen or more guests in the room'. He reinforces the point a few pages later, drawing attention to Margaret's dislike of references to her 'Clan' or 'Set': 'She maintains – and she is clearly right in doing so – that she possesses a multitude of friends of different ages and interests. There is nothing clannish about her personal relations outside the Palace, because the motivating point of her philosophy of living is that she enjoys contact with many different worlds.'

None of the pictures in Winn's book shows the Princess with a cigarette: once again, however, he feels compelled to nod at the reality revealed in the public prints. 'Whereas her maternal grandmother at her age could only smoke in private, Queen Mary's grand-daughter now occasionally smokes in public. The Queen Mother's only reaction was to suggest that the Princess in future always uses a holder.' Pitkin follows suit, reassuring her fans that 'she does not smoke a great many'.

Even at this young age, Margaret was living through a number of parallel realities.

At the time, smoking was perfectly acceptable, but – Winn notwithstanding – the atmosphere of decadent self-indulgence in the Princess's social life, laced with the possibility of illicit romance, encouraged editors to send teams of reporters and photographers to stalk the streets of Soho and theatreland in search of pictures of 'the Margaret Set'. They knew that their ration-restricted readership delighted in the vicarious excitement to be had from following Margaret's progress. The Set was usually happy to oblige. It was a relationship whose rules evolved in a way generally understood and accepted by both sides, though one important exception came on the Princess's 21st birthday.

For her coming-of-age celebrations the Set, including Billy Wallace and the Earl of Dalkeith, decamped to Balmoral. With the King and Queen in residence, there was no possibility that the party would co-operate with the pursuing press pack, who were left scouring the Scottish moors for glimpses of their quarry at the end of a long lens. The elaborate game of hide and seek was described by one high-minded observer as 'pathetic and unseemly', but the young people (including Princess Elizabeth) enjoyed themselves hugely, even penning a song for the occasion, set to the tune of 'The Teddy Bears' Picnic':

> *If you go up to the hills today,*
> *You're in for a big surprise.*
> *If you go up to the hills today,*
> *You'd better go in disguise.*
> *For all the Press that ever there was*
> *Will gather there for certain because*
> *Today's the day that somebody has a birthday ...*

And, with a pointed reference to the prominence of the *Daily Express* team, employees of Lord Beaverbrook, the next verse includes the lines:

> *Peeking time for Beaver Boys,*
> *A lovely time for Beaver Boys,*
> *Clicking their cameras all the time,*
> *As they ruin our holiday ...* [31]

The newspapers also felt aggrieved. Having fêted the fairy Princess for the previous four years, why should they suddenly be excluded from

---

31 The only reference to these incidents in Pitkin's year book for 1951 is a mention of 'more and more reporters from all over the world 'haunting the moor and Balmoral Castle. 'The Princess was not allowed much privacy,' the text adds primly.

this special occasion? Did the royal family not owe it to the public to offer them some access, however limited, to such a notable event in the life of a public figure? Hypocrisy was rampant on both sides. The press were mainly annoyed to have been robbed of a great story and the family itself seems to have missed the point altogether. Access, they decreed, would remain on their terms.

This discordant episode, in the summer of 1951, is one of the defining moments in public perceptions of the monarchy – a moment at which the media realised that it was still regarded by the royals as a shabby supplicant, doomed to hang about outside the Palace gate. If Margaret deigned to invite them to draw near from time to time, all well and good. Otherwise, they had better remember their place. What marked the Princess out was that, unlike other family members, she found it irresistibly stimulating to step outside the glass curtain; but when she tried to regain her privacy the curtain provided no protection at all: publicity and privacy made uneasy partners.

Nothing changed immediately, of course, but the shape of the future relationship between media and monarchy was being sketched out. Princess Margaret would be one of the victims; so, too, in her time, would Princess Diana: and eventually the monarchy would find itself in jeopardy.

Blissfully ignorant of these problems, the nation approached the coronation of Queen Elizabeth II with a real sense of hope. What better opportunity could there be to shake off the long, dreary post-war hangover? Or as she herself put it in her broadcast that evening, 'I am sure that this, my Coronation, is not the symbol of a power and splendour that are gone but a declaration of our hopes for the future.' Yet it seems utterly predictable that the Establishment should at first have resisted the idea of allowing cameras inside Westminster Abbey for the service: the objectors included the Queen herself.[32] In the end the Palace gave in, although certain parts of the service, like the Anointing, were thought to be too sacred to be sullied by the public gaze.

---

32 Ben Pimlott records a memo from John Colville, formerly Elizabeth's Private Secretary, but by now one of the Prime Minister's Principal Private Secretaries, to Churchill: 'Live television would not only add considerably to the strain on the Queen (who does not herself want TV) but would mean that any mistakes, unintentional incidents or undignified behaviour by spectators would be seen by millions of people.' It's not clear what Colville expected the distinguished congregation to get up to.

The ceremony was intensely real for the millions watching and listening at home and around the world even if, as *The Times* reported, the television pictures took some getting used to: the paper noted that viewers might have had some difficulty grasping the fact that what they were seeing was 'not a news film, but historic events unfolding'. The success of the event was a testament to the connectedness of the people with its royal family.

For once, the Queen's sister had a minor role to play. That no doubt explains why she was emboldened, during a pause in the proceedings, to approach Group-Captain Peter Townsend, place her hands lightly on his medalled chest and remove a fateful piece of fluff.

The incident was not picked up by the cameras. Townsend was not even on the radar of the British press, which was still absorbed by Margaret's frequent appearances with one (or more) of the upper-class young men who made up her Set. Only four days earlier, on 29 May, the *Daily Mirror* had shown her arriving at an 'amateur charity performance of a Gay Nineties comedy in which "her friend Mr Billy Wallace" took the part of a Guards officer'. While on 1 June the same paper carried a lengthy diary story about another putative suitor, Robin McEwen. The piece is full of delicious hints: McEwen is one of the Princess's 'special personal friends', and 'closest and most consistent friends'. The writer clinches his speculation with a ritual denial – 'There is no suggestion, as far as I know, of any romance between the Princess and Mr McEwen (a Roman Catholic). Such a question would bring up immense difficulties.' McEwen joined a roll-call of aristocratic partners identified by journalists purportedly in the know.

On coronation day itself the only personal insight into Margaret's behaviour in the *Daily Express* coverage was that the Princess seemed to find her coronet uncomfortable, at one point 'poking at it' as if she expected it to fall off.

The *Daily Mirror* was no more revealing, although afterwards its correspondent Audrey Whiting was one of a surprising number who claimed to have seen the lover's touch. (She was convinced that only a woman would have noticed such a fleeting moment of intimacy. Several of her male competitors begged to differ.) Whiting asked one of her neighbours the identity of the handsome RAF officer with pilot's wings and was told, 'He's Group-Captain Peter Townsend, and the King adores him.' She thought to herself, 'Somebody else adores him.'

At the time, she did not share this insight with the readers of her paper: the only intimate touch she chose to mention was one between the Queen and the Duke of Edinburgh while her maid, Bobo, combed her hair.

As with the Abdication crisis, it took the American newspapers to break the news of this royal romance. The story in the *Journal American* of New York was a sensation, immediately recycled almost everywhere – apart from the country where it happened. It was still possible for the United Kingdom, for all its sophistication, to remain insulated inside a communications cordon sanitaire. It would be a further 11 days before the *People* became the first British newspaper to relay the story of the romance, and then only in a typically hypocritical and roundabout way. The sheer cant of the exercise still takes the breath away: generously printing the 'scandalous rumours' that had appeared in the United States and Europe for the sole purpose of allowing the Palace to rebut them. 'The story is, of course, utterly untrue,' the paper hastened to ensure its readers, lying through its teeth. 'It is quite unthinkable that a Royal Princess, third in line of succession to the throne, should even contemplate marriage with a man who has been through the divorce courts twice.'

Margaret may have been a royal princess, but she was also the official plaything of the press. The birth of Prince Charles (in 1948) and Princess Anne (1950) had secured the succession, condemning the Queen's sister even more firmly to that hinterland between significance and celebrity. Her love for Peter Townsend brought the inherent illogicality of her position into the open for the first time. On the one hand, the adoration of a beautiful young woman for a war hero was the very stuff of the tabloid world-view. On the other, the highly unsuitable affair between a senior member of the royal family and a twice-divorced older man was a shocking betrayal of the system which had created them both and on which they both relied for their status.

Something had to be done. Townsend, as a comparatively humble equerry (to all intents and purposes, a servant) was promptly despatched overseas – out of sight, if never out of mind. The American press were enthralled at this evidence of the brutal British class system at work: 'Princess Meg's Beau Banished', they cried, 'Queen Exiles RAF Ace Linked to Princess Meg'.

Knowing as little as, or even less than, usual, the newspapers in Britain began a two-year orgy of speculation. In the face of total silence from the Palace, where Sir Richard Colville was living up to his nickname of 'The Abominable No Man', competing titles felt free to chase every passing rumour and to pontificate about what should be done. They lined up for or against the marriage, often invoking the haunted figure of the Duke of Windsor to illustrate their fantasies, since he really had been exiled for love. Each simply picked which sort of Margaret they wished to embrace and proceeded accordingly, using her plight to make the appropriate points. The *People*, which might have been expected to opt for the love angle, felt compelled instead to stick to the high moral tone it had adopted in breaking the story. 'A marriage would fly in the face of Royal and Christian tradition,' the paper opined loftily. The *Manchester Guardian* sympathised with Margaret, largely because of the hypocrisy of her oppressors, many of whom were divorced themselves.

And the public? The *Daily Mirror* ran a poll in which 97 per cent of the respondents voted for romance. The paper was severely censured by the Press Council for its pains, which only served to demonstrate how rattled the Establishment was. The spectacle of Margaret's private life as a proper subject for every passing pundit was alarming and strenuous efforts were made to prevent the argument being lost by default. As a counterbalance to the sentimental preference for a romantic outcome, a succession of ponderous interventions warned that the relationship with Townsend could threaten the monarchy, the Church, social stability, or all three. *The Times*, edited by Sir William Haley (who had been in charge of the BBC until 1952[33]) issued its gravest admonition just as the Townsend crisis came to a climax. His leader inveighed against 'the odious whipping up' of public emotion for the purpose of selling newspapers: and he reminded his readers of the Queen's position as 'the symbol of every side of society, its universal representative in whom her people see their better selves ideally reflected: and since part of their ideal is of family life, the Queen's family has its own part in the reflection'.

The risks were obvious. If the personal problems of the Queen's sister could be bandied about with as little respect as the football scores or the price of cigarettes, how long would it be before the press

---

33 Shortly before taking up the job of Director-General in 1944, Haley promised to provide broadcasting for 'all classes of listener equally'. He went on, 'This does not mean it shall remain passive regarding the distribution of those classes. [The BBC] cannot abandon the educative task ... to improve cultural and ethical standards.' Not a man to mess with.

was emboldened to cast its net more widely, to take in the rest of the royal family – even the Queen herself? What made them all so nervous – the Palace, *The Times* and the Church (the Archbishop of Canterbury was unyielding in his opposition to the idea of marriage) – was that Margaret was a creature over whom they could exercise no kind of control, other than by appealing to her princessly instincts. She was living life according to her own whims, in a way that offered a radical vision of what sort of person a royal personage might be. The evident reality of her frustrated passion stood in contrast to the dry determinations of her critics and therein lay the danger.

The tragicomic consequences of these contradictions were manna for the press of the day and for generations of subsequent chroniclers of the Princess's life.[34] Ahead of Margaret's 25th birthday – the day when she would, by law, be free to decide for herself – 300 journalists and photographers descended on Balmoral. Despite the Daily Mirror's plea – 'Come on Margaret! Please make up your mind!' – 21 August came and went with no decision. One strong hint, however, came in an article by Godfrey Winn in *Picture Post* – seen by some as an early example of a member of the royal family 'using' a friendly journalist. 'Do not imagine', Winn wrote, 'that this fairy-story princess in real life would exchange the destiny that is hers by birth and upbringing for

---

34 There is no dispute about the couple's first meeting: Townsend was appointed an equerry by George VI in 1944, when Margaret was 14, and thought her an 'unremarkable' little girl, apart from her dark-blue eyes and her nice line in repartee. But when did things get serious? Like all other commentators, biographers have felt free to speculate at will. Noel Botham (*The Untold Story*, 1994) opts for an adolescent infatuation which flowered during the royal family's tour of Africa in February 1947, when Margaret (only just 16 years old) often went riding with Townsend. Nigel Dempster (*A Life Unfulfilled*, 1981) has the intensity of Margaret's feelings in full flow by the autumn of the same year. Theo Aronson (*Princess Margaret – A Biography*, 1997) opts for September 1948, when Margaret represented her father at the installation of Queen Juliana of the Netherlands. Christopher Warwick (*A Life of Contrasts*, 2000) tends to agree that 'a certain chemistry' was at work by then. As for Peter Townsend himself (*Time and Chance*, 1978), he claims that it wasn't until 1952 that he and Margaret 'found increasing solace' in each other's company. One of the most explicit descriptions, however, is in Willi Frischauer's book *Margaret, Princess Without a Cause*, 1977): 'Had I not the testimony of some of Margaret's early confidants, I needed only study photographs of her and Peter together in South Africa, he looking at her in his boyish manner, she almost transfixed, lowering her eyes and blushing (even in black and white). Yes, it was all happening on this tour – not the ripe joy of adult passion but the enticing, bitter-sweet taste of young love.' He comments 'Because it was not seemly for a girl of seventeen to be involved – and with a married man twice her age – the beginning of her love story has been post-dated like a dubious cheque, and the period of her affair put with skilful obfuscation at a much later date ... when everything was presumably all right.' Whoever is right, it is staggering that a public figure under such intense scrutiny could conceal a passionate relationship for so long. And that the truth has remained so hazy for half a century.

any other kind of future in the whole wide world.' This was consistent with a remark reported by Winn when he met Margaret five years earlier: 'I cannot imagine anything more wonderful than being who I am.' (Whoever that was.)

By the autumn the journalistic noise had reached a crescendo and at last, on 31 October, Margaret's decision was made public. She would let Townsend go. Was her act of abnegation from a sense of duty, or through an unwillingness to lose her title, status and income? I have been told that Townsend himself had been worn down by the intense pressure and was ready to walk away. 'There are too many forces against it,' he felt. Later he wrote that he thought he had been treated like 'a political deportee' and that he was discomfited by the bald lies about him issued by the Palace. Margaret's official statement – in which she spoke of being strengthened by Townsend's unfailing support and devotion – said that she was 'mindful of the Church's teaching that Christian marriage is indissoluble, and conscious of the Commonwealth', and so had 'resolved to put these considerations before any other'.[35] Noël Coward wrote in his diary, 'This is a fine slap in the chops for the bloody press which has been persecuting her for so long.'

So many elements of what happened now seem shocking and reprehensible: the fact that the Palace felt the need to trick Margaret by sending Townsend abroad while she was out of the country; that the couple were strung along for two years, believing that there might be a happy ending; that divorced politicians like Anthony Eden put pressure on Margaret not to damage the institution of marriage – nobody emerges from the affair with much credit. By the time it was over Margaret had been cast as the martyr – the Princess who felt compelled to sacrifice happiness for duty, like some heroine from Racine.[36] Yet her close friends are not convinced that the marriage would have been a success and believe that Margaret may have been

---

35 Willi Frischauer's book, written only twenty years later, was sceptical: 'The tear-stained view of a broken romance dims powers of analysis. If Margaret had been so mindful of the Church's teaching, someone asked rudely, what had she been doing playing around with a married man all these years? Was it only now that she had become conscious of the Commonwealth?'

36 There was a touching scene at Kensington Palace 40 years later, when Margaret met Peter for the last time. Townsend's wife was supposed to come too and Margaret invited a few other friends because she didn't want to 'feel like a gooseberry'. In the event Mrs Townsend stayed away. At the end of the meal the Princess asked one of the guests to take a last picture of her with Peter.

more aware than she seemed of the risks of an unhappy match. One told me, 'They were definitely in love, but he was really too old for her – too charming, nice and gentle.'

If Margaret was hurting, she certainly did not pine: another friend said, 'Somehow she shrugged him off. She's got a very curious heart – once something comes to an end she is amazing about putting it to one side. She does a lot of discounting of grief. How much that costs her, I never know.' Within a matter of weeks (according to one account) she was engaged to a long-time admirer, Billy Wallace, on the grounds that it was 'better to marry someone one at least liked' than to end up on the shelf. (Wallace then made the tactical error of having a holiday fling on a Caribbean island and confessing it to Margaret. The engagement did not survive this outburst of honesty.)

For the press it mattered little whether the picture of the inconsolable lover was accurate or not. The doomed romance merely added to her celebrity attraction. And as the dust of the Townsend affair settled, it became clear that the wellspring of public respect for the monarchy as a whole had been depleted. Destroying young love is not exactly the best public relations. Like Diana thirty years later, Margaret seemed more alive, more attractive and more relevant than the rest of the royal family, even if her character was flawed. Unintentionally, she had transferred some of their reality on to herself.

A few dissident souls were already at work with their undermining tools: the Townsend débâcle inspired a *New Statesman* article by Malcolm Muggeridge entitled 'Royal Soap Opera', which started, 'There are probably quite a lot of people – more than might be supposed – who, like myself, feel that another newspaper photograph of the Royal Family will be more than they can bear. Even Princess Anne, a doubtless estimable child, becomes abhorrent by repetition.'

Muggeridge's views were well-known but evidence soon began to accumulate that the authority of the monarchy itself had been weakened. Less than 18 months after Margaret's split from Townsend, press speculation touched the Queen herself. Goaded as usual by an American newspaper, the taciturn Sir Richard Colville was moved to issue a formal denial of a story that the Duke of Edinburgh had had secret meetings with an unnamed woman. 'It is quite untrue that there is any rift between the Queen and the Duke,' Colville said. 'Rift Far-Fetched, Royal Aides Say' was how this came out in the United States. British editors were furious that their transatlantic competitors had managed to coax Colville from his habitual scornful silence and several retaliated by splashing the rift denial on their own front pages. It emerged that, rift or not, Prince Philip had remained in Gibraltar for ten days at the end of a five-month world tour: the *Mirror* helpfully advised him, 'Fly Home, Philip!' to kill the 'ridiculous and baseless' rumours. While the *Sunday Pictorial* wondered, 'How can you expect youngsters to understand that Daddy is so near, yet cannot come home?' This was new territory: direct criticism of the monarch's own family.

More was to follow. An edition of the erudite journal *National and English Review* published a series of articles on the future of the monarchy. One, by Lord Altrincham (who later gave up his title to become plain John Grigg, historian of note), caused a furore. Monarchy, he suggested, required its leading figures to perform 'the seemingly impossible task of being at once ordinary and extraordinary'. He accepted that the Queen was held in high regard, but warned that, as she grew older and 'lost the bloom of youth', she would need to do and say things to justify public esteem. He didn't think it would be easy, in view of her presentational shortcomings: 'Her present style of speaking ... is frankly a "pain in the neck"'; 'Like her mother, she appears to be unable to string even a few sentences together without a written text'. 'The personality conveyed by the utterances which are put into her mouth is that of a priggish schoolgirl, captain of the hockey team, a prefect, and a recent candidate for confirmation'. For his frankness he was slapped in the street by a member of the League of Empire Loyalists; his assailant was taken to court, but fined a token 20 shillings (£1) by a sympathetic magistrate.

The attitude of the BBC was instructive. Not only did the Corporation black all coverage of His Lordship's article (Independent Television News, not yet two years old, was happy to hear Altrincham expound his views in an interview with Robin Day), but the outspoken peer was also dropped from BBC Radio's *Any Questions* programme. When a BBC radio comedian risked a feeble joke about Margaret and Peter – its punchline was 'they had tea together. Again' – it attracted widespread attention. In 1957 the Corporation remained locked into its deferential relationship with the monarchy and with other national institutions, very much as Lord Reith had decreed three decades and a world war earlier.

Not for much longer. Britain's reputation, as well as the standing of its institutions, had taken a further battering with the Suez adventure, while the Russian invasion of Hungary brought home the powerlessness of once-great nations. A German magazine published a cartoon showing the Queen sharing a bath with her sister and saying, 'Margaret, could you not do something to distract the horrid world press from our Suez débâcle?' The critic Kenneth Tynan, writing in the same year, detected the sea change. 'The ivory tower has collapsed for good,' he wrote. 'Britain's angry young men may be jejune and strident, but they are involved in the only belief that matters: that life begins tomorrow.' That Christmas the Queen made her own tentative steps towards that new tomorrow: she broadcast her first televised message to the nation.

To be at once ordinary and extraordinary ... Princess Margaret was about to attempt the greatest juggling act of her life. This determinedly royal figure had fallen for a commoner, plain Antony Armstrong-Jones, and she had managed to do so under the noses of the newspapers. It must have been exhilarating to slip into his apartment in Pimlico or the flat he rented in Rotherhithe, overhanging the Thames, and live the life of an ordinary young lover for a few ecstatic months. Except that Tony, throughout their relationship and marriage, always called her ma'am, and many found that extraordinary indeed.[37] The two were formally introduced at a dinner party in February 1958. Armstrong-Jones was a fashionable young photographer with artistic

---

37 The maintenance by the Princess of this and other formalities (the bow or curtsy) applied to all and sundry, including her children, and remained in force until her death. Her daughter-in-law habitually greeted her 'Good morning, Your Royal Highness'. It spoke to me of insecurity – a need to be reminded, every minute of every day, that 'royalness' had not deserted her. Those who loved her saw it differently: it was purely, they said, a question of courtesy and tradition. One of her friends told me she found it very touching that 'great, dignified, magnanimous men' should acknowledge the Queen's sister with a small inclination of the head. The same source admitted that Margaret could seem priggish and disdainful of those she met – but explained that this, too, was a defence mechanism. 'If she didn't want to get involved with some crashing bore, or someone who came up and called her "Margaret", she just gave them a blank stare which acted like a polythene curtain between them.' In his autobiography the writer Quentin Crewe – whose wife was a close friend of the Princess – wrote, 'When she and Tony first came to our parties, it was entertaining to watch the reaction of other guests. Some, like Dr Johnson meeting Queen Anne, would bow so low that they could see back between their legs. Others would say aggressively: "I'm not going to call you Ma'am, you know." ' Considering the same phenomenon many years later, the *Guardian*'s Jonathan Freedland offered a less generous picture: 'Margaret comes over as a spoiled Elizabeth Bott character, or the overweight girl in *Charlie and the Chocolate Factory* crying, "I want it, I want it, I want it!" '

tastes, just the kind of character to intrigue the Princess. The occasion went well. Margaret's biographer Theo Aronson says Armstrong-Jones treated her with 'the right blend of deference and daring'; he bowed to the extraordinary and excited the ordinary in her. Almost exactly two years later they broke the news of their engagement and took almost everyone completely by surprise.

In the meantime the reporters who wondered why she was sometimes a less visible feature on the social scenery nodded wisely and explained that she was still in mourning for her lost love and possibly meeting him in secret. In any case there were plenty of sightings with her old Set, like the rehabilitated Billy Wallace. When she was seen in public with her lover, nobody noticed: he was the photographer, wasn't he?[38] What more natural than that he should attend royal functions – and even that he should be invited to Balmoral for the Princess's 29th birthday? The photograph released afterwards was evidence that he had merely been fulfilling his professional duties.

The newspapers should not have reproached themselves too much: even those close to her were kept in the dark. One told me that the rumour of an engagement reached a number of her friends on a skiing party in St Moritz: each wrote down on a slip of paper the name of a possible candidate. There were no correct answers. The same friend told me that, at about the same time, she had arranged a dinner for Margaret and rang Armstrong-Jones as someone the Princess might like to meet. 'Who else is coming?' he enquired casually. When he heard who was guest of honour, he went away to 'look at his diary' and returned to say that, regrettably, he was already booked. The subterfuge must have magnified the excitement of the relationship. Ned Sherrin quotes some delightful North American headlines when the news broke: 'Meg to wed court Fotog' (*New York Daily News*); 'She'll be the most famous Jones of all' (*Toronto Star*); 'He really clicked' (*Journal American*).

Once the engagement had been announced, a week after the birth of Prince Andrew in February 1960, Tony was – in effect – taken away to Buckingham Palace and locked up for the duration. This was

---

38 In his autobiography Ned Sherrin quotes the apocryphal story of Harold Macmillan being summoned to Sandringham, unaware that the engagement is about to be announced. He finds an anxious tableau and wonders why the Queen is frozen and fretful, the Duke pacing and swearing, Princess Margaret sobbing and the Queen Mother imbibing a large gin. Suddenly he spots a shrinking figure he recognises as a photographer. 'My God,' he says, 'the press are here already!'

uncharted territory and the Palace wanted to make sure that nothing went wrong. Perhaps they hoped that the interloper would absorb the royal gene, ensuring that he would become attuned to the niceties of the way things were done in royal circles.

Princess Margaret's perennial problem – what was she for? – now had a new dimension: how was the nation supposed to deal with her new husband? On the face of it, marrying a man from the 'real world' intensified her connectedness to the rest of us. Yet, from the start, she made it plain that she intended to maintain her royal status, with no concession to the background of the man she had chosen.

Tony was an irresistible target for some sections of Fleet Street. He was a photo-journalist, 'one of them', who had gone over to the other side. Snide observers wondered how much money he was making from stories about his engagement illustrated with his own photographs. The *Daily Mirror*, for which he had never worked, tried to speed him on his way by describing him as 'the former photographer'. Guerrilla warfare by the gossip writers did achieve one notable scalp when the couple's best man, Jeremy Fry, was forced to step down 'through ill-health' in the face of a rash of scurrilous stories about his past. This sort of coverage was still the exception. It was much more common to read the warm endorsements of his many friends (so many that Sheila Logue, in the magazine *Punch*, was moved to boast, 'I am the only Fleet Street journalist who isn't a personal friend of Antony Armstrong-Jones').

In May 1960 the vast majority of the population, too, was unmoved by questions about Princess Margaret's equivocal position. As Bernard Levin observed in his review of the Sixties (*The Pendulum Years*): 'Millions, unskilled at reading between the lines of the gossip-columnists' code, suspected little of what was going on, and for them the marriage took place in an atmosphere of metaphorical orange-blossom that had not been seen in Britain for decades.' Just as it had been for the coronation, London was packed with people anxious to see the happy ending to the royal fairy story. The television audience reached 300 million. And when the married couple drove to Tower Pier to join the Royal Yacht, crowds pressed around the car and delivered a spontaneous ovation. For Levin it was 'the high point of that ancient adulation of royalty that had caused so many stern moralists to declare that it was nationally unhealthy'. In true Levinesque style he continues, quoting the angry young playwright John Osborne: 'The moralists who thought of the Monarchy as "the gold filling in a mouth of decay" did not make entirely clear if what they were advocating was extraction of the teeth and their replacement by some kind of Scandinavian plastic ones.'

The couple were away for 40 days. When they returned Margaret was the proud owner of a plot of land on the island of Mustique and the monarchy had gained a new brand of critic – emboldened by the 'ordinariness' of the royal couple to attack the monarchy head on: if they (or at least Tony) intended to be part of the real world, why should they be protected from its less pleasant manifestations? Questions were asked in Parliament about the cost of the honeymoon – £1000 a day (about £13,000 at today's values); about the increase in Princess Margaret's Civil List allowance from £6000 (£76,000) to £15,000 (£189,000); about the cost of refurbishing their Kensington Palace home: £6000; and, in due course about the provision of a far plusher set of apartments on which the taxpayer was asked to spend a sum equivalent to £600,000 forty years later. It was open season on the couple's expenditure, thus establishing that, in principle, the Civil List, and the finances of all the royals, could and should be questioned, just as if they were local council officials or MPs.

Margaret was beginning to act as the Trojan Horse – offering the family's enemies access to the fortress in which they had sheltered for so long. *The Economist* quoted Walter Bagehot: that a wise court is one 'which stands aloof from the rest of the London world, and which has but slender relations with the more amusing parts of it ... for the light nothings of the drawing-room and the grave things of the office are as different from one another as two human occupations can be'. Standing aloof was not what Margaret and Tony had in mind. They were ready to take up starring roles in the Swinging Sixties.

Matters were not improved by Tony's acquisition of a title – the Earl of Snowdon – nor by his decision to continue his career in the press piranha pond, with the inevitable jealousy and resentment this caused. How dare he strut around royal palaces, living off the fat of the land? But then again, was it not outrageous that he should shamelessly exploit his position to grab lucrative jobs? The cliché 'no-win situation' could have been invented for him.

The language of these attacks was usually constrained, but tempers were lost when Snowdon was appointed 'artistic adviser' to the new *Sunday Times* colour magazine early in 1962.[39] The *Observer* assailed its rival and in particular its Canadian proprietor, Roy (later Lord) Thomson: 'It will inevitably seem unfair to rival newspapers and magazines that the Queen's close relative is used for the enlargement and enrichment of the Thomson empire.' In case this was thought to be mere professional griping, the *Observer* also warned the royal family against allowing themselves to be associated with Thomson's 'expansionist aims'. 'To use the fame of the monarchy to put money into the hands of a private firm is a doubtful procedure,' said David Astor, the *Observer*'s owner, in a television interview. The *Daily Mirror* chipped in that the family was beginning to look like something from 'Walt Disney land' and its columnist Cassandra (William Connor) offered to sign up Princess Margaret as a women's features editor. The *Sunday Times* appointment also produced what was probably the first caricature of the royal family: a *Spectator* cartoon by Trog (Walter Fawkes) of the 'Snowdon family-album', featuring snaps of corgis and royal hands waving from Rolls-Royces. If the Palace had a strategy for dealing with all this, nobody noticed: indeed, the Queen had given permission for her brother-in-law to take the job.

Between official engagements and Snowdon's work, the couple immersed themselves in the London scene with abandon. The candle of their unique celebrity attracted every pretty moth in town – Mary Quant, Vidal Sassoon, Edna O'Brien, Peter Sellers, Rudolf Nureyev, the Beatles: they were the icons' icons. If the Fifties had been more stifling in Britain than anywhere in the world, the sense of release in the Sixties was more explosive. Ned Sherrin reckoned that the marriage compounded the belief that anyone could get anywhere: 'Exciting jobs were in anyone's reach. With a handsome face and social manner the commonest in the land could gain access to the most select circles. The way was being prepared for the barbers, models, graphic designers,

---

39 The first issue appeared on 4 February 1962. It bore the legend 'A Sharp Glance At The Mood of Britain', and showed a series of pictures of Jean Shrimpton in a Mary Quant dress, photographed by David Bailey. Inside were short profiles of 'People of the 60s' like Quant herself and the artist Peter Blake along with a professional footballer ('good-looking, shrewd, self-deprecating – a product of the New Wave'), a young industrialist ('tough, fluent, incisive') and a milkman's son from Liverpool who is quoted as saying, 'We'll never get an adequate system of education until someone takes a damn great hammer to the idea of Oxbridge as a glorified finishing school.' One of the featured People sums up the Mood: 'What do you need to be of the Sixties? First, you should be under 30. Second, you should be in tune with your times.' Margaret and Tony, admittedly, were 31, but allowances could be made for royalty.

footballers and pop singers, the new rich about to become the new fashionable.'

The same social stirrings were throwing up a variety of threats to the stability of the British Establishment, from the dissident Labour MP Willie Hamilton, campaigning for grace and favour homes to be handed over to the homeless, to the new scourge of satire, sweeping from the stage, to the magazine stands and finally to the airwaves. And there, prominent among the highly visible, brightly coloured, potential targets for the new predators, were the Snowdons.

When *Beyond the Fringe* arrived in London in May 1961, Alan Bennett, Peter Cook, Dudley Moore and Jonathan Miller, fresh from their university capers, showed a wider audience that subjects like religion, patriotism, sexual taboos and capital punishment were no longer off limits. Royalty was a rare exception. In a recent BBC interview Miller said that the royal family would have been an impossible target for *Beyond the Fringe*. 'Most of us would have imitated royalty as part of the funny stuff that any irreverent young men would have done at that time, but it simply wasn't allowed – even if we had been inclined. There were long extensions and tentacles from the Thirties world of deference which were still operative.'

Within six months *Private Eye* had staggered on to the streets. Its third issue, in November, showed a sexy girl in a Father Christmas outfit, and a speech bubble offering mock praise to the new glitterati, including Snowdon. (Soon, the *Eye* was ready to decry the Snowdons as the 'highest-paid performing dwarfs in Europe'.) A year later, *That Was the Week That Was, TW3*, swung the first satirical sledgehammer at the polite façade of television's traditional respect for national institutions and within a few weeks was transmitting a joke (told by David Frost) about the Queen, sinking along with the Royal Barge.

And now the Queen, smiling radiantly, is swimming for her life ... Her Majesty is wearing a pale blue taffeta dress with matching lace ... And Lord Snowdon has just taken a colour photograph. And what a gesture – the Band of the Royal Marines have just struck up 'God Save the Queen'.

According to *TW3*'s producer, Ned Sherrin, it was Princess Margaret herself who wondered why the royal family had been excluded from the programme's attentions. The sketch was hardly the stuff of revolution, but it came only 18 months or so after the *Beyond the Fringe* team had decided it was too risky to venture on to this territory at all. One crucial difference was the role of the Lord Chamberlain – the chief officer of the royal household – who wielded the power of censorship over stage performances, but not over television. The best (or worst) he could do was to insist that the Royal Barge sketch could not be adapted for a West End revue. The director remarked, 'It seems strange to me that millions of people can see it on television, but hundreds are forbidden to see it in the theatre.' Moreover, that edition of *TW3* received far fewer than the usual weekly crop of complaints from viewers: a mere 47, and only 36 about the Royal Barge. Three times as many people called in to express their approval, which is probably because they worked out that the Queen was not the real target: it was really about the blind, unreasoning respect in which royalty was held. The Lord Chamberlain continued to exercise his powers (reluctantly, according to Ben Pimlott) until 1968, though unfortunately those powers did not extend where they were really needed – to television.

The first few years of the Snowdons' marriage coincided with this period of transition from deference towards the royal family, to the modern free-for-all. But for the moment – even while the satirists were beginning to assail the fortress from beyond the walls[40] – the couple's reputation with the general citizenry inside reached extraordinary heights. Christopher Booker, first editor of *Private Eye* and one of the creators of *TW3* and its successors, looked back at the Sixties in *The Neophiliacs* (1969). Lord Snowdon and Princess Margaret, he wrote, were the stars of the New Aristocracy. 'The popular press was beside itself with the gay, "irreverent" guests who, it was reported, were more or less regularly received at Kensington Palace – Peter Sellers, Spike Milligan, David Hockney, Mark Boxer, Bernard Levin, Jonathan Miller, Kenneth Tynan.' Booker quotes a feature in one magazine about 'The Pacesetter Princess'; and another in the *Sunday Mirror* on 'The Little White Room' in the South London dockland where ' "Tony and Margaret" had spent happy, informal evenings away from the pomp in the early days of their marriage'. Even the *Spectator* commissioned a piece by the head of an avant-garde art gallery, full of such phrases as 'tough resilience' and 'direct but spontaneous curiosity'.[41]

---

40 The most consistently savage treatment of the royal family was still some years ahead – with the advent of *Spitting Image* in 1984.

Public obsession with the couple reached its pinnacle in 1965 with their coast-to-coast tour of the United States. From San Francisco and Los Angeles, to Washington and New York they were treated – well, like royalty.[42] The highlight was a White House reception given by President Johnson. Most Americans, though, made little distinction between Princess Margaret ('Cable Car Serenade for Madcap Meg') and other New Aristocrats, like the model Jean Shrimpton ('Now that Shrimp Look Sets New York Staring'). The trip also served to crystallise growing discontent over the extent to which the British taxpayer was subsidising their activities.

Willie Hamilton, the veteran Scottish Labour MP, was making a career for himself highlighting royal spending: Princess Margaret was his cause célèbre. For Hamilton and other critics it was obvious that the Foreign Office had been duped into paying the bills for the American tour, on the basis of a handful of spurious 'official engagements' absorbing no more than 48 hours in three weeks. The MP's book My Queen and I drips with sarcasm: 'Of course, the Princess's trendy husband, Lord Snowdon, would have to go too, with his valet.' Margaret herself was aided by a retinue of 11 including a hairdresser and two maids. 'The event was utterly typical of our Margaret's haughty lifestyle,' Hamilton thunders. 'For her the people of Britain must seem like so many milch-cows.' The total bill was £30,000 (now £325,000), causing the Sunday Express columnist John Gordon to expostulate, 'Leaving New York after her holiday frolic among the tinsel princes and princesses of Hollywood, Princess Margaret said: "We hope we can come back again." Before the next time comes, I hope I won't be considered discourteous or disloyal if I ask: "Who paid for this fantastic tour?" For fantastic it certainly was.'

The left-wing press was openly dubious by now about the ratio between public works and private pleasure in the Princess's programme. This appeared in the New Statesman: 'Some members of the Government, I hear, feel that the Snowdons ought to be given a straight choice between being royal – with all the duties and obligations this

---

41 Elsewhere in his book the same author notes a defining feature of the New Aristocracy as their rejection of 'fuss' and 'ceremony': Tony, for instance, was 'impatient with pomp'. Another common factor was their highly professional attitude to their work. Thus Snowdon ran his life on 'pure, high-octane, nervous energy, rattling leisure into work and work into leisure'.

42 Buckingham Palace drew huge crowds in the same month – but the screaming youngsters were not interested in the Queen or the Duke: the Beatles were due to receive their MBEs. The occasion marked another dipping of a royal toe into the celebrity pool.

implies – or accepting a strictly private status. I've little doubt that the second would be in the best interests of the royal family as a whole.[43] Even the Establishment *Sunday Telegraph* joined in with a more measured piece about the 'ambiguities' of the visit. As so often, it was Princess Margaret and her husband who had tempted the dissidents to new acts of boldness.

This was a critical period, as a prescient book called *The Royals*, published in 1966, made clear.

> *In a world which is bubbling with pink-scented, synthetic heroes and heroines, 'pop' stars, screen and TV idols, all avid for the headlines, their images pressured into public notice by powerful publicity machines, the Queen, and the Royals she represents, face a problem which is not easy to solve. How far can they concede to the demands of an age dedicated to advertising and public relations … and still retain the aura of majesty and mystique which has, until now, always clung to royalty in this country? To what extent can they permit themselves to compete with the popular idols of the day, when they know that the popular idols are here today and gone tomorrow, and are as good only as their next film, play or song, whereas the Royals are here for good?*

The authors, Leonard Moseley and Robert Haswell, laid much of the blame at the door of the Palace and staff who know 'as much about public relations as a Hottentot'.

Christopher Booker's *The Neophiliacs* ends in 1968 – year of student revolution and political assassination, by which time 'Tony's and Margaret's' marriage was also a war zone.[44] Her biographers have now reached a measure of agreement that her first brief affair, with one of her daughter's godfathers, Anthony Barton, took place in 1966 and was to some extent engineered by her husband to give him more freedom. Her second romance was with Robin Douglas-Home, nephew of the

---

43 The Earl of Wessex and his wife, Edward and Sophie, were given just such an ultimatum 35 years later. They opted for opening hospitals rather than earning a living.

44 Margaret's friends resent the way in which she has borne so much of the responsibility for the collapse of the marriage, pointing out that Tony was capable of many small acts of cruelty. One story concerned her love of play-acting: country-house weekends often included the making of short films, with Tony enjoying the role of the Great Director. Despite her pleading, he would sometimes simply refuse to let his wife take part – even when it came to a spoof advertisement for Wills' cigarettes. 'But I'm the only one who smokes,' she protested.

recently defeated Conservative Prime Minister. This brief relationship was extremely important to her, though like other painful events in her life, her feelings had to be discounted when Douglas-Home, part-time nightclub pianist and fulltime charmer, committed suicide the following year. One of her friends asked her how she had managed to look so cheerful at a public appearance on the same day. 'Oh well, Robin's dead now,' she replied.

It was at this point that the papers felt brave enough to discuss openly a possible rift in Margaret's marriage: the spur was her admission to the King Edward VII hospital in London – her first time as an in-patient. Taken with the rumours about Douglas-Home, and Snowdon's very frequent absences on photographic assignments, it wasn't hard to concoct stories of a rift. As an antidote, elaborate reunions were staged and duly reported: some readers may well have been reassured. But once again, the characters were play-acting – and the royal reporters might as well have been theatre critics. The parallels with the treatment twenty years later of Charles and Diana are compelling – certainly in terms of the pain and unpleasantness on all sides, which were supposed to remain hidden under the greasepaint. The twin tracks of a deteriorating private relationship and the need to maintain some sort of harmony in public imposed an immense strain. Diana made herself sick and grew thin: Margaret put on weight and began to look like what she was – a woman drowning her sorrows in Famous Grouse.

In 1970, the *Private Eye* cover showed the couple being driven through the crowds. She is saying, 'What's all this about us rowing in public?' He replies, 'Shut up you fat bitch and keep smiling.'

Robert Lacey, in *Majesty*, describes Margaret's emotional life at this time as being 'keyed to a neurotic pitch', so much so that psychiatric help was called in.

Marriage had not resolved but had intensified her problems of identity ... On the one hand she revelled in the irreverent company Snowdon had kept before his marriage. On the other, she insisted on royalty's right to be bowed to, or to decide when she was tired and the party must end. Snowdon, himself highly strung, declined to hide his annoyance at the demands his wife made on him. Annoyance led to unrestrained disagreement, blazing rows even, and, increasingly, to a separate social life.

For a few short years Margaret had been able to be both the fairy Princess of the people's imagination (or of the media's construction) and at the same time the real woman she wanted to be. The balancing act was so expertly executed that her rapid fall from grace was peculiarly shocking – even if everyone assumed that her station in life would provide her with a safety net. However, while she was going through her vertiginous routines, it gradually became more and more difficult for the other senior members of the family to stay out of the limelight.

In 1968 the *Daily Express* published an affectionate picture of the Queen, taken four years earlier, in bed with the baby Edward. Even though the media-hating Sir Richard Colville had finally retired as Press Secretary, the Palace protested – but with the photographs already in the hands of *Paris Match* and *Life* in the United States resistance was futile: the cordon sanitaire could protect the family no longer. Like aspiring pop stars, they steeled themselves to put on a show in front of the masses, whatever the risk to their image.

It was in this atmosphere that the televising of Charles's investiture as Prince of Wales (under Snowdon's direction) was devised. The Prince had never been heard to utter a broadcast word before he reached the age of 20 and had only rarely been seen in public: now he was to be subjected to a series of interviews, one conducted by David Frost.

Most daringly, the Queen gave permission for the making of an intimate television portrait: *The Royal Family*. The ninety-minute production, promoted by Colville's successor, William Heseltine, was partly supposed to counter the perceived dullness of the Queen's inner circle (not least by comparison with Margaret and Tony); and – with so many 'misleading' reports in the air – to meet television on its own terms. The film – which showed the Queen buying sweets at the Balmoral village shop and the Duke barbecuing sausages – was watched by 68 per cent of the population on either BBC or ITV. The reality of royal life that was supposed to be revealed now looks artificial and staged, and Margaret is reduced to bit parts in just three brief scenes.[45] But in front of that huge audience, the film undoubtedly served a purpose: it started to reshape popular perception. Unfortunately,

---

45 She follows three paces behind the Queen into a box at Covent Garden, mingles with Olympic athletes at a Palace reception (along with every other royal) and is part of the Christmas family gathering at Sandringham. Altogether, we hear her speak about 25 words. This seems a modest contribution for such a high-profile figure, but her scene-stealing propensity will have been on the minds of all concerned. It is intriguing to note that the film remains to this day under strict copyright and control. Permission to show extracts is rarely granted.

the new perception carried risks all of its own. If the royals were normal, why did they deserve abnormal degrees of respect?

Television itself did not race to exploit this breakthrough: for several years the medium remained diffident, confining anything that might be considered disrespectful to comedy programmes. The first edition of *The Goodies* in November 1970 included an elaborate sketch about the family's financial problems. Having redeemed the Crown Jewels from a pawnshop, the Duke of Edinburgh, armed with a polo stick, tries to smuggle them back into the Tower of London – and that's where Tim Brooke-Taylor, Graeme Garden and Bill Oddie come in.

Bill: So the ones in the Tower are really fakes?
Tim: That's right, they put the replicas there. But now they're back in the money, what with their television appearances and selling Balmoral to the Burtons, they decided to get the real ones out of pawn, and then they tried to put them back ... (realisation) and – and we stopped them!

The Goodies sketch drew on stories that the Palace itself, in the new spirit of transparency, had drawn to the public's attention: a year earlier the Duke of Edinburgh had appeared on the NBC programme *Meet the Press* and admitted that the royal family was heading for a financial black hole. In his jovial fashion he mused about a possible move to 'smaller premises' and wondered whether he might have to give up polo.[46] Consequently, this was now a perfectly permissible subject for debate, but the real venom on royal spending was reserved for Princess Margaret. In 1972, long political negotiations over the up-rating of the Civil List ended with the award to the Princess of £35,000 (up from £15,000 at her marriage and worth £270,000 today). In vain was it pointed out that she had fulfilled 117 public engagements in 1970: public sympathy was evaporating fast. Her purchase in 1972 of a new Rolls-Royce aroused considerable comment, not least because of

---

46 Papers released in 2002 under the 30-year rule reveal the intensity of the secret discussions between the Palace and the incoming Heath government in 1970. Palace officials fought hard to have the royal income index-linked to avoid unseemly annual disputes, but Downing Street resisted, preferring to leave the decision to a regular parliamentary vote. The same papers reveal another reason why the Queen was anxious to avoid high-profile debates on the Civil List: civil servants told Heath that the Palace was worried 'lest the Queen's popularity should diminish in her later middle age and that a review might fall just when her popularity was at its nadir'. This demonstrates an unusual level of awareness about the vagaries of public opinion in a mass-media age.

the expensive alterations she ordered: for some reason the Princess insisted that the highly polished woodwork should be given a matt finish and that the side-indicators should be removed. The following year it emerged that her latest trip to Mustique had been partly funded by the Foreign Office. All she had to do to justify a £3000 expenses bill was to carry out a short official visit to the British Virgin Islands.

To the frustration of her enemies, the mainstream British press still held back from the sort of vituperative commentary they would have liked to see. Willie Hamilton scornfully quotes the *Daily Mail* of 12 March 1973:

Here, amid the still of the tropic Caribbean night, a clear and resonant voice could be heard singing that old hit tune 'Walk On By' – to the vocal accompaniment of local islanders. The singer? A very tanned and relaxed Princess Margaret performing happily away – the high point of an impromptu cabaret at a party this week-end marking the end of her month-long stay in Mustique. The previous night the Princess – looking noticeably younger than her 42 years – had been the mainstay of a 'Jump Up', local jargon for a festive dancing party.

Hamilton, however, drew comfort from the fact that one opinion poll after another confirmed that public support for the Princess really was on the wane. By September 1973 she occupied joint bottom place (with Princess Anne) in the *Sunday Mirror*'s royal popularity table. Hamilton's book, written two years later, goes on, 'She makes no attempt to conceal her expensive, extravagant irrelevance and it is impossible to make out any honest case for her being much use to anybody.' The Princess, at the age of just 43, had entered the third phase of her media image. From the nation's favourite child, by way of international celebrity, she was becoming a reviled sybarite. Was this manifestation any more real than the others?

———

Television remained tame and unthreatening, but newspapers growled more menacingly. The picture that comes to mind is that of a school of scavenger fish, circling patiently, scenting blood but waiting for the opportunity to pounce. Margaret was not the sort of woman to back away into the shadows to avoid the threat or – like her niece, Anne – to contemplate a change of image. Was she not still the sister of the

Queen? She had fought hard and made sacrifices to hang on to her title – Her Royal Highness – and she had no intention of making concessions now. Margaret's biographer, Christopher Warwick, seems surprised that she attracted so much hostile attention, when other family members also took regular holidays: the Kents to the ski slopes and Princess Alice by slow boat to the Caribbean. Was it merely because she was newsier and had a higher profile than her more junior cousins, he wondered, or was she perceived to move in a racier, more hedonistic set? The truth is that she had set herself in a different league. She was a royal accident waiting to happen.

Margaret first met Roddy Llewellyn in September 1973, the month of the *Sunday Mirror* poll and shortly after her last family holiday with Tony: he, in turn, had already met the woman who would become his second wife, Lucy Lindsay-Hogg. Their private lives had now diverged completely, but separation was still no more than gossip and rumour in the press. Roddy, not yet 27 years old, was a drifter, a figure from the minor aristocracy who in earlier years would certainly have been despatched to the colonies 'to make a man of him'. (Indeed, one of his sporadic occupations was in Southern Rhodesia.) Within months of the meeting, Margaret had transported him to Mustique, where he mooched happily on the beach and discovered a taste for gardening. On their return (on separate flights) the relationship blossomed for a time before Llewellyn began to feel the strain: an intense, secret sexual relationship combined with the 'proper' job that had been provided for him in the City were beyond his capacity to handle. His sudden departure on the hippie trail to India (though he never got further than Turkey) left Margaret in despair and suffering a nervous collapse.[47]

At the start of the following year (1975) the *News of the World* published – on two successive Sundays – details of the breakdown of the royal marriage. Both Roddy Llewellyn and Tony's earlier lover,

---

47 This is another of those events to split the Princess's biographers. Noel Botham leads the way in asserting that she suffered a breakdown, though he goes on, 'Some people claimed inaccurately that she had taken a handful of sleeping tablets because Roddy had walked out on her.' The official version by Christopher Warwick is non-committal: 'The Princess suffered what some have described as a nervous breakdown and others as attempted suicide.' Warwick declares that no one who knew her believed she was intent on ending it all. Nigel Dempster downplays the whole incident still further: 'She took a handful of fairly innocuous sleeping-pills, the after effect of which caused her to cancel a couple of engagements.' Theo Aronson is not so sure: 'A rumour began to circulate that she had tried to commit suicide … a friend was probably right to describe it as a *cri de coeur* rather than a serious attempt to take her life.' The schedule of her brushes with illness published at the time of her death reads 'November 1974: heavy cold'.

Jackie Rufus-Isaacs, were named in the articles. Yet still there was no official acknowledgement of what was happening, despite *Private Eye*'s continual snapping at the couple's heels and the more delicate jibes of gossip writers like Nigel Dempster.

It was not until February 1976 that a decade or more of cant, deceit and dishonest reporting were finally swept away. The *News of the World*, this time, managed to smuggle a reporter on to Mustique and his photograph of Margaret and a bare-chested Roddy at a wooden table on the beach broke the last taboo. It seems completely appropriate that this snap revealing the 'truth' about the Princess's affair drew its potency from being doctored: other friends sitting at the table were simply cropped to create the Caribbean love nest of the paper's (and, no doubt, the readers') lurid imagination.

Margaret could now be painted openly as a rich woman idling away her middle age with a toyboy. Which, in a sense, she was. As she prepared to return to Britain, the press was in a ferment of excitement and moral indignation. Soon reporters and photographers were laying siege to the Wiltshire farm where Llewellyn and his friends had established an upper-class commune, offering untold sums for the inside story of sex with the Queen's sister. Lord Snowdon certainly moved quickly to occupy the moral high ground, by demanding a formal separation, and on 17 March the *Daily Express* felt bold enough to proclaim 'Margaret and Tony Set to Part', though the scoop was probably less the result of journalistic endeavour than the fact that the paper's proprietor, Jocelyn Stevens, had been advising the Queen on a separation statement.

Two days later Kensington Palace announced that by mutual agreement the couple had decided to live apart, adding that there were no plans for divorce.[48]

Who knows what damage these events caused to the standing of the rest of the royal family? And it wasn't over yet. In 1977 Willi Frischauer wrote the closing paragraph of his biography, *Margaret, Princess Without a Cause*: 'Whether on duty or on holiday, alone or in company, separated, divorced or remarried (as she may be sooner than many think) she remains a colourful character actress on the royal

---

48 The notion of 'burying bad news', familiar to a twenty-first century readership, has a long pedigree. The separation was made public on the day that Harold Wilson announced his resignation as Prime Minister – with Wilson apparently doing the decent thing by timing his news to help the Palace. In the event, the plan backfired. It was the Labour leader's departure that was buried.

stage. And liable, at any time, to steal the show.' The hint of remarriage was the only thing he got wrong. For a start, the relationship between Margaret and Roddy survived for four more years and never ceased to provoke the press, like a lure to a bird of prey.

Ben Pimlott believes that the Margaret story 'became the highway to a new, more raucous kind of press voyeurism, which combined the snobbish, the coy, and the explicitly sexual'. Competition between popular newspapers, as so often before, was one of the important factors, especially the *Daily Mail* (enduring another down-swing in its fortunes) and the *Daily Express* – with the new young tabloids greedy for titbits from the royal table.[49] In an echo of an earlier age, the *Sun* soon demanded that Margaret 'Give Up Roddy!' or be expunged from the Civil List.

The scene was set for the next huge story: finding a bride for Prince Charles. And even respectable papers now felt at liberty to speculate about his romantic intentions with all the confidence of real insiders – Davina Sheffield, Sabrina Guinness, Lady Cecily Kerr, Lady Jane Wellesley: bartered-brides-to-be is how the Prince's biographer, Jonathan Dimbleby, describes them. Charles is quoted as saying that when 10,000 people turned up to watch him go to church with Lady Jane (the Duke of Wellington's daughter), he wondered whether he should do the decent thing and propose. The Palace press secretary at the time, Ronald Allison, said that not a single day of his five-year tenure of office (1973–8) passed without a query about whom Charles would marry.

By late 1980 Lady Diana Spencer had appeared on the scene and the press excitement was stoked up in a way not seen since the Townsend days. The siege of the Spencer household drove Diana's mother to demand, 'Is it fair to ask any human being, regardless of circum-stances, to be treated this way?' A royal group, including the Queen and Prince Charles, passed a crowd of reporters and asked them to wish their editors 'a thoroughly nasty New Year'. All this, though not her responsibility, was part of Margaret's inheritance. Through her the royal family had supped with the devil – and found that the spoon was never long enough.

The republican-minded journalist Jonathan Freedland thinks that

---

49 Rupert Murdoch bought the *Sun* newspaper in 1969, and put the first Page Three girl on display the following year. The *Daily Star*'s arrival in 1978 was followed by the takeover of the *Daily Mirror* by Robert Maxwell in 1984.

Palace officials may well have believed, especially in the early years, that she could be a decoy: 'While the press attack her, they leave us alone.' What they failed to realise was that their willingness to allow Margaret to be demonised meant that a taboo had been broken. 'They should have been very alarmed,' Freedland said.

The family knew that it could no longer rely on the citizenry to behave like subjects: the residual respect in which the monarchy had been held for so long attached increasingly to the Queen herself, and the Queen alone. But Diana's appearance offered an alluring opportunity – the chance to create a new princess and a new fairy tale. The process both attracted and repelled the rest of the family: they enjoyed the reflected glory (the royal wedding was watched by a worldwide audience of 750 million), but then found they couldn't compete with the new star, any more than they had been able to match the glamour of the Margaret Set. Most of their own attempts to harness the media turned out disastrously, from the excruciating interview given by Charles on his engagement, to *It's a Royal Knockout* (1987) – the nadir of the fortunes of the minor royals as celebrities.[50] It was entirely appropriate that the puncturing of the synthetic love story was played out this time on television, as first Charles (in the autumn of 1994) and then Diana (a year later) revealed how unreal the whole charade had been – each seeking public support and understanding for his or her version of the truth. Diana's death was the sort of melodramatic climax that none of her press pursuers, in their most productive dreams, could have invented. Her trick, of course, was to die young.

***

And Margaret? She lived on to see herself obliterated from the public consciousness.

---

50 1983–4 was a bumper year for royal-media relations. Here are a few choice quotes: Princess Diana – 'I simply treat the press like children'; Princess Anne – 'When they have nothing better to do, they just make up a story'; Prince Andrew – 'The papers are "daily rags" full of the latest rubbish'; Prince Edward – 'If I have to cancel this holiday because of you people, I will make sure that you never forget it'; Prince Charles – 'If you don't lose yourselves before long, I shall lose my temper'. The best moment came when Prince Andrew, on a visit to a construction site, turned a paint spray on his tormentors, who didn't get the joke. Princess Margaret had her own contretemps – with Boy George. He claimed that she had refused to be photographed with him and had called him 'that over-made-up tart'. Boy George, in a huff, said he didn't want to talk to her anyway and – for good measure – he earned more money for the country than she did. Kensington Palace issued a furious denial, but a newspaper poll found that 65 per cent of its readers supported the singer.

As Willi Frischauer points out in his 1977 biography, the acres of newsprint expended on the exploits of the Princess and the Gardener created the impression that she, by associating with a manifestly unsuitable young man, had been responsible for bringing her own marriage to an end. The reality was much more complicated, but nobody was really interested. That must have hurt. Margaret and Tony were both determined, independent people with a hunger for life (including sex) and a strong streak of selfishness. Each was capable of awful behaviour, particularly towards the other.[51] And once the initial attraction between them had died away, they were exposed to the fact that they were living in someone else's dream. Divorce was only a matter of time, since the old solid conventions had been demolished, including society's attitude to marriage. The decree nisi was pronounced in May 1978 while Margaret was in hospital suffering from hepatitis.

A flurry of books appeared trying to make sense of her life[52] (nearly all concluding that it had been a disappointment), but once Diana was on the scene, the media – for the most part – lost interest: Margaret complained bitterly that the press made up stories about her and paid no attention to the public functions she continued to fulfil: looking at the list of her engagements for the 12 months from August 1983, the total of 164 looks impressive. But the list is deceptive. The Princess was working on only 95 days in the year – not many for someone aged 53 – and 17 of the events were packed into three days of another Foreign Office-funded trip, this time to St Kitts, en route for a month in Mustique.

From time to time rumours circulated about some new relationship, but towards the end only regular health scares brought Margaret's name to the fore. A fourth image of the Princess began to take shape – that of the sad old woman, plagued by lung damage and strokes, becoming more and more demanding of the royal niceties as she

---

51 Margaret's allies say that, once the separation had been formally announced, Tony showed no immediate inclination to move out of Kensington Palace. 'It was like a Chekhov play,' I was told by one friend. 'Margaret had a letter from Roddy saying that he was leaving, and she was so upset that she wouldn't let me go. At one point, I was sitting on a chair outside the bedroom, and Tony paced up and down without speaking, just to discomfit me. It was a nightmare.'

52 My favourite oddity is the 1979 tome *Margaret: the Tragic Princess* by James Brough, which suggests that Margaret's behaviour had an exotic cause – the disease of royal madness, porphyria. Brough did not reveal the name of the journalist who consulted the unnamed specialist who confirmed this theory on the condition of what the Americans call 'deniability'. You can see why.

became less and less central to the royal family's activities. What survived was the sense of duty to her sister: hence her outrage at the behaviour of the Duchess of York, especially the toe-sucking pictures: 'Clearly you have never considered the damage you are causing us all. How dare you discredit us like this?' Some commentators thought it pure hypocrisy, but such a thought will never have crossed her mind. She was a proper princess, daughter of a king-emperor, sister of a queen. This, in her own mind, gave her – and had always given her – the right to be naughty without losing respect. Fergie was an interloper who neither merited nor managed to earn that respect.

The most dramatic scene of Margaret's final act was played out near the end of her life – the scalding of her feet in the bathroom of her property – Les Jolies Eaux (on this occasion inaptly named) on Mustique. The sequence of events that day is like something from the pen of Roald Dahl in one of his darker moods. Her son David, to whom she had made a gift of the house to avoid death duties some years earlier, had decided to sell the place. During that final Mustique holiday in March 1999 she sat by the pool and was forced to watch prospective buyers prying and poking around her beloved home. Later, feeling miserable and low, she may well have turned to a faithful friend, Famous Grouse. At some stage she mistook the shower controls for the tap leading directly from the hot-water geyser and before she realised what was happening was standing in boiling water. The resulting damage was not merely painful and debilitating, it was a further humiliation, and she never really recovered.

As early as 1969 – and largely provoked by the Princess's antics – Bernard Levin felt able to declare that the cult of monarchy had withered and died. He drew attention to the collapse of a project to publish a magazine devoted entirely to the royal family, *Majesty*, and applauded 'the way in which a healthily sceptical maturity stole upon the country in the Sixties'. As evidence he noted that the BBC had 'ceased to give minor news of the royal family precedence in their news bulletins over major matters of domestic or international affairs'. Yet somehow the cult survived – its demise delayed by what Jonathan Freedland calls a quirk of fate. 'The Margarets and Dianas were unable to have the lasting political effect they should have done: the inevitable discarding of the monarchical idea has been delayed by about half a century because – in the Queen – the Monarchy happened to produce an exemplary, unimpeachable, doughty and reliable woman who single-handedly propped up the edifice.' Margaret, according to Freedland, was simply a warning sign that the family failed to spot.

What she herself thought about such weighty matters may never be known, even though the Princess had one private occupation that did not often feature in the gossip columns. She kept a diary. Somewhere in Kensington Palace are the volumes, written purely for her own satisfaction, that could tell a story or two. They date back as far as the war, and events like the VE-Day revels outside Buckingham Palace, but she continued to write what a friend called 'great swaths' about her experiences in later life: after a dinner party, for instance, she would jot down her impressions of the people she'd met. The friend described the Princess's style as 'funny and well-informed'. From a woman who tended to speak her mind anyway the results would be interesting.

Towards the end, Princess Margaret was merely one of the 'minor royals' who – according to the republicans on the *Guardian* newspaper – were dragging the monarchy down. Yet the paper's huge on-line poll, conducted by YouGov in December 2001, did produce a residue of support for her. Of the sample, 10 per cent thought she was 'hard-working', 6 per cent felt she was in touch with the concerns of every-day life in Britain and 13 per cent, with their rose-tinted spectacles in place, were prepared to state that she was still a 'good ambassador for Britain'. One in five, though, had no view one way or the other about a woman who used to be universally adored. Even ascribed celebrity can run out.

A telling article appeared in the *Mail on Sunday* newspaper a couple of weeks after her death. The paper reported that the Duke of Edinburgh had conspicuously failed to rush to his wife's side when her sister died. Instead, he was, apparently, disporting himself with a much younger woman at a farm on the Sandringham estate. Anyone ploughing through the two-page account of the 'Intriguing Royal Liaison' between the 80-year-old Duke and Lady Penny Romsey would have been in no doubt about its implication: the Queen's consort had, over many years, been unfaithful to his wife. He had even deserted the Queen Mother's 100th birthday celebrations to be with his 'friend'. This struck a chord with me: in November 1957 Margaret played truant from the Queen's tenth wedding anniversary ball, preferring a trip to the theatre with her friends. Then, at a time when a third of the population believed that the Queen was chosen by God, the raising of eyebrows was discreet. Now, no holds are barred. In reality the royal family, then as now, is no different from most other families, except that they have always lived in glass houses – and Margaret was the first to find throwing stones irresistible.

Her penalty was to lose all protection from media assault. On the first anniversary of her death, ITV broadcast a scabrous account of her life, portraying her as a serial adultress, who was encouraged to have a lesbian affair to avoid the risk of unwanted pregnancy.

John Yorke, executive producer of *EastEnders*, wrote an essay at the time of the Jubilee comparing the Palace to a set of soap scriptwriters. In this analysis the deaths of Margaret and the Queen Mother gave the Jubilee an extra narrative drive: 'The destruction of a dynasty followed by death, followed by rebirth, is an almost perfect narrative arc; the more hideous and painful the journey, the greater the sense of joy at its happy end. And, as with other soaps, it is at such moments that the royal family generates its biggest ratings.' Margaret might have had a wry smile at her final role as a bit-part player in the longest-running soap of them all.

An alternative view came from the writer Francis Wheen. 'It would have been better if Princess Margaret had been the older sister,' he told the *Independent*, 'because that would certainly have destroyed the monarchy.'

TWO

Charles Saatchi –
A Merchant of Dreams

Princess Margaret's adult life was a public relations disaster. The ineptitude of the Palace publicity machine – indeed its contempt for publicity – left the Princess exposed to high risk and with her royal assets largely unexploited. Ironically, the decline of her reputation coincided with the growth of an industry designed to turn fading products into best-sellers. Who knows what an adman might not have achieved with the Margaret brand?

Advertising, in coronation year, was at a low ebb. The persistent blight of rationing in the post-war years offered few enough opportunities for product promotion. But there was a bigger problem. Successive Chancellors of the Exchequer had committed themselves to protecting sterling from the rampaging dollar. One imperative was to boost exports, but in the debilitated state of the economy that meant suppressing home demand. In the circumstances it was obviously perverse for advertising to encourage consumption. Hugh Dalton's discouraging idea was that only 50 per cent of a firm's advertising expenditure would be allowable against tax. In 1948 his successor, Sir Stafford Cripps, persuaded larger firms to accept a 15 per cent reduction in their advertising budgets for a range of products including fuel, alcohol, tobacco and luxury goods.

Shops, in any case, had not changed much since the pre-war years. Local businesses, often individually run, dominated the market, served by a strong system of wholesale suppliers – so price competition and the opportunities for advertising were limited. Instead, shopkeepers built up real relationships with their customers. Our family would never have thought of being unfaithful to Holland and Barrett in Bishops Stortford, part of a small chain of grocery stores (and forerunner of the modern health-food outlets of the same name). We knew all the staff by name, particularly Bob Payne behind the meat and cheese counter. Bob and his colleagues were the main sources of advice for my mother and other shoppers, and much more reliable than any advertisement. Once my mother had made her choices (or left a list behind the counter) the goods would be assembled and delivered by van or bicycle later in the afternoon. (The restoration of home deliveries by some modern stores is a tribute to the social and commercial importance of such personal contacts – lost in the intervening years.) There was a large 'provision merchants' at the other end of the town, owned by J. Sainsbury, but we never went there.[53]

Once the food reached our home, it was stored away in the larder, a cool, dark space with meat safe and breadbin; metal gauze covered the window to keep the flies out; the floors were of red brick. The lack of a refrigerator made trips to the shops almost a daily necessity – and the complete shutdown on Sundays (not to mention early closing on Wednesday afternoons) required proper planning. Shopping, in other words, was something you had to think about, but in return you were rewarded with a range of personal and social contacts.

---

53 Bishops Stortford's shopping is concentrated on North Street and South Street, linked by Potter Street and the Market Square. Sainsbury's is one of only six companies still operating (roughly) on the same site as in coronation year. The others (based on a comparison of 1952 and 2002 town plans) are a stationers (Boardmans), the *Herts and Essex Newspaper*, the Stort Service Station, Dorringtons Bakery and an outfitters called Carr and Bury, whose owners were good friends of our family. Many of the changes revealed by the lists are unsurprising. In 1952 there were two estate agents. Now there are nine, along with a batch of building societies, charity shops, card and craft shops, and fast food outlets. The main absentees from those days are three seed merchants, a saddlery, a store selling ropes and tents, and two firms specialising in television and radios. The old Holland and Barrett is long gone, but a modern Holland and Barrett Health outlet has replaced the dry cleaners we used to use.

The United States, by this stage, had already had years of advertising experience, both on television and radio, even if it was frequently by way of programme sponsorship, rather than free-standing product promotion.[54] By 1951 there were no fewer than 100 television stations across the country and naturally they only survived by milking as much money as possible from commercials. Their techniques were unbelievably crude. Cowboy films would be faded out every fifteen minutes so that an attractive young woman could laud the benefits of a new cleaning fluid. 'Yes, it's quite an exciting film, isn't it. But before we go on, I'm sure you'll want to hear about ...' So great was the leverage of the advertisers that if necessary a comedian performing live could be dipped out, even if it meant missing his punchline.

Britain, at the time, was protected from (or missed out on, depending on your point of view) the wonders of broadcast advertising. When the House of Lords, in 1952, discussed the possibility of programme sponsorship on the BBC, as a way of injecting more money into television production, Lord Reith compared the idea variously to smallpox, bubonic plague and the black death. It was a political non-starter. One MP explained, 'We are a much more mature and sophisticated people' (than the Americans, obviously). Consequently, viewers (on the single channel) continued to watch their Westerns without interruption and, for a few more years, consumers maintained that direct connection between purchaser and product, without the filter of the copywriter's craft.

The restrictions on advertising budgets were lifted only gradually and it wasn't until 1959 that expenditure overtook the levels achieved in 1938. However, the removal of controls on hire-purchase agreements in 1954 opened the way for real growth in consumer spending. Macmillan's Conservative government, elected in 1951, had promised 300,000 new homes a year and hit the target for the first time in

---

54 In 1952 Alistair Cooke became the presenter of *Omnibus* – the first serious cultural programme on the American networks – but even this highbrow show was discreetly supported by companies like Greyhound Buses and Willys Overland Motors. Some sponsorship was more blatant. One of Cooke's contemporaries, Raymond Gram Swing, earned a fortune through the connection of his radio news programme with the General Cigar Company, while *Camel News Caravan* ran from 1948 to 1956, purveying serious news alongside regular recommendations of the eponymous cigarette. One of the stars of this sort of tie-in was Betty Furness. Not only was she the 'spokesperson' for Westinghouse Appliances on the drama programme *Studio One*, but also during three successive political conventions in 1952, 1956 and 1960. Her early appearances went out live and once she was famously unable to remove an 'easy-to-remove' vacuum cleaner hose. Westinghouse were not amused, but her fans loved her for it. Later she turned gamekeeper and became head of the Consumer Protection Board for New York State.

coronation year. This building programme spurred many people to buy things they'd never needed – or which had never been available – before. Instead of inheriting furniture and equipment in the traditional way, new council tenants were enjoying the vivid experience of creating their own homes. A television was always a high priority. Ownership of TV sets rose from 53 per cent in 1957 to 78 per cent in 1960.

The new prosperity and optimism reopened the door to the advertisers – but unfortunately for the newspaper industry, newsprint was still rationed (and remained so until December 1956). Many popular papers were still running eight-page editions and the scope for selling more ads was limited. This made commercial television's arrival in 1955 extremely timely. To begin with only 200,000 homes could receive the new services, but three new transmitters in the following year made ITV available to 60 per cent of the population and before long advertisers began to show a serious interest in the medium. The ITV network was completed by 1962, a year in which Britain came second only to the United States in its total national expenditure on advertising, though the Americans still spent almost ten times as much.

To start with, copywriters and creative teams were schooled in the written word, and their early work often sounded wooden and stilted. Nonetheless the commercials were saved by their novelty value. A pattern soon emerged: the biggest advertisers were Unilever, Beechams, Thomas Hedley (a subsidiary of Procter and Gamble) and Imperial Tobacco; Cadbury, Mars and Nestlé followed close behind. Margarine, toothpaste, detergents and cigarettes were the most familiar products on view – everyday high-volume items, given an unfussy treatment.[55]

What appealed to the advertisers was that consumers would give their undivided attention to a television ad, rather than being distracted by the welter of information on the page of a newspaper or magazine. A survey in the early 1960s, reported by Jeremy Tunstall in his book *The Advertising Man*, offers an insight into other perceived benefits of the new medium: 'Young housewives – whom many advertisers are especially keen to reach – are strongly represented among television viewers. Another important advantage of television is

---

55 In 1960, 40 per cent of all television advertising was on food and drink, 19 per cent on household items like soap and detergents, 10 per cent on toiletries and cosmetics, 7 per cent on medicines and 6 per cent on tobacco. Household appliances, radio and music equipment, and cars came to just 11 per cent in total.

that it impresses retailers and encourages them to stock the advertiser's goods. Retailers take note of a manufacturer who advertises on television because this gives him the reputation of being dynamic and up-to-date.'

Often the slogans were identical: 'Persil Washes Whiter!' The tone was generally utilitarian and unimaginative, stressing how well the item did the job it was supposed to do. A copy of the *Evening Standard* during the Suez crisis includes:

To a mother – whiteness matters ... a woman chooses Persil to keep family coloured things bright, woollens and fine things soft and new. For best results use Persil in your washing machine; it's best in it and safe for it.

Gordon's Gin ... for a reviving 'Gin and Lime': Some say 'Gimlet', some say 'Gin and Lime' – but all agree that this refreshing favourite is all the more heartening if you make it correctly ... thus: half-fill shaker with ice, add ²/₃ Gordon's gin, ¹/₃ Lime Juice, and a small dash of bitters; shake well, top up with soda water.

Teals Silicone Wax – SHINIEST FLOOR POLISH OF ALL TIME means over 47% more shine on your floors ... WITH NO HARD RUBBING.

Playtex – The bra that launched the American look. Fits and feels as if fashioned for you alone. Never before such heavenly comfort.

There is nothing fancy about the simple line drawings and informative text, no jokes or subtleties, and certainly no requirement for the reader or viewer to puzzle over the meaning. The British advertising industry was still in its awkward adolescence. Eight of the top 18 agencies (in 1962) were subsidiaries of American companies and the biggest boasted just £16 million (£200 million today) of billings.

In the summer of 1960 Charles Saatchi, aged 17, left Christ's College, Finchley in north London, with no qualifications and a taste for partying. One of his first jobs was in an advertising agency, but he hated it, probably because he was expected to perform menial tasks of the 'bra that launched the American look' type. He soon left and drifted through the next few years with no real sense of purpose.

As an avid admirer of American television programmes, it was no surprise that he should gravitate to the United States, where he absorbed the culture and, naturally, the advertisements that peppered every show. Being a boy with no intellectual pretensions, he was not offended by the low taste on display. He is said to have been strongly taken by the work of Bill Bernbach, one of the founding fathers of modern advertising and the man who made the Volkswagen Beetle one of the most recognisable brands in the world by stressing the smallness of the car in a society where big had always been beautiful. Bernbach is credited with many bons mots, too: 'If you stand for something, you will always find some people for you and some against you. If you stand for nothing, you will find nobody against you and nobody for you.'

This turned out not to be a maxim appropriate to Saatchi himself – a man who, having made his creative name with campaigns for the Health Education Council's anti-smoking drive, went on to be hailed for his promotion of Silk Cut cigarettes. One of the most extraordinary things about Charles Saatchi was the impossibility of finding out what he thought about anything – apart from a badly drafted piece of copy. Then everyone knew straight away and in terms not suitable for small children.

Charles is one of the great proselytisers for the unreality of the modern age. He and his brother Maurice took the British advertising industry by the scruff of its neck and transformed the art of persuasion into one of the driving forces of the economy; they then helped to elevate Margaret Thatcher to high office, not out of a sense of political purpose (as far as one can tell) but because – like Everest – she was there; their plans for world domination of the service sector were breathtaking, but turned out to be based on financial smoke and mirrors; and, as a sideline, Charles became one of the key figures in the development of modern art, but in such a whimsical and unpredictable way that no one can be quite sure if he himself always knew what he was doing. His own view, as expressed to the New York Times, is that his character is profoundly uncomplicated: 'There are no hidden depths.' Even that statement begs not to be taken at face value.

In his personal behaviour, too, Charles Saatchi seems to have cultivated the sense of being not quite real. By deciding not to meet clients, never to attend board meetings and not to accept interview requests, he gradually became an insubstantial figure – like one of those mad movie scientists who invents an invisibility potion and can only be seen when he lights a cigarette.[56] A copyrighter called Tony Brignull, writing in the *Guardian*, reckoned that Saatchi's hermit-like behaviour was 'not shyness alone, but calculated to preserve the value of his currency: the less they see, the more they value.'[57] But one of the Saatchis' biographers, Ivan Fallon, takes a different view about the level of premeditation involved. In his analysis, Charles was not particularly keen on meeting people, found he could get away with not doing so and only later realised that his absences could be put to positive advantage.

The air of uncertainty is compounded by the meagre number of solid facts about the brothers' background and upbringing. It was known that their parents, Nathan and Daisy, were prosperous Iraqi Jews who emigrated to Britain, but few details were ever made available. The brothers were perfectly happy for profilers to state – incorrectly – that their parents had left Iraq before or during the war, implying that they themselves were British born and bred. In fact, Charles and Maurice were both born in Baghdad. Charles was four by the time the family left Iraq for good in 1947; Maurice was a baby. The first substantial book about them – *The Saatchi & Saatchi Story* by Philip Kleinman (1987) – dealt with their origins in a single line: they were 'the middle two sons of an Iraqi Jewish businessman settled in North London'. That was true, but not very illuminating.

The full story is rather inspiring. Nathan, their father, was a successful Baghdad merchant importing textiles, mainly from Manchester, and selling them throughout the Middle East. But he had the foresight to realise, ahead of time, that sentiment in post-war Iraq was turning against the Jews. In 1946 he resolved to move himself and his entrepreneurial skills to London. He purchased wool and textile

56 Or, in the 1933 film starring Claude Rains, if his body happens to be wrapped in bandages with dark glasses to cover the eye sockets. Rains's character in the film, Jack Griffin, goes to a secluded village to continue his researches into the drug which has made him invisible. This (according to one film guide) 'subsequently arouses the curiosity of the nosy locals. As Griffin continues his experiments, he begins to suffer from drug-induced megalomania, which eventually becomes full-blown madness. He begins to terrorize the countryside – first playing pranks, and then turning to murder.' Saatchi's eccentricities developed along rather less antisocial lines – like pretending to be the cleaner polishing partitions, in order to avoid coming face to face with a client. And the nearest he came to murder was throwing a chair at his brother during an office row.

57 This is quoted by Rita Hatton and John A. Walker in their polemical pamphlet *Supercollector – a critique of Charles Saatchi*. Not many art collectors can have provoked such an elaborate investigation: it reminds me of the sort of documents produced during periods of internecine feuding within the old Labour Party – only much more elegantly presented.

mills in Britain to form the basis of a new business, and found a home in Hampstead, before returning to collect Daisy and the children. They left Baghdad shortly before the introduction of stringent anti-Jewish laws. If they'd waited two more years, all their assets would have been confiscated.

In Britain, Nathan's business had its ups and downs, but by 1954 he was able to buy a large house in Highgate where Charles and Maurice grew up. Nathan lived to be 92 and an obituary in a Jewish journal said that – despite his success – he never really shook off the loneliness of the immigrant life, nor the longing to return to his roots. He comforted himself by becoming a pillar of the Spanish and Portuguese Jewish communities in London. But he certainly provided his family with a prosperous and stable upbringing.

The sons of the family – even the oldest brother David, who was ten when he left his homeland and spoke no English – had none of their father's difficulties with assimilation. Charles's birthplace, and the disruption caused by the move to London, has never been part of what film scriptwriters might call his back-story. None of the books written about him mentions his pre-secondary schooling and the writers are compelled to pick up his undistinguished scholastic career when he was already in his mid-teens. The teachers consulted by Ivan Fallon could remember no redeeming academic feature and no interest shown by Charles in sport or any other school activities. The activities he did enjoy were not on the Christ's College, Finchley curriculum, like his passion for collecting – Superman comics and jukeboxes were two early obsessions. He loved playing cards and boardgames, too. Almost no photographs have been published of his childhood – a rare reticence in this celebrity age.

For the first few years after leaving school, Charles must have been a worry to his parents: he was a natural recruit to the Swinging Sixties, grew his hair long, wore blue jeans as soon as they hit the streets (in 1960), gatecrashed parties and drove motorbikes and sportscars. Some of the time he was unemployed, though he also attended a design college in London. This skimpy list of activities is recycled, in one form or another, by all those who write about Charles. It's all there is to cover the formative period of his life from the ages of 17 to 22.

Maurice has hardly been more forthcoming: he told a business biographer, Alison Fendley, 'I had a very nice, upper-middle-class upbringing in a very nice house in Hampstead. It was all very good and very happy, and very nice.' An uninformative masterpiece. But Maurice has an admirable record of educational achievement to speak for him – from grammar school to the London School of Economics, where he won the Sociology Prize in his final year.

No, there is something striking about the way the brothers have wished to draw a veil over their private lives and to banish all curiosity about their exotic origins. Maurice is said to have told one of their Jewish contemporaries, the broadcasting executive Michael Green, that they had escaped from 'the ghetto' and so should he. Charles reportedly tried to have a reference to his family as 'Iraqi Jews' removed from a book about the advertising industry. This bashfulness has allowed Saatchi watchers free rein to speculate on the significance of their background: perhaps the spirit of the bazaar was bred in the bone – maybe, subconsciously, they were driven by the immigrant's urge to succeed in an alien land?

It was not that they didn't get on with their parents – indeed, both boys lived happily at home until they were married, in Charles's case, when he was 29. And when Maurice and he were rich, they established a synagogue in honour of Nathan and Daisy, even though they themselves were not religiously inclined and both married outside the faith. Such evidence of filial devotion is understated and mostly undeclared: it's as if it suited them to emerge from nowhere as fully-fledged advertising executives.

The story of the creation of the brothers' agency Saatchi & Saatchi was, in its own way, another fairy tale, and like all good fairy tales it has grown and developed in the telling, embellished with fascinating and sometimes fictitious details. The first brass plate bearing the company name was fixed outside their new office in London's Golden Square in the summer of 1970.[58] The name gave the enterprise a head start: 'Saatchi', the Iraqi word for watchmaker, was distinctive in its own right, but it had also become well-known in the advertising business – thanks to a subtle programme of self-promotion carried out by Charles.

---

58 One of the main claims to fame of Golden Square was as the focus of the cholera epidemic of 1854. The epidemiological studies of Dr John Snow identified the Broad Street water pump as the source of infected water and led to great improvements in public health. Surely no one could equate the spread of advertising in the past three decades with the blight of a disease like cholera.

He had finally settled down to a proper job in 1965, taken on by an American-owned agency as a junior copywriter. The atmosphere, according to one of his colleagues, was uninspiring, but he found himself among young people bursting with creative energy. Their bosses proved to be allergic to some of their more radical ideas – and within a year Charles, along with his art director partner Ross Cramer, had moved on to more congenial pastures: the agency Collett Dickinson Pearce (CDP) was keener on Cramer than Saatchi, but accepted that the two men came as a team and Charles began to blossom, both creatively and as a rising star of the London scene. He favoured flashy suits, grew his dark, curly hair to gypsy lengths and drove fast cars, trading them in like library books when a new model caught his eye. By 1968 he had graduated to a Rolls-Royce Corniche.

In fact, one of the most striking campaigns conducted by the Cramer-Saatchi duo was on behalf of the Ford Motor Company – and it brought Charles an early taste of controversy. They chose to sing the praises of Ford's top model – the Executive – by comparing it with its much more expensive competitors, the Jaguar, Rover and Mercedes. This comparative advertising (a polite name for 'knocking copy') was common in the United States but frowned upon in Britain: one problem was the Trade Mark Act of 1938, which made it an offence to exploit another company's marque in an advertisement. The new breed of admen thought this restriction was ridiculous, and set about the task of pushing back the legal barriers and the industry's own codes of self-regulation. Wasn't it obvious that the comparative merit of similar products was exactly what prospective purchasers needed to know? An advertiser's duty was to his client, not to the objective truth. Like a barrister, his task was always to make the best of the case on offer, often weaving fantasy from humble reality. In that respect deriding the opposition was just another weapon in the copywriter's armoury.

The sort of audacity displayed by Saatchi and Cramer, combined with a fresh approach to the artistic possibilities of the advertisement, soon boosted their bargaining power. Within a year or so at CDP, Saatchi asked for – and was awarded – a 150 per cent pay rise to £9000 (now worth about £90,000). He was still only 24 years old. Living at home, and with few expenses apart from his cars, he soon featured in the *Evening Standard* as one of the highest-earning young men in the country.

Before long, he and Cramer were emboldened to set up in business on their own, not as a full-scale agency, but as a creative consultancy. They took on a handful of like-minded young colleagues, and also developed working relationships with the film-makers David Puttnam and Alan Parker. In theory, the consultancy hired out its teams to advertising agencies, but one of its most important contracts was directly with a client: the Health Education Council. Charles was instrumental in developing a series of anti-smoking advertisements, which caused a considerable stir (and even persuaded him to reduce his personal consumption for a time – an unusual example of an adman being convinced by his own copy). One showed a picture of a stained hand being scrubbed by a nailbrush with the caption 'You can't scrub your lungs clean'. Another showed a stream of tar being poured into a saucer, demonstrating the contents of a smoker's lungs.

Cramer Saatchi started winning awards and public attention. Ivan Fallon notes that the images produced for the anti-smoking campaign gave rise to one of the handful of direct quotes given by Saatchi to a national newspaper (the *Sun*): 'Of course they're shocking. But the truth is shocking. What we did was dig out as many facts as possible about what smoking can do to you, and present them baldly, ruthlessly, clinically.' When interviewers came to meet the two men it was Cramer who did most of the talking: one writer noted that Saatchi offered only the occasional interjection 'with affable indifference'. Yet for all his laconic behaviour in company, Charles was working assiduously behind the scenes on developing his image.

The trade journal *Campaign*, given a new lease of life in 1968 by Michael Heseltine's Haymarket Publishing group, was beginning to reflect the ambitions of the industry and was quick to capitalise on newsworthy figures like Charles Saatchi. This was not just because the firm had recently taken on a new graduate trainee – Charles's younger brother Maurice. The Cramer Saatchi partnership made waves and, whenever it did so, *Campaign* was the first to know. When Saatchi had no stories about himself to sell, he passed on news or gossip about other firms, and in return was able to rely on the best possible coverage for his own efforts.[59] It was the sort of long-term

---

59 Philip Kleinman's book *The Saatchi & Saatchi Story* includes a delightful anecdote: a rumour started to circulate that the firm had insured its creative talent like a football team – and that anyone poaching a member of staff would have to pay a transfer fee. There was no evidence for this and Kleinman says it was pure invention. Naturally, the Saatchis did nothing to put matters straight.

project of which modern publicists, like Max Clifford, would have been proud. Charles was creating a myth.

When Charles and Maurice set up shop together, Ross Cramer left to pursue a separate career in TV commercials. The brothers were on their own, but with the great advantage that everyone connected with advertising, including important potential clients, knew (or thought they knew) that they were dealing with a firm at the cutting edge. In case anyone missed the point, Saatchi & Saatchi took out a full-page advertisement in the *Sunday Times*. The piece was laid out, without illustration, like a news story. It was headed 'Why I think it's time for a new kind of advertising'. How many of the 4 million readers of the paper, apart from industry insiders, would have ploughed their way through 1500 or so closely argued words is highly debatable, but as a show of bravado it was impressive. In retrospect, it doesn't seem surprising that neither brother should have put his name to the piece. It was signed instead by one of their young colleagues, Jeremy Sinclair, who had apparently had nothing whatsoever to do with its creation. *Campaign* duly obliged with a follow-up front-page story: 'Saatchi starts agency with £1 million'. This figure for their billings included the Health Education Council account and work for the Family Planning Association, featuring another attention-grabbing advertisement: the pregnant man.

The picture of a morose-looking man – his hand resting on a distended stomach – and the caption 'Would you be more careful if it was you that got pregnant?' – tickled Fleet Street's fancy. As it happens, it made no obvious difference to the sexual behaviour of boys and girls with sex on their minds. A review of the official statistics shows that the number of under-16 pregnancies rose from 7713 in 1970 (the year the advertisement first appeared) to 8825 the following year and peaked at 9702 in 1973. Ten years later the total was still over 9000. That was hardly the point. The agency had created something that had an integral value of its own, beyond the utilitarian purpose for which the clients had paid. It was on a higher plane of reality than the earnest public health workers could have hoped to achieve with their own efforts.

News of the pregnant man spread far and wide, even earning a cherished spot in *Time* magazine. This unprecedented publicity re-inforced the industry view of the new agency's potential and of Charles Saatchi's creative brilliance. The fact that the ad had actually been created by one of the teams transferred from the old partnership, Jeremy Sinclair and Bill Atherton, was another minor, and irrelevant, detail. The pregnant man became inextricably linked to the Saatchi name, consolidating their grip on the industry's collective imagination.

A steady accretion of anecdotes gave the new agency the colourful appearance of a coral reef on a sterile ocean bed. Which other company would have dared to pull the 'bustling office' stunt? Hoping to snare a valuable new client, the brothers thought that important visitors might be deterred by the small size of their operation and staff were asked to invite their friends round to make up the numbers. When the scene still looked insufficiently frantic, passers-by were dragged in from the street outside on the promise of a fiver. All they had to do was look busy. The Saatchis were manufacturing illusions, and not just on billboards and television screens.

Any publicity would do. If it involved tales of Charles's febrile temper, the richness of the profanities with which he heaped scorn on hapless employees, or the physical violence (in the form of hurled chairs) meted out against Maurice, that was fine. He had every right to be impatient, his colleagues let it be known, because he was Charles – exceptional, visionary, courageous, terrible, unbearable and just plain different. (All those adjectives appear in a single paragraph of Ivan Fallon's book, used by Saatchi's friends to express their bewilderment and admiration.) You couldn't, as they say, have made it up: but you could certainly exploit it and they did. With Maurice – the consummate businessman – keeping the financial ship afloat and Tim Bell as a super-salesman (soon to become known as 'the third brother', or sometimes 'the ampersand') Saatchi & Saatchi was ready to take on all comers. Charles, who had remodelled himself with a new neat haircut, sober suits and club ties (that spiteful competitors hinted he had no right to wear), was the creative one. Practically an artist. The clients loved it.

They were operating in an industry, as the estate agents might say, with scope for redevelopment. Some 600 firms, mostly small and unknown, jostled for business, none had more than 5 per cent of the market and many were financially weak. *The Persuasion Industry*, written in 1965, describes the British advertising community as riven by chronic insecurity, and a prey to 'silliness, assertiveness and anxiety'. It goes on, 'The other fact about the advertising business which struck us repeatedly was its surprising loneliness and isolation. Just as the agencies exist at the whim of their clients, so advertising men themselves seem to form a strange inner society of their own. More than in most careers, they form a sort of self-perpetuating clique, with its own gossip, its own brand of humour, its own distinct view of life.'

The brothers seem to have been immune to these weaknesses. Over the period of Saatchi & Saatchi's gestation and infancy (1966–74), the Institute of Practitioners in Advertising reported a drop in overall employment among its members from 20,000 to 14,000. The worst year of all was 1971. All of which makes the brothers' achievements more remarkable. As Edward Heath's Conservative government stumbled into the oil crisis, the miners' strike, the three-day week and rampant inflation, the Saatchis were in expansionist mood. In 1974 they achieved billings worth £10.8 million (£64 million today) with profits of £190,000 (more than £1 million). The stock market collapse that followed Labour's election victories in 1974 marked a brief hiatus, but soon – and even though national advertising expenditure remained in decline for a decade – their business went into overdrive.

They never let themselves be deflected by mundane perceptions of reality – or what other people might think of them. Ignoring the usual niceties, Maurice would simply write to his rivals and ask if they'd like to be taken over. His hit rate may have been low and he had to put up with regular dollops of disdain from his outraged correspondents. But it didn't need many positive responses to keep the company growing, and the sense of a thrusting and dynamic operation was enhanced by Charles's carefully planted stories: one suggested that the brothers were about to buy an agency in the United States; another that they were about to set up a French subsidiary. Neither happened immediately, but the impression that they *might* have happened had the desired effect.

After a number of small acquisitions, they contrived a merger with a much larger company, Garland-Compton. This was a breakthrough. Saatchi's new partners had strong marketing expertise, a number of desirable clients including Procter and Gamble – the world's biggest advertiser – and a listing on the stock market. Logic dictated that Garland-Compton would be the dominant partner, or an equal, at least. That is certainly what its executives expected: many seem to have believed that their 70-year-old company was simply buying in a little creative talent. But after the completion of a complex financial deal Charles (nobody doubts it was he) put the story rather differently to his old friends at *Campaign*: 'Saatchi swallows up the Compton Group'. Dismayed Compton bosses cried foul, but nobody else cared. The widely accepted 'reality' was that Britain's most aggressive agency had scored a takeover coup. The formal name of the group was Saatchi & Saatchi Garland-Compton, but somehow the two last words fell swiftly into disuse.

One important outcome of the deal was that the brothers now had access to stock market funds and that in turn opened up the possibility of using their quoted shares to pursue their expansion plans. Coverage of their activities in the financial press raised their profile among clients, who flocked to the new group. For several years this combination of organic growth and acquisition seemed unstoppable and in 1979 they achieved Charles's declared (and much derided) ambition of becoming Britain's number one agency. It had been one of the quickest rises to market leadership in British commercial history. And that was only a staging post on the road to world domination. In 1986, after acquiring 37 more companies – and with the United States at their feet – they could claim to run the biggest advertising empire in the world.

Neither Charles nor Maurice had given any hint of a pressing interest in party politics when – in the spring of 1978 – they won the contract to sell Mrs Thatcher's Conservative party to the nation. As entrepreneurs, they probably resented Labour's punitive taxation rates, but the tax regime had hardly held them back in their drive for market domination.

Political advertising had been a powerful force in the United States since 1952, when the Republicans introduced the idea of saturation election advertising: one agency alone produced 49 television films and 29 radio ads, and paid for 130 station-break spots on the eve of polling day. It seemed to work. Dwight D. Eisenhower won at a canter, but it took a long time for party strategists in Britain to learn the lesson. The politicians you saw – in the Tory victories of 1951 and 1955 – were more or less the politicians you got, even if Churchill in 1951 was somewhat larger than life. It was not until the end of the decade that the Conservatives took the radical step of hiring an advertising agency. Its remit was to find ways of associating the party with prosperity and opportunity ahead of the 1959 election. This was reasonably controversial at the time: in their satirical social survey *To England with Love*, David Frost and Antony Jay reckoned it was absurd for the Tories to hire Colman, Prentis and Varley – because the party was itself no better than an advertising agency (for Government policies). 'It was like J. Walter Thompson hiring Ogilvy and Mather.'

The election result quelled the critics and persuaded some high-minded souls at Labour headquarters that they should dip a toe into this promotional pond. Until then, they had shared the disdain for advertising felt by the serial presidential loser Adlai Stevenson. In 1956, after his second defeat by Eisenhower, he growled, 'The idea that you can merchandise candidates for high office like breakfast cereal … is the ultimate indignity to the democratic process.' He had right, but not history, on his side.

The process of moving from simple messages and political talking heads to more glossy production styles was slow. Labour, in particular, relied on the voluntary contributions of sympathetic admen. There were setbacks, too. The most memorable billboard image of the 1970 campaign was Labour's derisive dismissal of 'Yesterday's Men' to characterise the Tory Party. Labour lost. Four years later, Ted Heath's Conservatives turned Harold Wilson into a puppet throwing away pound notes. The Conservatives lost.

Soon afterwards, Ted Heath stepped down as Tory leader – making way for the little-known former Education Minister, Margaret Thatcher. Despite the economic quagmire into which Labour had strayed, it was by no means certain that she could lead her party to victory. Conservative Central Office chose Saatchi & Saatchi to run their campaign: Gordon Reece, Mrs Thatcher's PR guru, had been looking for a firm that was hungry for success. As Reece explained to Ivan Fallon, 'You wanted somebody who said, God! We could get really famous if we did this properly.' Reece's Labour opposite number wrote to Callaghan, 'Significantly, in appointing Saatchi & Saatchi, the Conservative Party have moved away from the more traditional, staid advertising agencies they have used in the past, and chosen an agency which has a reputation for being aggressive, publicity conscious, energetic and creative. Their work may even be considered controversial.' If that's what the Tories hoped for, they weren't disappointed.

The relationship got off to a sticky start. No one expected Charles to attend the initial meeting with Reece and the party hierarchy: that was Maurice's job. Unfortunately, Maurice turned up late and Tim

Bell, who was to become most closely involved with the party, was away on holiday. The firm still got the contract, though. Fallon reports that when Reece visited the Saatchi offices to finalise the details (Charles being absent), Maurice accepted with the words, 'We are all Conservatives.' Political passion or pragmatic politeness? Maurice was, after all, a smooth operator touting for business. Looking back, Fallon believes that if Labour had asked first, the Saatchis would certainly have agreed to work for Callaghan. 'If anything, Charles might have been more comfortable in the Labour camp,' he told me. 'Even Maurice wasn't very political, despite having worked for Michael Heseltine.'

Revealingly, when the Saatchis asked Central Office to define the characteristics of the new Conservatism, they were told that nothing had ever been written down – or at least not in a form that an advertising man could sell. None of what would become trademark policies like privatisation, council house sales or trade union reform was yet fully formed. This was the quandary and the challenge: what exactly was the product? Between them – and making considerable use of focus groups – the members of the Saatchi team came up with a few simple concepts: freedom, choice, opportunity, minimum interference by the state. They waited for someone at Central Office to decry this crude simplification, but everyone seemed happy with it. The basic tenets of Thatcherism were laid down as much by Charles and his creative colleagues as by any political philosophers.

It had been generally assumed that Callaghan would go to the country in the autumn of 1978, but he surprised everyone by holding on until the following year.[60] It was a mistake. The union troubles of that winter of discontent offered the advertisers a wealth of new material. It had already been agreed that they would make liberal use of knocking copy. The aim, according to David Butler and Dennis Kavanagh in their review of the election, was to make people dissatisfied with the Labour government. Charles and his copywriters

---

60 I can vividly remember the September day on which Callaghan was due to speak to the TUC conference in Brighton and – we all assumed – to announce the dissolution of Parliament. As one of the BBC's political/industrial correspondents attending the conference, I was eagerly looking forward to reporting on this dramatic event. But Callaghan was working to a different script. It was a complete shock when he said he intended to soldier on – a shock probably unrepeatable in these days of spin and leak. I was to spend my next six months traipsing from one picket line to the next, as workers at companies like Ford smashed through the government's income policy. Public sector workers followed suit and I covered one of the most bizarre stories of the winter – the non-burial of corpses in Liverpool. Even the dead conspired to wreck Labour's reputation.

developed an eye-catching poster campaign: 'Educashun isn't working'; 'Britain isn't getting any better'; 'Cheer up, they can't last for ever'.

When Callaghan dropped his non-election bombshell, they began all over again – with the message 'Time for a change'. The Saatchis soon demonstrated that their knack of grabbing any passing publicity had not deserted them. One poster bearing the caption 'Labour Isn't Working' showed a queue of (purportedly) unemployed people snaking away into the middle distance. Labour protested loudly: these people weren't unemployed, they were employees of Saatchi & Saatchi! The charge could be flatly denied – because the figures portrayed were really members of Hendon Young Conservatives. The press coverage of this spat – according to Butler and Kavanagh – was worth £2 million to the Tories.[61] More than twenty years later (in 2002) a survey by *PR Week* placed 'Labour Isn't Working' at number 16 in the list of all-time great publicity campaigns.

The Saatchis broke new ground from the start, as they coaxed British politics from the Dark Ages into the bright lights of the modern media. Their first party political broadcast – trailed by tantalising titbits in the tabloid press about a 'not-to-be-missed TV event' at nine that night – had Britain going backwards under Labour: people walking backwards across Waterloo bridge, a British airliner taking off in reverse. Tim Bell's campaign films were equally highly polished. One featured the 'international prosperity race', in which our European competitors raced ahead of a British runner weighed down by taxation, inflation and unemployment. Another had a couple in the dock, found guilty of wanting better schooling for their children and a home of their own. The final film put Mrs Thatcher in front of the camera in her office.

The exercise was regarded as a creative triumph, yet audience appreciation figures gave the Conservative election broadcasts the lowest rating of the three main parties. No one could explain this, but it soon ceased to matter when Margaret Thatcher swept to victory on 4 May 1979. Saatchi & Saatchi, the firm with a hard-to-forget name, was once again associated in people's minds with (the Tory) success. Who could tell how many swing voters had been lured away from Labour by those

---

61 Reality, as this row swirled round in the media, was a flexible item. The main complainant, the Chancellor Denis Healey, had got the right idea but the wrong advert. Another Tory broadcast had indeed been shot using members of the Saatchi staff outside their Charlotte Street offices.

glossy films? Nobody cared, any more than they cared if the portrayal of the Tories credited them with a much more coherent philosophy than they really possessed. Mrs Thatcher was in Downing Street and Saatchi & Saatchi collected all the available kudos. (Lord King, the Tory-appointed chairman of British Airways, switched his company's lucrative advertising contract to Saatchi & Saatchi in 1983. Success breeds success.) In her book *The Inside Story*, Alison Fendley reports that Maurice Saatchi ascribed the firm's international expansion to the Tories. 'We owe them everything, Charles and I. Before Mrs Thatcher hired us, nobody had ever heard of us. Certainly not in America.' (When, in 2002, a panel of experts sat down to choose one significant figure to represent each year of Elizabeth's reign, Charles Saatchi was the 1979 selection.)

In the losers' camp, another professional advertising man warned Labour that they had better take heed of what had happened. It was not a question of Tory policies being sold like soap powder, but the Saatchis had produced the cohesion needed 'first to create a professional communications strategy and then to make it work'. Labour took a long time to absorb that message and lost some more elections in the process.[62] But Peter Mandelson, and the other designers of new Labour, understood it very well. Often what you have to say is less important than the consistency with which you say it.

Back in 1979 Charles doubtless bathed in the reflected glory, but he did so in private. He was nowhere to be seen when Mrs Thatcher made a visitation to the firm's offices during the campaign: and even when the new Prime Minister gave a celebration party in Downing Street, only one Saatchi was present.[63]

---

62 The Conservatives would probably have won the 1983 election with no advertising at all, but the Saatchis, once again, enjoyed the benefit of being on the winning side – as they did for the third time in 1987. This time, however, they were outshone by Labour's campaign, fell out with the party chairman, Lord Tebbit, and almost got the sack. But to their own surprise they were back in 1992 and came up with the slogan 'Labour's Tax Bombshell'. This clever suggestion of a threat to middle-class incomes did serious damage to Neil Kinnock. Soon afterwards John Major rewarded Maurice with a peerage. Charles might have received a gong, too, if anyone could ever have found him.

63 Cecil – now Lord – Parkinson was party chairman during the 1983 campaign and began to wonder if Charles really existed. When they finally met for lunch, he likened Charles to a human deer: 'charming but tentative. He keeps his eye on you until he starts to relax.' There is no record of any face-to-face Charles/Thatcher meetings. Doris, the first Mrs Saatchi, later produced a theory to explain his behaviour: 'I'd say that his extreme regard for privacy and withdrawal from the public eye has something to do with the fact that his family were immigrants, escaping persecution.'

During this period the balance of power between the two brothers was shifting: Maurice, with his corporate expertise and eye for detail, was the driving force. Charles, whose attention span was notoriously brief, was never seen at the inevitable board meetings or City presentations. He even found it hard to sit through a whole film or play. What he really liked was playing games. Chess, scrabble, poker, snooker – all shared the benefit of a defined (short) timescale and a clear outcome in which he was very often able to end up a winner. He enjoyed tennis, too, and in Ivan Fallon's description played with a ferocity out of all proportion to his skill. The idea of a slower second serve, to guard against the risk of a double fault, never occurred to him. The same sort of spirit under-lay his business ambitions, but luckily those around him, especially Maurice, were on hand to do the donkey work of putting dreams into practice.

For the four main biographers of the brothers (it's tempting to see them as modern gospel writers, with their tales of triumph, disaster and redemption laced through with parables and prayers to Mammon), amateur psychoanalysis of Charles is part of the fun. Charles's passion for collecting is a particularly fruitful area: at one end of the scale he continued to hunt for rare Superman comics, but he also had garages full of cars. This interest in assembling sets of things reached its apotheosis when he discovered modern art.[64]

The interest was fuelled by his American wife, Doris, whom he met at a copywriters' desk in the mid-Sixties and married in 1973. If she had been passionate about ceramic pots, or art deco mirrors, or postage stamps, Charles could surely have become one of the world's great dealers in pots, mirrors or stamps. But art it was, and above all (at first) the art produced by the minimalists of New York. It started with a drawing by Sol LeWitt, bought for £100 in 1970. But did he really like the works of LeWitt, Dan Flavin, Donald Judd and Carl Andre (the man whose firebricks sculpture raised so many 'Is It Art?'

---

64 Amateur analysts love this obsessive-compulsive behaviour, which is supposed to reflect a mind grappling to impose order on a threatening and confusing world. For their benefit, I pass on one of Ivan Fallon's stories: after an enjoyable night at a West End club, Charles insisted that his staff track down records of every piece of music played by the band. Some had to be shipped in from New York. Fallon also has a theory about Charles's unconventional behaviour: that he may have suffered from undiagnosed dyslexia – a condition in which problems of attention and memory, as well as temper and impatience, often figure.

hackles when it was re-created for the Tate Gallery some years later)?[65] Or did he – right from the start – sense the investment potential of a group of artists with almost no following in Britain? Was it mere chance that his entry into the art market happened to coincide with the introduction of the Times-Sotheby Index, the first explicit attempt to provide investors with a guide to the movement of prices? The index used a complex logarithmic formula to calculate the investment value of different kinds of art: perhaps Charles noted that early twentieth-century works, by painters like Picasso, Braque and Chagall, had shown one of the steepest increases: it had risen 29-fold between 1950 and 1969, compared with the Impressionists (up 17.5 times) and English watercolours (up 12 times). If money had been his motive, new American art would have looked like another exciting investment opportunity.

Many of the minimalist pieces were still comparatively cheap – compared with the longer established pop art of Andy Warhol, which already attracted huge international interest and prices to match. Saatchi's critics, like the authors of the Leninist diatribe *Supercollector*, have identified plenty of unattractive explanations for Charles's move into the art market. They quote the psychoanalyst Anthony Storr: 'Social prestige and status will accrue to any collector who may be poorly educated and associated with a trade generally held in low esteem.' And they add on their own account, 'It is a fascinating hobby for those who are not first-order creators like artists.'

The implication is that Saatchi and his wife had a premeditated plan to make money out of art and the early evidence for that is by no means clear-cut. Motives are notoriously hard to pin down. He undoubtedly tracked trends with all the assiduity of a stock market speculator – from pop art and minimalism, through photo-realism, neo-expressionism and the trans-avant-garde. As his hobby developed and grew into a serious preoccupation, he ceased to be a mere enthusiast: by his purchases – and sales – he started to influence the market in a way not matched by any other British collector. And that,

---

65 Minimalism stresses the idea of reducing a work of art to the minimum number of colours, values, shapes, lines and textures. No attempt is made to represent or symbolise any other object or experience. Flavin, for example, exploited the effects of fluorescent light when he hung a single glowing tube on the wall at about a 45-degree angle, and called it *Diagonal of Personal Ecstasy*. As for the firebricks, the secretive Andre was keen to stress the importance of the number involved: 120. 'One hundred and twenty', he explained, 'is the number richest in factors. Arithmetic is only the scaffolding or armature of my work.'

in the eyes of his critics, was his crime – that he distorted the natural development of art in this country. Among the specific charges:

1   that he bought in bulk (and without critical judgement), thereby forcing up prices artificially so that he could sell at an inflated profit at his leisure;
2   that he could ruin an artist's reputation by off-loading his work without warning;
3   that by loaning items from his own collection to public galleries in which he had an interest, he raised the profile of 'his' artists to his financial benefit;
4   that Doris wrote favourable magazine reviews of the couple's favoured artists;
5   that the Saatchi Collection became a hotchpotch of haphazard items, more like an art supermarket than a 'proper' gallery;
6   that Charles used company money to buy works of art (though Saatchi argued that the corporate purchases – some 200 works – had all been sold off by 1992, making a £15 million profit for shareholders);
7   and, finally, that he was really a bit of a philistine who treated canvases and sculptures like tins of beans. He was, in short, little more than a dealer (and that was not a compliment).

The Julian Schnabel affair was a classic of its kind.

Schnabel hailed from Texas but worked in New York, where he held his first one-man show in 1979, at around the time the Saatchis began to take an interest in him.[66] They were too late to pick up any of the works on display, but over the next couple of years they bought his output in quantity and prices started to rise steeply, towards $50,000 and beyond. By 1982, Charles had also become a leading figure in a

---

66 Schnabel is one of the subjects covered – scathingly – by the distinguished critic Robert Hughes in his collected essays *Nothing If Not Critical*: 'Schnabel is a most eclectic artist; what you see in his paintings is what he was looking at last.' While the website of DJT Fine Art describes him thus: 'Probably the most exhibited, financially successful and aggressively self-promoting American artist of his generation,' who 'emerged suddenly in the late 1970s as a leading and controversial figure within a movement labelled New Image. He produced paintings and prints, and his brash, appropriative style, which shows an awareness of Expressionism, combined huge scale, often garish colours and obscure textual reference.' He often used tarpaulin instead of canvas, and one of his techniques involved broken crockery. The website reviewer comments tartly that this was 'typical of what some critics regarded as his attention-seeking devices'. Saatchi's attention was well and truly caught.

group of high-value donors at the Tate Gallery – the Patrons of New Art. Before long, the Tate was mounting an exhibition of Schnabel's work and, by great good fortune, Saatchi was on hand to offer several pieces from his own collection – nine of the eleven exhibits, in fact. (This happy state of affairs might have produced a wry smile from Schnabel himself – a man with a lively sense of irony: he once told an interviewer, 'I do dream about art, and images come to me in dreams. I am definitely hoping to be in touch with my subconscious. I expect a call any minute.')

In the wake of the rumbling criticism that followed the Tate exhibition, Saatchi resigned his Patrons post, but Schnabel's reputation went from strength to strength. When Charles sold two of his works a decade later, they fetched record prices – over $300,000. Schnabel, in turn, was irritated to see his early efforts dispersed in this way. By the end of the exercise Charles had managed to upset almost everybody – yet from his own point of view he had done nothing wrong. He had encouraged an up-and-coming artist, enabled that artist's work to be seen by a wider public, allowed a public gallery to benefit from his generosity and sold a few pictures in order to keep his collection moving with the times. What was wrong with that?

A similar row developed over the Whitechapel Gallery in London, of which Charles was a trustee. Was it a coincidence that artists scheduled for future exhibitions should find themselves – shortly beforehand – taken up by the Saatchi Collection? Was he using his inside knowledge to stock up with works that were about to receive a blast of publicity and a consequent boost to their market value? These rumours dogged his footsteps throughout the Eighties and, in due course, he left the Whitechapel, too. There seems no doubt that the decision to establish his own gallery grew from his frustration at the way the art world seemed determined to deal with him.[67]

The allegations against him were reinforced by another (typical)

---

67 One art critic, who for obvious reasons prefers to remain anonymous, likens Charles's experiences to those of Melmotte, the Jewish outsider who tries to buy his way into London society in Trollope's *The Way We Live Now*. To start with, Melmotte makes waves by refusing to accept convention, secure in the knowledge that money speaks louder than manners. But having bought himself a seat in the House of Commons, he suffers a hideous embarrassment: nobody had warned him that MPs never rise to speak without doffing their top hats. Bemused and resentful, he accedes. That, my friendly critic suggests, is what Charles must have felt when he was forced to give up his honorary posts for failing to observe the niceties.

Saatchi oddity – his deep reluctance to talk about his collection, even after setting up his eponymous gallery in north London. It was one of the biggest private galleries anywhere and still only had room to house a fraction of the works he owned at any one time. You might have expected the owner to be intensely proud of such a space, happy to share his enthusiasm with art lovers. You'd be wrong. One art critic told me the bizarre lengths to which Charles would go to *avoid* a conversation about the works on display: 'Sometimes he was there when I arrived, a black figure in the blanched white gallery. We circled round each other, knowing that there was no way out for either of us. In desperation, he would ring the office on his mobile phone, even though it was only a few yards away, rather than be forced to strike up a conversation.' Another regular visitor said that it was much more normal for Saatchi not to be visible at all.

What could explain this diffidence? A writer who knows him better than most told me, 'I always got the feeling that he was worried about being found out. He feared that he wouldn't be able to hold his own with a serious art critic – that he might be exposed as a shallow person with no formal artistic education.' This same source, however, felt that Charles had been maligned by his enemies: 'You don't build a collection like this by accident. He has an incredible eye, and he's always feeling his way to the outer edge of where things are going. He will walk round a gallery and in a nanosecond see everything he needs to see, but he is physically incapable of standing in front of a painting and looking at it for any length of time. And he's just not interested in explaining himself.' No wonder some artists feel their work might as well be on a supermarket shelf, as he sweeps in, casts a peremptory eye across the fruits of their labour and – like some latter-day Roman emperor – signals success or failure with a flick of his chequebook before driving off in a Bentley convertible.

For the first few years of the Gallery's existence, Charles and Doris continued to concentrate on their American interests. The space was huge – three times the size of the Whitechapel. It was also highly original, built inside the shell of an old industrial unit, with the old loading dock converted into a spacious reception area. The architect (Max Gordon) retained the outline of the original building, complete with the original steelwork exposed in the roof: the walls were matt white, the floors grey. Nothing like it had been seen in Britain before and, at 30,000 square feet, there was room to display even the largest piece of minimalist art. The critic Brian Sewell may have deplored the contents as 'spiritually arid and draining to the soul', but the gallery proved an inspiration to the next generation of British artists – not just because of the unique array of iconic works, but because of the concept of the gallery itself. At various times it boasted 15 Warhols, 27 Schnabels and industrial quantities of other highly rated American work. The notion of placing modern art in redundant commercial buildings caught on quickly, and before long shops, warehouses, factories and even a power station were being given new leases of life.

Three years later, in 1988, a group of art students from Goldsmiths' College took the unusual step of organising their own independent exhibition. They called it 'Freeze' . One of their tutors, Michael Craig-Martin, says that the choice of location – a derelict site in south London – was an unspoken tribute to the Saatchi project, as were the scale and scope of 'Freeze'. Damien Hirst confirms this, in Gordon Burn's book of conversations with the artist, *On the Way to Work*: 'When I was an art student I went down to look at his space and I just f***ing wanted one. I mean, art looks great in there.'

At the time, Craig-Martin was taken aback by the brash self-confidence of his students, among whom Hirst was prominent: he sensed that they were impatient to get their work out into the market without jumping through the conventional hoops – the laborious preparation of a body of work and the thankless task of persuading a gallery to display it. They showed considerable enterprise: a meticulous mailing list, a professionally produced catalogue and some eye-catching work combined to ensure maximum attention for 'Freeze'. Hirst took the trouble to press-gang the exhibitions secretary of the Royal Academy – a sceptical Norman Rosenthal – into joining him in a long taxi ride into the wilderness south of the river. Rosenthal liked what he saw, but – to his later regret – bought nothing. Plenty of others did and this taste of commercial success left its mark on the exhibitors. Charles Saatchi himself, in one of his rare interviews some time later, declared that these young artists could be 'perceived as part of the Thatcherist legacy', with 'an entrepreneurial spirit that is very new for British artists, and indeed unique throughout the world'. He meant it as a compliment, no doubt, though it opened the artists to the criticism that they had been too ready to sell out to the art Establishment. It might look like self-help and individual initiative but weren't 'real' artists supposed to be hungry until they were old or dead?[68]

Hirst's next move, along with two others, was to open 'Building One' in a former biscuit factory in Bermondsey. At its second exhibition Saatchi arrived and behaved (according to Michael Craig-Martin) like a child in a sweetshop. He was immediately drawn to the rotting cow's head and the flies immolating themselves on an Insectocutor, which Hirst called *A Thousand Years*, and which he bought for £4000. Soon afterwards Saatchi told the *Independent* newspaper that he believed Hirst was set for great things and explained, 'His work is deeply affecting and disturbing. That usually means something.'

At about the same time he snapped up Rachel Whiteread's *Ghost*, the plaster cast of an inside-out room – its negative space. Once he had discovered what was becoming available on his doorstep, he never looked back. As Craig-Martin put it, this was the sort of original work he'd always assumed was only available overseas. Charles started to collect paintings, sculptures and installations as if they were Superman comics: naturally he was on hand when Damien Hirst needed financial help to create his vision of a shark in formaldehyde – *The Physical Impossibility of Death in the Mind of Someone Living*. He commissioned the work for an estimated £50,000, which paid for the creature to be caught and shipped from the far side of the world. It was the start of a fruitful – if fiery – relationship between the two. In Hirst's conversations with Gordon Burn, many of the underlying tensions are on display. Burn suggests to Hirst that he was instrumental in Saatchi's decision to move out of American art. 'Nah, it was wedge,' Hirst replies. 'Money. He couldn't afford it. And the market was going down. He buys cheap and he sells expensive. So that was what he did. Then he bought cheap the English and he's going to sell it expensive. That's what he does.' Was Hirst happy about that? 'I don't give a shit. He's got a fabulous space. He buys a lot, and he gets a lot of people to see it.'

By 1992 Saatchi was ready to stage an exhibition in his own gallery, and its title – 'Young British Artists' – became the banner under which Hirst and his contemporaries rallied. The shark was the star attraction

---

68 In his book *Blimey*, the artist and writer Matthew Collings offers a wry interpretation of his own: 'Part of the mythology of the Young British Artists is that they were oppressed by Thatcher's Britain and were rebels against the dominant culture. But sometimes people argue the opposite, that being enterprising and entrepreneurial and putting on luxury entertainment exhibitions in spaces that were previously warehouses but had become available because of the recession is not really revolutionary.'

and turned Hirst into an instant celebrity. Other 'YBA' shows followed, often with pieces in irredeemably bad taste: the child mannequins with penis noses, a frozen head made with the artist's own blood, the female sex organs garnished with elephant dung, the blown-up photos of topless midgets. It could have been designed as a permanent publicity drive to keep BritArt, as it came to be known, in the public eye.

At the height of his new collecting mania, Saatchi was reputed to be visiting a dozen galleries and workshops between breakfast and lunch. The works (by his standards) were mostly cheap and the market in any case was depressed by a new recession. He scoured the small ads in magazines like *Time Out* in search of artists he might have missed and was prepared to delve deep into the least fashionable corners of the city in pursuit of a bargain. Speaking a decade later, Sarah Lucas still talks with bemusement about the day that a man she had never met called at her exhibition ('Penis Nailed to a Board') and bought a number of items. A few days later a team of professional art removers in overalls and white gloves arrived to pick up Charles Saatchi's purchases. 'It was hilarious,' she says.

What was he up to? In 1992 he broke the habit of half a lifetime and actually answered some questions posed by a journalist. The *Independent* article bears the headline, 'A very private collector: Charles Saatchi, Britain's leading modern art collector, talks (but only "a little") to Dalya Alberge.' He told Alberge, firmly, that he just liked art. 'My art collecting has nothing to do with price,' he insisted. 'If I was buying for investment, I would be doing it very differently. A lot of the work I buy isn't saleable. But if I'm wearing my sensible hat, I like to feel that if I buy six works, and five prove mistakes, at least there is one that is a success.' And elsewhere in the interview, when asked about the selling spree he had undertaken after 1989, he replied, that 'the market was overheated and it was a good time to sell'.

That sounded very much like an investor – a dealer – speaking: he had a freedom to sell as he pleased, in a way that was not available to public galleries like the Tate, which are compelled to hold on to their purchases for several years. As Saatchi built up his holding of BritArt, dozens of works from his original collection were disposed of, often at a huge profit. One close observer of the art scene told me that a private operator like Saatchi had other advantages: 'A public gallery has to hold the exhibitions it has announced, even if things go wrong – they can't get the pictures they want, for instance, or transport and insurance costs are prohibitive. Saatchi can simply change what he's doing at the last moment, or cancel the event altogether.' In the early heady years of BritArt, that was rarely a problem he experienced. Each new show brought an intensification of media interest and in 1993 Rachel Whiteread became the first of the YBAs to win the Turner Prize with another monumental sculpture, *House*.

The following year's Turner Prize-giving was notable for the extra-ordinary fact that Charles Saatchi stood up in public and made a short speech: 'I'm not sure what today's young artists are putting in their porridge, but it seems to be working,' he said. 'They are pro-ducing the most striking new art being made anywhere in the universe. And if sometimes that work is tasteless and cynical and uncouth, it's because sometimes we all are.' He may have been speaking a truth he himself did not recognise. One later Turner Prizewinner has been quoted as saying, 'A lot of artists are producing what is known as Saatchi art. You know it's Saatchi art because it's one-off shockers. Something designed to attract his attention. And these artists are getting cynical. Some of them with works already in his collection produce half-hearted crap knowing he'll take it off their hands. And he does.'

Saatchi's BritArtistic progress reached a triumphant/outrageous climax with the 1997 exhibition 'Sensation', which was staged not at his own Gallery, but at the Royal Academy in Piccadilly. It was he who made the initial approach: he told Norman Rosenthal that he wanted to 'sort out' his huge collection and present its highlights to a wider audience. Nothing like this had ever been attempted before, but in the planning process it emerged that if 'Sensation' were truly to represent the best of BritArt, some glaring gaps would have to be plugged – artists like Mat Collishaw and Gillian Wearing, who had never been on Charles's shopping list. Saatchi steadfastly refused to borrow from other collectors to fill those gaps: he had to own every-thing. He had no choice but to go on a last-minute shopping spree, which included his first Tracey Emin installation – the tent bearing the embroidered names of all the people with whom she'd ever slept. He paid ten times what the work had originally cost. (Saatchi had always turned up his nose at Emin, and – before 'Sensation' – she was just as disdainful of him. Afterwards she became one of his favoured artists, and she somehow managed to overcome her principled reluctance to sell to the man who had helped put Margaret Thatcher in power and therefore, indirectly, had been responsible for the sinking of the *Belgrano*.)

Among the items ensuring sensational coverage, and the resignation of some outraged academicians, were Hirst's sliced-open animals and a portrait of Myra Hindley (by Marcus Harvey) made up from countless children's handprints, which was helpfully defaced by angry members of the public, thus guaranteeing extended coverage on television and in the press.[69]

In the construction of the show, Charles could often be seen 'padding around in a pair of antique Chinese slippers, obsessing over the details of traffic-flow and lighting', in the *Guardian*'s description. Others noted his eccentric behaviour, practically living in the gallery, oblivious to the dishevelment of his clothes or indeed anything but the inch-perfect placement of the exhibits. When the show opened, predictably, he was nowhere to be seen. But then he didn't need to be seen. 'Sensation' attracted 300,000 visitors, all of whom will have noted the show's subtitle – 'Young British Artists from the Saatchi Collection' and drawn their own conclusions from where they found themselves: inside the portals of the British art Establishment. It was, de facto, a benediction of Charles Saatchi and his achievements. It also gave solid substance to a body of work which, in the eyes of large chunks of the population (including some of the artists) wasn't art at all. And some of those in the art world saw 'Sensation' as a full-stop. RIP BritArt, 1988–97.

Saatchi didn't stop buying. He picked up Tracey Emin's unmade bed in 1999 for £150,000; the following year he paid £500,000 for the

---

69 Those unkind enough to suggest that Charles might have been instrumental in promoting his own scandals for PR purposes felt their point was proved when 'Sensation' was shipped to New York. This time it was Chris Ofili's dung-splattered *Holy Virgin Mary* that provoked a headline storm, especially when it was taken up as a cause célèbre by Mayor Giuliani. His threat to 'put them out of business' ensured that the show would gain maximum attention. Critically, however, reactions in the US were more mixed. One commentator posted a five-part indictment on the Internet of Saatchi's recipe for success: '1 massive amounts of capital, 2 clever manipulation of the media taste for outrage, 3 packaging nationalism as a brand name (e.g. Young British Artists), 4 a moribund but aristocratic economy that funnels talent into anachronistic endeavours, that is, art-making, and 5 an aesthetic of decadence unique to a fading empire that also happens to suit the taste of an enervated avant-garde.' Another accused Saatchi and the auction house Christie's, which supported the show, of 'using a publicly supported space (Brooklyn Art Museum) to raise the value of objects that offend many people who are taxed to support that museum'. And this time the publicity game backfired, when museum directors in Australia and Japan cancelled their plans to take the show, to avoid becoming embroiled in a blasphemy scandal.

Chapman brothers' vision of *Hell*; and soon thereafter he invested £1 million in Hirst's *Hymn* – based (rather too closely for comfort) on an enlarged plastic anatomical figure on sale for £14.99 in toyshops. This last featured in a follow-up exhibition to 'Sensation', entitled – anagrammatically – 'Ant Noises'. At the same time he continued to search assiduously for the next Damien Hirst or Rachel Whiteread in the lofts and warehouses of east London, sometimes with the help of 'sniffer dogs' who scoured the city on his behalf for the scent of fresh talent.

All the difficult questions remained unanswered. The historian Lisa Jardine was granted an audience after 'Sensation' and concluded in the *Daily Telegraph* that, like other art lovers before him, Charles might be doomed to be misunderstood and maligned: '... the same art experts who deplore Saatchi's influence on the art market will soon have absorbed his star finds – Damien Hirst and Rachel Whiteread – into the British Art "tradition". They will also conveniently have forgotten the crucial role played in forming that tradition by the vigorously entrepreneurial collector.'

Saatchi's backing for artists like Damien Hirst had been triumphantly vindicated, but was Hirst's celebrity achieved by him, or attributed to him by Saatchi's purchasing power? Was Charles the benign benefactor who nurtured an incipient artistic revival? Or did he create the illusion of a new artistic movement with all the wily deviousness of the adman – and with the ultimate aim of advancing his own personal interests? Should the whole thing be dubbed 'advertisingism', to borrow Matthew Collings's coinage, because it 'compresses information, making it ironic, flat, abstract and popular'?

Certainly the leading young artists had started work before Saatchi found them; a number of significant developments took place without Saatchi's involvement – like the 1995 exhibition 'Brilliant', which introduced New York to the work of the YBAs and gave BritArt an international dimension; and there were other important players, notably Jay Jopling. If Saatchi was the Supercollector, Jopling was the Supersalesman: his White Cube Gallery in St James's and its later counterpart in east London, became the focal points of the movement, while his negotiating skills helped to push the prices of top-rated artists to astronomical levels. Yet Saatchi's readiness to pay (as well as elevating the value of his existing holdings) was a vital part of the equation. In a BBC 2 retrospective of BritArt in 2002, a number of leading figures conceded that Charles Saatchi was the most important collector of their work.[70]

The cool and far from adoring assessment of an artist-critic like Matthew Collings runs as follows: 'If there were to be a leader of the YBA semi-movement, it would be Charles Saatchi, which isn't surprising since he is an advertising guy. ... Damien Hirst is a kind of rival king, or partner king, in the eyes of the public. But within the art world the perception of Hirst wavers and changes a lot, whereas the perception of Saatchi never changes – he is the ultimate power.' Hirst himself seems deeply ambivalent. 'I think he's a generous guy,' he tells Gordon Burn. 'He's generous to artists. He's a cut-throat businessman. He's childish. I love him. Child*like*. I bet as a businessman he's childish. But as an art collector, he's childlike. So that's the side I see of him.'

If anything, Hirst sympathises with Saatchi's plight. He sees his sometime sponsor as 'addicted to shopping' and 'addicted to things' – and judges that he was just unfortunate to pick art as his most important 'thing', because his desire to control it could never be satisfied. 'He's being dragged around on a leash. Art's dragging him round on a leash, and he doesn't know it. Or maybe he does know it. But there's no way he'll stop.'

For Charles Saatchi's critics, however, that interpretation is far too generous. For them, he is an arch manipulator and they produce the example of New Neurotic Realism to support their case. This name appeared in a book published by the Saatchi Gallery in 1998 and was much discussed in the press. Eventually, an NNR exhibition opened at the Gallery and much critical effort was devoted to analysing whether the works on offer really amounted to a discrete artistic movement worthy of its own '-ism'. Unkind souls decided that NNR wasn't real at all – that it was simply a way of packaging and marketing a disparate group of artists in whom Saatchi had taken an interest. In *Supercollector*, Rita Hatton and John A. Walker are adamant: Saatchi was not simply responding to what was happening in new art, he was influencing its very formation – and he had the power to invent whole

70 The excellent three-part series produced by Vanessa Engle included interviews with the entire cast list of the BritArt phenomenon – apart from Charles Saatchi. Instead, he was portrayed as a computer-game Pacman figure, his jaw opening and shutting to consume everything in sight. After watching the programmes, I heard from Engle that Damien Hirst and Jay Jopling had also refused interviews – but there was plenty of library material to cover their absence. In Saatchi's case there was almost none.

movements that went on to become part of the history of art. The second – promised – exhibition of New Neurotic Realists never took place. The movement turned out not to be real at all.

The ambivalence of the art world towards Charles Saatchi remains unresolved. Matthew Collings, whose books offer some trenchant views of the last decade's developments, accepts that, after a moderate artistic flowering of the Fifties and Sixties, featuring genuine stars like Francis Bacon, Lucien Freud and David Hockney, there had been a fallow period in Britain. To that extent the revival of interest in modern art in the Nineties – egged on by Saatchi and others – was welcome. Charles had 'innovated finding art to be glamorous instead of obscure or boring, which no one in Britain had thought of before'. But this was a very different cultural flowering. Collings describes the Fifties as an authentic period when 'authenticity was valued for itself'.

By comparison, he regards BritArt as operating in a vacuum of values, with no political, cultural or moral standpoint. In this interpretation it is an ideal celebrity activity, in which being a famous artist is a full and sufficient reason for commanding huge prices, being celebrated in high-powered exhibitions and winning the Turner Prize. 'Art', Collings told me, 'is usually a very vivid expression of the unconscious of the times, so the fact that art is hollow and playful and empty of values is not surprising: it's a product of society.' In a recent Prospect debate (with Brian Sewell) he elaborated on the celebrity theme: 'The new art's "ideas" aren't really ideas at all. It is popular because it's scandalous, and scandal is something our age finds fascinating, though in a distanced, emotionally vacant way.' And he picks on Tracey Emin as evidence of the damage that celebrity can do: 'She has become the most popular sign of the decline of something that might originally have been creative (that is, the whole YBA phenomenon) into something that is too easy. The point of art is that it should make demands on you.'

In this sense Charles Saatchi has been a powerful catalyst of the celebrity tendency in modern art. One critic pointed out that a leading BritArt figure, Sam Taylor-Wood – a photographer married to the gallery-owner Jay Jopling – had become the protégée of Elton John. What more proof was needed that contemporary art had become little more than an extension of the glamour business? And that it might well turn out to be considerably less enduring than one of Elton's hits? Taylor-Wood, who has appeared 30 times in the pages of *Vogue*, was described in one newspaper profile as having put art into the A List, but the reverse is just as true.

Saatchi's merchant instinct surely helped to instil in young artists the notion of the value of their work. They might cavil and resist (on grounds of artistic integrity), but usually, in the end, the sums of money available in the transatlantic market that Saatchi had helped to create were simply irresistible.[71] Damien Hirst put the matter simply. When Gordon Burn asked about the £1 million Saatchi paid for *Hymn*, Hirst replied, 'A million pounds ... I'd sell my f***ing granny for a million pounds. A lot of what I say is hypocritical, but I think with a benchmark of a million pounds you owe it to everyone around you and behind you to take the money.' No one can gainsay the reality of £1 million.

The Tate Modern in London has emerged as a temple to the new religion and its enormous drawing power – 5 million visitors in the first year – proves that contemporary art has been elevated to a level of public consciousness perhaps never seen in Britain before. Yet Saatchi has kept the place at arm's length. He was asked to offer some of his Hirsts on loan for the Tate Modern's opening, but refused; and the media were happy to latch on to the idea that he regarded the Tate's director, Sir Nicholas Serota, as a rival. This theory was given added weight when it emerged that Saatchi had applied for planning permission to develop the old GLC (Greater London Council) building, by Westminster Bridge, as an alternative South Bank attraction, where there would be room to do justice to the scope of his collection. For some time no one could work out whether he really meant it, or whether it was another piece of Saatchi propaganda (an echo of the old *Campaign* days), designed to annoy, to titivate or to act as a way of prefiguring some possible future reality – on the old Saatchi & Saatchi principle that saying something was true tended to make it so. Even when the north London space was closed and sold to developers, the doubts lingered until the builders moved in to the new space.

After such a career, it's small wonder that Charles Saatchi, the invisible weaver of illusions, is rarely taken at face value. When he

---

71 An artists' collective called 'Bank' used to publish a tabloid-style magazine: one issue showed a small girl in pyjamas wagging her finger at the camera. The text ran 'Last night a young six-year-old girl had a message for megabucks-advertising tycoon Charles Saatchi. Lucy Tidmans, who is dying of an incurable disease, said in a stuttering voice, "Ad Man, you're a bad man!" She may be short in years, but young Lucy's message came across loud and clear. "It's not fair that this man with all his money should dominate our visual culture,"she continued. And finally in one last heartbreaking statement, she added, "If I were going to grow up I would not like to live in such an unfair world." '

donated nearly a hundred works to the Arts Council, the unbelievers dismissed it as a clear-out of items that he no longer had room to store; when he offered pieces to the NHS (including *Hymn*), they hinted at ulterior motives and decried his lack of sensitivity;[72] and when he established a series of bursaries for London art students, they concluded that he was involved in a crude attempt to buy up the next generation of YBAs, and/or to acquire some interesting new work on the cheap. The notion of the Saatchi 'museum' on the South Bank produced another wave of cynicism. The motive was easy to find, they said: Charles was jealous of Serota's success with Tate Modern and needed to find a way of undermining him.

A mile or so downriver Serota, in a tone of weary resignation, has admitted that the Tate is jealous of Saatchi. He told the BBC that there were real weaknesses in his collection: he had to be able to justify every purchase and was always vulnerable to being outbid by a private collector. Maybe Saatchi would help out with some donations for posterity? Serota, with a smile, replied, 'I've no idea at all. Charles is wonderfully enigmatic about these things.'

Any such co-operation became less likely than ever when Saatchi launched a vicious verbal assault on the 2002 nominees for the Tate's Turner Prize. He described the work as 'pseudo-controversial rehashed claptrap' and condemned the way the Prize had veered towards what he called 'empty art'. Saatchi also told the *Sunday Telegraph* that the Turner Prize committee (chaired by Serota) 'had no idea what constituted cutting-edge art'. He was particularly upset that the Chapman brothers, Dino and Jake, were not represented on the shortlist, though that obviously had nothing to do with the fact that he had just paid £1 million for 'twenty-four hand-carved ethnographic carvings based on McDonald's hamburgers'.

These comments provided a further justification for his County Hall project, though Saatchi himself tended to offer other, more philan-thropic, motives for the move. In another of his sparse public statements he said, 'I don't want the artists I believe in having to wait until they are pensioners before the public has a chance to see their

---

72 It was felt, for instance, that a work by Carina Weidle showing decapitated chickens was not an ideal therapeutic aid; *Ointment* by Robert Wilson fared better – a still life of sausage, fried egg, mushrooms and baked beans. As for *Hymn* – by far the most expensive item on the list – the suggestion was that the row over its provenance had reduced its value sharply and that Saatchi was worried about depressing the Damien Hirst market in which he was so heavily invested.

works.' He has also acknowledged the commercial logic of setting up a site next to a popular tourist attraction like the London Eye. Nobody was in any doubt that any Saatchi gallery, even one charging for entry, would be a strong competitor for public spaces like Tate Modern.

The *Supercollector* snipers have a simple solution to Charles's monopolistic position. 'If nationalisation should ever again become popular with a Labour government, the Saatchi collection would be a prime candidate and the gallery entrance charge could then be abolished.' They shouldn't hold their breaths.

Maybe 'museum' was exactly the right word for Charles's new project: a building to celebrate the past. One argument runs that both he and Young British Art were a phenomenon of the Nineties, and that the more fashionable they became, the less substantial they seemed. By this reckoning the 'movement' suffered a grievous blow when it was taken up as part of Cool Britannia by Tony Blair's new Labour Party.[73] This was the unambiguous verdict of Ivan Massow, as he prepared to jump ship from his post as Chairman of the Institute of Contemporary Art (having already fallen seriously out of love with the Labour Party):

> *Yes, for a brief moment, concept art brought the UK a reputation for being cutting-edge (and Tony Blair duly jumped on the bandwagon, stuffing No. 10 with works by Hirst, Rachel Whiteread and Angus Fairhurst) but, having made its point, broken the mould and, for a while, raced ahead of the international arts scene, the British arts world is now in danger of disappearing up its own arse. Most concept art I see now is pretentious, self-indulgent, craftless tat that I wouldn't accept even as a gift. It is the product of over-indulged, middle-class (barely concealed behind mockney accents), bloated egos who patronise real people with fake understanding.*

And about Saatchi himself he wrote that he was 'one of the elite who have invested so much of their reputation defending this kind of art that they are unable to criticise it'.

Even for students of celebrity the rapid absorption of the BritArt stars into the cultural Establishment has been startling. Many are now rich, and just as well-known for associating with the rest of the rich

---

73 The 'new' favoured by Labour has never been formally adopted into its title. The word hangs around on the periphery, to be taken up or set aside depending on the circumstances (and the audience). 'Old' Labour figures like Tony Benn insist that it has no more substance as a movement than, say, New Neurotic Realism.

and famous – musicians, models, fashion designers and sporting stars – as they are for anything they might produce with brush, camera, cattle or the contents of waste-paper bins. This carries the obvious risk that the currency of their fame – the art that shocked and scandalised Nineties Britain – could be devalued.

Charles Saatchi may not care. He did not get where he is today by worrying about what people think about him.[74] His passion for go-karting has probably helped to relieve some irritations (if such there have been). And in any case, approaching 60, something rather remarkable started to happen to him: from time to time he was seen in public and didn't even seem to mind when his photograph appeared in the popular press. The spur for this uncharacteristic behaviour was Nigella Lawson, cook, superwoman and widow of the journalist John Diamond. Saatchi was a family friend and scrabble partner, but after Diamond's death from cancer, he and Nigella were drawn together; in due course they became what one commentator called 'a platinum couple', a celebrity pairing to outshine even the more exotic relationships of gilded London society. Gossip writers went into raptures. Rory Ross of the *Evening Standard* suggested that Nigella was not an obvious choice for Charles. 'Unlike the first two Mrs Saatchis,' he wrote, 'who are socially-marginal, low profile, cool American blondes, Nigella is a self-assertive, well-connected, raven-tressed, damask-skinned beauty.'

The first two Mrs Saatchis would surely never have tempted Charles into the pages of OK magazine, to be seen strolling on white sands, even managing a glimmer of a smile. 'Celebrities fly away to beat winter blues,' OK reports. 'Nigella, 41, looked happier than she has for months as she frolicked in the sea during a rare holiday on the paradise island of Mauritius with a close friend, advertising tycoon Charles Saatchi.' According to OK, Charles (58) too was escaping from a difficult year, marred by a messy divorce from his second wife, Kay, and 'forced to pay £1 million legal fees as the couple fought over ownership of their £100 million art collection'. The two wandered off into an Indian Ocean sunset and nobody was ready to predict whether this was real, or just Saatchi tweaking the media's tail yet again.

---

74 In his *Independent* interview of 1992, Dalya Alberge asked him whether he minded the carping of his critics. 'I don't care,' he replied. But she thought the words were spoken 'with just a little too much emphasis'.

Many observers believe that, although Maurice has always handled the business side of their working lives, Charles has never ceased to push and goad from behind the scenes. He has been the grit in the Saatchi oyster and to very good effect: through most of their lives the two men have been able to paper over any cracks between the real world and the reality they contrived to make the rest of us believe in. Only once did they fail to mind the gap and, when they fell, the fall was swift and spectacular.[75]

Striving to be the biggest agency in the world, they had taken considerable financial risks. Many of their acquisitions were made by means of deferred payments: a typical deal would be for an initial investment of $30 million, followed by a similar amount to be paid over a number of years – but only if agreed profit levels were reached. The benefit for the brothers was that staff of the new company had to strive to 'earn out' the balance of the purchase price. The downside was that in due course the huge bonuses had to be paid, which was fine – provided the parent company continued to grow. Many of the takeovers also involved rights issues of new shares – and again, while the company was on the up this presented no problems. By 1986 the group's share price had risen to a staggering £56.

But once Saatchi & Saatchi had started down this course, the commitments entered into made it impossible to turn back. And the brothers' vision of continuous growth blinded them to the warning signs. Fired by the ideas of Ted (Theodore) Levitt from Harvard Business School, they had become converted to the principle of globalisation, 'learning to operate as if the world was one large market'. In the Saatchis' case this involved not just gobbling up advertising agencies, but expanding their operations into related services, like business consultancy, direct marketing and public relations. (The 1988 annual report registered their activities under no fewer than 17 separate headings.) Until 1986 there was scarcely a blip in their astonishing progress, though they made plenty of enemies. A ruthless determination to finalise deals often meant breaking the usual codes of behaviour in Madison Avenue and there were many longing to see them come to grief. Clients, for instance, were outraged at the Saatchis' habit of

75 My edition of Ivan Fallon's book, published in 1988, is entitled *The Brothers, The Rise and Rise of Saatchi & Saatchi*. By the time the US edition was published later the same year, that seemed a touch optimistic: the American title was, *The Brothers, The Saatchi & Saatchi Story*. Before the end of the year a new UK version had to be rushed out: it had become *The Brothers, The Rise and Fall of Saatchi & Saatchi*.

spending millions to woo or pacify managers in their target companies. David Ogilvy, one of the founding fathers of the American industry, published an updated version of his *Confessions of an Advertising Man* in 1988 and, with all the finality of an Old Testament prophet, decried 'the emergence of megalomaniacs whose mind-set is more financial than creative. They are building empires by buying up other agencies, to the consternation of their clients. They have never heard of the South Sea Bubble.' He didn't need to name the guilty men.

It turned out to be a prophetic pronouncement and a series of crises loomed, which would undermine the Saatchis' aura of invincibility. Not quite a South Sea Bubble, perhaps, but a dizzy decline from grace. Important American clients began to desert them. In London they tried – and failed – to take over the struggling Midland Bank and then the blue-chip merchant bank, Hill Samuel. For many this vaulting ambition was the proof that the brothers had been taken in by their own illusions. The stock market crash of October 1987 dealt them a devastating blow. By 1989 they were issuing their first profit warnings after 18 years of continuous growth; by 1991 their share price had shed most of its value and, to make matters much worse, they had lost their number one spot; by 1993 they had dropped to number seven in the agency league table; by 1994, under extreme pressure from angry investors, the brothers had lost control of their beloved company. Charles was compelled to give up his post as lifetime president. In 23 years, depending on whose figures you believe, he had attended one board meeting, or none at all.

Reality had finally caught up with the Saatchis, but reality couldn't hold them. By 1995 they were back in business, first as the New Saatchi Agency and subsequently as M & C Saatchi. Or rather Maurice was back in business. Charles was busy with the things that Charles did, well away from where all the business was taking place. The new company's first birthday party, held at the Saatchi Gallery, attracted the Prime Minister John Major and many of his Cabinet, but not the elder Saatchi. He stayed at home, to prove that nothing had changed.

In the year 2000, after just five years' operations, M & C Saatchi overtook the old Saatchi empire in the listings league table. And in 2002 the following line appeared on the industry's website: 'Saatchi & Saatchi tops all the agencies and London tables at £52,750,000.' They were number one again.

THREE

Elizabeth and Delia – Imaginary Cooks

Delia Smith is a woman whose name is synonymous with real cooking that anyone can try – or perhaps eponymous is a better word, since 'Delia' now appears in the Collins Dictionary as both adjective and noun: 'doing a Delia' or a 'Delia dish' are now part of our cultural heritage. The *Guardian* newspaper thought the word indicated 'a style of sensible, perhaps unambitious, English cooking, proof against cock-ups'. In the introduction to one of her latest blockbuster cookbooks, Smith gives her own interpretation of the Delia effect, proclaiming a culinary crusade against the risk that we may lose 'something very precious … a reverence for simple, natural ingredients and the joy and pleasure they can bring to everyday life'.

Can this be the same Delia Smith who once published a book called *How to Cheat at Cooking*? It was her first attempt, admittedly, but as her biographer Alison Bowyer says, 'If Delia's fans were to read it today they would no doubt be aghast to see Delia Smith cheerfully advocating the use of packet sauce mixes and instant mashed potato.' ('Mash Means Smash', model Martians told us, in a memorable advertising catchphrase.) The slim volume was published in 1971. Its recipes were designed to appeal to an upwardly mobile generation that had come through the carefree Sixties, bought a flat or house, wanted to 'entertain', but didn't have the time or knowledge to do the job properly. What should they do? They should remember that 'there are more important things in life than cooking', said the 30-year-old Delia: 'The flood of cookery manuals, part-works and tele-virtuosi seem to have convinced us all that we need to be frightfully painstaking cooks.' The truth, she suggested, was that clever shopping, artful use of pre-prepared materials and judicious presentation could obviate the need for taking pains. On supermarket goods:

> *A little tarting up by you of the tinned, packeted, frozen or dehydrated product will take care of your creative instincts and probably enable you to pass it off as something you created from scratch.*

On equipment:

> *Have lots of intriguing jars for your herbs and spices ... (they'll look very phoney if they're choc-a-bloc full, so never quite fill them up) ... you must have plenty of top-drawer cook-books placed in full view (needless to say keep* this one *well hidden).*

On frozen goods:

> *Good freezer standbys are frozen potted shrimps, ratatouille (Findus) and baby onions in cream sauce (Birds Eye) – both can be poured over chops or steak to give them an edge.*

Soups were to be made by buying packets or tins and adding a pinch of creative ingenuity – wine, cream, herbs or croutons. For sheer gall, my favourite recipe is 'Baked Fish Fingers': the cook was invited to pour tinned tomatoes and mushrooms over fish fingers in a baking dish and sprinkle with cheese (though surely it would take an inert or inebriated guest not to notice the tell-tale shapes on his plate).

Whom was the book aimed at? On one hand Delia was recommending that 'most canned foods are perfectly sound for periods longer than given in the chart' and 'if you see a cheap buy in a dented can, this is safe, provided there is no sign of rust or seepage from the seams'.[76] But she also suggested a list of shops providing a mail-order service for the hostess in extremis: Harrods, Selfridges, Fortnum and Mason, and the House of Floris for 'very special home-made chocolates'. It conjured up an unlikely target readership given to hoarding damaged cans of beans while maintaining an account at a Knightsbridge store.

The confusion reflects the social upheavals of the moment: by 1971 the new freedoms had given many of the burgeoning middle classes ideas above their station (and budget). One contemporary commentator thought that – for the first time since the eighteenth century – 'the art and craft of cooking seem to the British a natural topic of conversation among civilised people'. The trouble was that even civilised people often had nothing in their experience or background to realise their aspirations.

Delia Smith, whose father had been the manager of an ironmonger's shop in Bexleyheath, understood the problem. She arrived in London from the suburbs in 1960, with no qualifications and no obvious prospects. But within two years she had stumbled into a job at an eccentric restaurant called The Singing Chef, where the chef, Kenneth Toye, really did sing (on special occasions) and celebrity guests, like the guitarist Julian Bream, would sometimes strum for their supper. Delia Smith was enthused by the French menu, and would press Toye for the recipes to blanquette de veau, coq au vin and his signature dish, omelette soufflé flambé, which she jotted down in a notebook. Toye advised her to learn the business properly, starting as waitress and washer-up. She agreed, even though she was already holding down one day job as a hairdresser and another as a food stylist and make-up artist for television commercials. The effect of this frenetic activity was her rapid absorption into Swinging London, or at least its outer circle. Her Mary Quant bobbed hairdo was a badge of membership and any charms that Bexleyheath might once have possessed quickly faded.

None of the details of her early life – birthplace, schooling, even parents – merits a place in her *Who's Who* entry. The earliest reference is to the publication of the *How to Cheat* book when she was already 30 years old. It's as if the first 29 years of her life had never happened.

---

76 Elizabeth David rarely resorted to cans, dented or otherwise. The collection of articles published in 1984 as *An Omelette and a Glass of Wine* includes a 1960 *Spectator* piece beginning, 'It isn't only the expense, the monotony and the false tastes of the food inside most tins and jars and packages which turn me every day more against them. The amount of space they take up, the clutter they make and the performance of opening the things also seem to me unnecessarily exasperating.'

In due course she took a job as a cook at a private house in Harley Street and spent her free time researching eighteenth-century English cuisine in libraries. The meals she cooked for her employers were based on books by contemporary cooks like Elizabeth David and Robert Carrier, because she was confident that they would work. (Slavish adherence to classic texts did cause one painful culinary crisis when she added – as instructed by a misprint in a Carrier menu – four tablespoons, rather than teaspoons, of chilli powder. This may help to explain her later assiduity in checking every minute detail of a dish, from ingredients to cooking times, several times over.) It was in her Harley Street garret that she wrote her first cookery column for the new *Mirror* magazine: kipper paté, beef in beer and cheesecake.

How to Cheat offers several glimpses of life in the circles in which she was moving: what to serve for pre-dinner drinks? 'Vermouth is a pretty safe bet. I'd be surprised if at least one guest didn't ask, "What is it?" so choose an example that will give you the chance to drop the name of your wine-merchant (don't say off-licence).' This was for people who wanted to pretend to a certain lifestyle – one which expressed their individuality, aspirations and self-regard – but who couldn't be bothered with the tedious business of creating an authentic culinary experience. But then in Britain, illusion and cooking have gone hand in hand throughout the post-war period.

Twenty years earlier Elizabeth David published her first volume, *A Book of Mediterranean Food*. It could hardly have been a more different publishing debut, yet it shared one characteristic with Delia Smith's *How to Cheat*: the dishes it offered were not what they seemed. For almost all her readers in 1951 the recipes were an impossible dream, using ingredients that couldn't be had for love nor money.

For a decade spanning the war, Elizabeth David had travelled, lived and worked around the Mediterranean, in Egypt, Greece, Italy and France. It was a period of romance, emotional turmoil and intense physical experience – a sharp contrast with the dreariness of the Britain to which she returned. In the freezing winter of 1946–7, bereft of coupons to buy warm clothing, she crouched in a draughty London flat and wrote down her memories of the food she had cooked and eaten in warmer times and climes. The first fruits of these labours came in the form of a series of escapist articles for *Harpers Bazaar* in 1949: one recipe for a 'Gourmet Picnic' was described by an admiring chef (quoted in the biography of Elizabeth David by Lisa Chaney) as pure fiction, since it required a range of unobtainable items – courgettes, peppers, aubergine, garlic, olive oil, anchovies, fresh pasta, almonds, raisins, garlic. 'Elizabeth made little concession to the current dearth,' Chaney writes, 'and gave only the occasional recommendation to her reader, such as "chopped chives, or the top of an onion or leek" instead of basil.'

If these magazine pieces read like romantic literature, *A Book of Mediterranean Food* was scarcely more realistic. One reviewer remarked on the author's unwillingness to make 'any ignoble compromises with expediency'. Elizabeth David herself wrote in the Preface to the 1955 edition, 'Even if people could not very often make the dishes here described, it was stimulating to think of them; to escape from the deadly boredom of queuing and the frustration of buying the weekly rations.' And in 1988, in yet another edition, she was ready to concede that the work had, in truth, been 'a personal antidote to the bleak conditions and acute food shortages. I see that it was also largely in a spirit of defiance', she admitted, 'that I wrote down those Mediterranean recipes.' So 'Turkish Stuffing for a Whole Roast Sheep', or 'Partridges Seasoned with Greek Mountain Herbs', satisfied the sagging spirit, if not the appetite.

The design expert Stephen Bayley interprets Elizabeth David's work as a vital piece of social commentary. In this context he quotes the words of the poet Kenneth Rexroth on post-war attitudes to eating out in 'an exhausted and demoralised culture':

> *How can they write or paint*
> *In a country where it*
> *Would be nicer to be*
> *Fed intravenously?*

'Mrs David's reaction to this civilisation of rissoles and beige soup', Bayley says, 'was to mouth the words lemon, garlic and oil as if they were pornography and to start on her heroic series of cookbooks which let the sun shine into a damp and dreary Britain.'[77]

But it was only after the end of rationing – and when *Mediterranean*

---

77 *Pace* Stephen Bayley, rissoles were one of my favourite childhood dishes. My mother used Fray Bentos corned beef mashed up with potatoes and parsley, and covered them in finely ground breadcrumbs. I can still recapture the smell of them cooking in her gnarled black frying pan. There were few concessions to modernity in her kitchen. The first gadget I ever saw was a patent potato peeler. The vegetables were placed in a special saucepan with a handle fixed into the lid and turning the handle rotated a set of grating arms. The operator required great manual strength and the results were patchy.

Food became one of the first cookbooks to come out in paperback (in 1954) – that Elizabeth David's ideas started to reach a wider, more practical, audience. Ironically, as Julian Barnes points out, 'by the time she was acknowledged as a defining cultural influence she had stopped writing the kind of books that made her one'. Nonetheless, works like *Italian Food* (1954), *Summer Cooking* (1955) and *French Provincial Cooking* (1960) made her (retrospectively) an icon of the new freedoms enjoyed by a more outward-looking, self-confident nation. Olivia Manning, reviewing *Italian Food*, described its potential readers as 'the New Poor' – those who would have had cooks and housekeepers before the war, but who now had to do their own cooking and shopping. Evelyn Waugh made *Italian Food* his 'Book of the Year'.

In due course the young Delia Smith would declare herself a fan of Elizabeth David because she '... seemed to epitomise my own instincts for simplicity and purity, matched with inventiveness', though she did allow herself to wonder whether David's obsession with foreign food might have contributed to the dire state of British cuisine. Thirty years later, looking back over a successful career, she upgraded her enthusiasm by several degrees. 'Elizabeth David was the biggest influence on anybody who was interested in cooking,' she said in a BBC documentary, *The Way We Cooked*. 'I just devoured Elizabeth David morning, noon and night. She was by my bed, she was in my bag in the train, wherever I was, I was reading Elizabeth David.'

Was the feeling mutual? Artemis Cooper, who wrote the authorised biography of David after her death, says that her subject decreed Delia Smith to be 'no great stylist', but someone 'whose understanding of cooking was based on solid principles and experience'. Elizabeth's friend and literary executor, Jill Norman, was not so sure: 'I don't ever remember her talking about Delia, but I think she found her boring.' Elizabeth only started to watch television in later life, Norman says, and used to enjoy sending up the TV cooks: 'She felt that you couldn't watch television and cook, whereas you could read a recipe and cook. And that television trivialised food and made it into entertainment rather than giving it a proper place in the culture.'

The two women, then, span the half-century: Elizabeth David representing the romanticised, craft traditions of the chef-as-creator – Delia Smith taking over as the champion of the television age, providing reliable recipes for the masses. Tom Jaine, former editor of the *Good Food Guide*, is intrigued by the comparison: 'What is really interesting about Elizabeth David is not her, but the reverence in which she is held. The same is true of Delia now.'

———

The ambivalence of the British, and more specifically the English, to good cooking is a commonplace verging on a cliché. But in the coronation era, at least, rationing and the absence of choice provided an excuse for the paucity of interest in raising standards.[78] As in other spheres of life, the siege mentality of the war years proved hard to shake off, despite the best efforts of a few evangelists. A London-based Frenchman, André Simon, had founded the Wine and Food Society in 1933, though its appeal was realistically limited to people of a certain social standing – those with a 'right understanding and appreciation of good food and wine'. In his comparative study of eating tastes in England and France *All Manners of Food*, Stephen Mennell reports that one of the Society's meetings was picketed by unemployed workers 'protesting at the luxury, waste and indulgence it represented'. But Simon continued undaunted on a mission to raise standards – partly for the better health and contentment of the consumer, and partly to encourage foreign visitors who, he reckoned, had always been deterred by 'the present deplorable state of the majority of country inns'.

Simon sustained his *Wine and Food Quarterly* throughout the war and in 1943 published a collection of essays from the journal under the emotive title *We Shall Eat and Drink Again*. The novelist E. M. Forster contributed an account of a journey from France back to his home country. After an early morning crossing, he settled down in the London train with a book, when a mournful cry echoed down the corridor: 'Porridges or prunes, sir? Porridges or prunes?'

That cry still rings in my memory. It is an epitome – not, indeed, of English food, but of the forces which drag it into the dirt. It voices the true spirit of gastronomic joylessness. Porridge fills the Englishman up, prunes clear him out, so their functions are opposed. But their spirit is the same: they eschew pleasure and consider delicacy immoral.

---

78 The Retail Price Index list of items considered essential in 1952 tells the story. Fresh fruit (1952): cooking apples, oranges, bananas; compared to 2002: cooking and dessert apples, pears, bananas, strawberries, grapes, oranges, grapefruit, avocado pears, peaches, organic fruit, kiwi fruit. Or bread (1952): large and small white loaves; (2002) large white loaves (sliced and unsliced) small brown loaf, large wholemeal loaf, bread rolls, pitta bread, French stick/baguette.

In furtherance of his reforming ambitions Simon started work before the war on *A Concise Encyclopaedia of Gastronomy*, which was finally completed in 1949. It is full of definitions, advice and recipes, and does not shrink from the magnitude of the task ahead – the education of an apathetic populace. Take this complaint by a contributor on the subject of vegetables:

> *The private gardener is obsessed by the photographs of the prize-winning sorts in the catalogues; the market grower selects for weight of crop and capacity to stand up to the journey to market. So we get Brussels sprouts that are but small cabbages and leeks that aim at being gate posts. The same desire for size causes vegetables to be kept back until they have passed the stage at which they should be eaten.*

After which, invariably, the monster specimens were 'boiled to death in plenty of fast boiling water'. No wonder there was so little public enthusiasm for good, healthy food. The food writer Philip Harben, soon to win fame and fortune as the first TV chef, noted in 1944 that pre-war diets for many had consisted of fish and chips, white bread, margarine (which in the 1930s had no vitamins), jam and cheap cakes. A shortage of money was one factor, he admitted, but some people ate such foodstuffs just because they liked them (better than soggy cabbage). Harben suggested that the wartime 'British Restaurants' should be perpetuated after the war as places where high-quality food would be available at communal meals. While John Fuller, another visionary quoted by Stephen Mennell, thought the Promenade concerts provided a useful model: might not a new generation of cooks inspire popular gastronomy for the masses, just as Sir Henry Wood had made music accessible to a wider public?

Such innovative ideas never took root, either because of the innate

---

79 In their satirical essays *To England with Love* David Frost and Antony Jay wrote, 'We [the English] have always felt that there was some correlation between our sterling qualities and our appalling food. For a hundred years, the abysmal boarding-school diet sent out clean-limbed, clear-eyed young Englishmen to deal with lesser breeds without the law. The Battle of Britain was won on the dining tables of Repton. Haute cuisine was for effete foreigners, hysterically obsessed with inessentials, like sex. France had Escoffier, England had King Alfred. For us, food was leathery meat, watery greens, leaden suet puddings, stewed tea, pink blancmange and tapioca. It was epitomised by the seaside boarding house waitress bending over a customer with the magic words, "Gravy, sir. One lump or two?" '

conservatism of the population, or the blight of rationing, or both.[79] It was the dogged tenacity of the bad old ways that inspired Raymond Postgate, in May 1950, to set up the Good Food Club. The Club got off to a queasy start. Readers were invited to contribute their opinions on restaurants in the columns of a newspaper – *The Leader* – which was closed down without warning soon afterwards. The operation moved to a sister title, *Lilliput*, but a new editor decided the articles and letters were not to his taste. In desperation Postgate decided to go it alone and, using the information collected by his correspondents, published the first *Good Food Guide* in 1951. Postgate's single-mindedness was remarkable. He admitted having invented a 'notional' organisation, since the Good Food Club had no premises, no subscription, no funds, no list of members and no staff. The concept, and its realisation, was in his own head. These days it would be called a 'virtual' club, the pen-and-paper equivalent of an Internet chat room. The chairman of the British Travel and Holidays Association, Sir Alexander Maxwell, provided a bracing foreword: 'The British have a reputation for being completely apathetic about food. ... The reward of apathy is to each the meal he deserves. ... Let us therefore awake anew to a proper appreciation of good food, seeing in the austerity of the times a challenge only to our ingenuity.'

In his own introduction, Postgate did not mince his words: 'For fifty years now complaints have been made against British cooking, and no improvement has resulted. Indeed, it is quite arguable that worse meals are served today in hotels and restaurants than were in Edwardian days.' He accepted that life for restaurateurs was not easy: 'Remember, in ordering your food, the particular shortages from which we still suffer. The most serious of these is the shortage of butcher's meat. Unfortunately, roasting and grilling, at which the British used to excel, call specially for butcher's meat, and innkeepers feel obliged to offer roasts and grills when they really have not got the materials.' His overall aim was to use the passion of his members (those who bought the book) to drive up standards, and the few hundred brief recommendations were intended to chivvy the restaurant trade into action:[80]

---

80 One of the most energetic recommenders was my father's old friend, the cricket broadcaster and wine buff, John Arlott. As far as I know, my father didn't play this game, but he records in his diary a lunch taken on a trip to Chelmsford in April 1952 at a hotel called the Saracen's Head: '4/- for kidney soup, fried fillet of plaice, chips; coffee.'

Blackpool – The Savoy Hotel: Luxury class hotel recently re-opened, re-equipped with care. Food and wines as good as you'd expect. Situated on the North Cliff near all that's going on in Blackpool. There's an air of aloofness and quiet luxury. Service equal to that of the pre-war days. Lunch, 5/6d, dinner 7/6d or à la carte.

Bath – Pratt's Hotel: Straightforward food; plenty of chicken to make up for unavoidable shortage of meat; eggs for breakfast, even when they're scarce; good coffee. Swiss chef.

Preston – Rowntree's Café: Preston is a desperate place for anyone who dares to want food after 7.30 p.m. This café is open until 10 p.m. The food is good, plain and well-cooked. Three-course meals from 2/6d to 5/-.

Nottingham – Victoria Station Hotel: Uninteresting surroundings, but quite a good meal – and if you're going to get in late, they'll put an appetising snack supper in your room, together with drinks (alcohol, hot milk), provided you give them advance warning.

Taunton – The Tudor House: This place received two young persons in hiking kit, sopping wet, bedraggled and impecunious looking, almost at closing time. Gave them with great pleasure soup, roast goose, sweet, coffee and dried them off.

Many of the favoured restaurants in the *Guide* boasted continental chefs – the Swiss were particularly prized. But Postgate advised those in search of a good English meal, especially outside London, to concentrate on the 'non-wine' meals: 'British cooking – so far as it has adapted itself at all to realities – is commonly intended for a country where drinks are not wine, but beer, tea, coffee and even cocoa: and that tea and coffee, through propaganda and fiscal favouritism, have been edging beer out.' The best bets for solid, reliable cooking, therefore, were breakfast and tea – high tea in the north of the country. 'Kippers, oatmealed herrings, kidney and bacon, porridge, butteries, bannocks,[81] black puddings, faggots, real marmalade – these are things you will not get outside Britain prepared as they should be prepared.' These items had one thing in common: their quality depended on the skill of the processor, rather than the talent of the chef.

81 For non-Scottish readers: Bannock – a flat oatmeal cake baked on a griddle; Buttery – a roll made with a buttery dough.

This was a deeply ingrained cultural fact of life. Stephen Mennell says that in the women's magazines of 1952 'there was little or no sign of French or any other foreign influence (save possibly a little American[82]), and still not much suggestion that readers and their families might actually *enjoy* cooking and eating'. The most exotic recipes were described as 'spicy', which was a 'cliché epithet for any dish containing virtually any flavouring beyond salt and pepper'. Small wonder that Raymond Postgate was so keen to highlight any evidence whatsoever of Continental influences at work.

The encroachment of such skills was slow and cautious, Elizabeth David notwithstanding. One entry in the 1953–4 *Guide* described the arrival of a French chef (and three female assistants) at the Corporation Hotel in Middlesborough, 'a Satanic town of steel mills' which had 'suffered gastronomically both from a tradition of grimness and from a long spell between the wars of unemployment'. Unfortunately, 'the habits of the citizens confine the chef to "very plain" meals'.

That coronation year edition does betray Postgate's guarded optimism about the progress that his readers had noticed – most spectacularly, a fall in the price of wine: 'Three years ago the great majority of hotels put 100%, or even more, mark-up on their wine-lists, and with blithe impudence asked 18/- or £1 for a common ordinaire' (more than £15 today:[83] Postgate would be depressed to know that – 50 years on – diners are still very familiar with equivalent prices for a 'common ordinaire'). In towns not covered by the *Guide*, readers were told to look for 'a clean-looking pub which has a menu outside', with an addendum for the benefit of foreigners that 'any respectable woman can go without hesitation into the Saloon Bar or Lounge of a clean English public-house and take her lunch. She need not even drink beer. Lemonades and such will be served to her with complete equanimity.'

The abiding problems were of restaurants that closed early and without possibility of reprieve, cold food and miserable service, and ersatz cream (one of Postgate's particular bugbears). Almost nothing opened on Sunday. A trip to a restaurant in 1953, in other words, was

---

82 The Wimpy, the first mass-produced American hamburger, was unveiled to a breathless British public at the Ideal Home Exhibition of 1953.

83 My recollection is that my family rarely drank wine, except at a hotel: then the usual choice was Chablis, Beaujolais or 'claret'. A hotel visit was a rarity, anyway, though my parents often went to the pubs in Bishops Stortford (none of which features in the *Good Food Guide*). Children were banned, of course, though at some point my sister and I reached the age where we could be left in the car with a packet of crisps and a bottle of lemonade with a straw.

not to be undertaken lightly or carelessly: it needed to be planned in advance – the Nag's Head at Harby in Nottinghamshire required six hours' notice of an intention to dine – and then carefully monitored. It was still common for unscrupulous chefs to brighten up their vegetables with bicarbonate of soda, and to deploy tinned and powdered items masquerading as the real thing.

In the 1955–6 *Guide*, Postgate could at last proclaim, 'Rationing is over.' But if that was a cause for celebration, club members were warned of the work that still needed to be done to stamp out bad practices for which there were no further excuses:

1   *The provision of any synthetic white substance as cream. When a 'cream substitute' is used, this should be clearly stated on the menu. I am not a lawyer, but I believe that to call such a substance 'cream' is a legally false description, but whose is the duty to enforce this I don't know, now there is no Ministry of Food.*

2   *The provision of margarine instead of butter, or a mixture of margarine and butter.*

Postgate conceded that margarine quality had improved, but gave a gutwrenching description of what happened whenever he was lured unknowingly into eating some: at three the following morning he was inevitably stricken with indigestion, with 'a stream, not of lava so much as of red-hot polish ... pouring from my tormented guts up my gullet to my mouth'.

As the decade proceeded, there were few signs of a reduction in Postgate's bile against the generality of 'British catering'. In 1957–8 he printed anonymous reports from members on 'a typical English meal': 'Soup from an American tin. Soggy steak from the Argentine. Synthetic cream and tinned Empire fruit. Tinned Coffee'. Then he capped it with a real horror he'd endured in a West Country establishment: 'Grapefruit cut in segments which were put back with all the pith left in, sour but heavily sugared. Minestrone which was some sliced vegetable in coloured water. Scampi, the Mediterranean fish but still tough and tasteless, served with "mayonnaise" poured out of a bottle into a sauceboat round the corner. Roast beef, cut thin, overcooked to brownness, lying in weak beef-extract gravy. ...' He added a vivid picture of a waiter grudgingly squeezing his sprouts so that the water drained away into the corner of the serving dish.

Postgate was still fulminating two years later, this time against the four main ways in which English chefs wrecked food: by overcooking it, failing to season it, salting and peppering it excessively and leaving it sodden in water. He demanded an end to false piecrusts, mock cream, adulterated butter, bottled mayonnaise, thin cold meat smothered in hot gravy and passed off as a roast, lousy coffee and sweaty, factory-made cheese. And he even gave way to sarcasm as he castigated the perpetrators of these misdeeds: 'The hotels concerned have not realised the war is over. This is probably wishful thinking on their part, for the war was a happy time for them. The consumer knew his place, and all a manager needed to do was to say, "Don't you know there's a war on?" at regular intervals.'

In 1961, in the *Guide*'s tenth anniversary edition, Raymond Postgate finally allowed himself a momentary burst of optimism and even a hint of self-congratulation on the achievements of his Club: 'Food in Britain is nothing like as bad as it was ten or so years ago. ...' Might people think he had gone soft? Just in case, he went on, 'but then it was intolerable in those days. There is still a lot of dreadful food served in this island, but at that time there was practically nothing else at all but dreadful food.' Egon Ronay was often prepared to be even ruder: his guide barked that 'what they do in Wales could be called gastronomic rape, except that they don't seem to derive any pleasure from it'.

It was in 1961, too, that food scientists invented a new way of aerating bread – the Chorleywood process – which ensured the dominance of the sliced white loaf in the British diet. And it wasn't until 1968 that government statisticians judged that 'a restaurant meal' was such a regular occurrence that it should become a component of the Retail Price Index.

During this decade of painfully slow progress in British gastronomy, Elizabeth David and a handful of other celebrated chefs like Robert Carrier were attempting to change public attitudes through their writing. The fact that their own influences were mainly from overseas is easily explained. As Tom Jaine, one of Postgate's successors, says, 'It's very difficult to write a book about English food that's sexy. It's difficult to tie down. England invented the steamed pudding, so we have a long tradition in puddings, but that doesn't make a very exciting book.' Elizabeth David did not do steamed puddings. The final section of *Mediterranean Food* ('A Few Sweets') contains such delights as 'Watermelons Stuffed with Blackberries', 'Apricot Soufflé' and 'Siphniac Honey Pie'.

In a collection of interviews published in 1966, Michael Bateman described this book as a devastating work, 'which burst like a firework on the post-war era of rationing' and which 'didn't even mention margarine'. At the time Bateman was writing, David was at the height of her fame and influence: he judged that she appealed on three levels – the romantic, by evoking memories of the pleasure of food, the scientific, through her scholarship and research, and the practical, because she had tested her recipes again and again to make sure they worked. She was hugely admired by professionals. In 1971 the *Good Food Guide* published a special *Dinner Party Book*, based on recipes gleaned from restaurants featured in the *Guide*. The introduction notes that one proprietor declined to co-operate on the grounds that 'he cooked most of the time from Elizabeth David, and did not wish to be accused of plagiarism'.

Despite her influence, and despite her best-sellers, she was never tempted to use television to put across her ideas. Small-screen cookery had become well-established since the 1946 debut of Philip Harben, a small round man with a spade beard and trademark stripy apron, though live programmes presented a particular challenge to the pioneering TV cooks. At the end of one show Harben went to the oven to retrieve a dish, looked up to the camera and said, 'Well, they're not quite ready yet. Goodbye everybody.'[84] The life of a celebrity chef was not especially glamorous, nor was the BBC overly generous: Harben often provided materials like meat and butter from his own ration allocation. Nonetheless, even in these early days, celebrity gave a huge boost to his book sales. 'The little box exalts people, turns them into gods. It makes graven images of them, or at least, grey flickering images,' Michael Bateman says. Harben 'became a Personality. A star, in fact.'

Stephen Mennell points out that Harben, who had a penchant for European cuisine, had to be careful not to move more quickly than his

---

84 The title of 'first television chef' is sometimes awarded to Marguerite Patten who, in later life, reflected wistfully that her stardom had come too soon: 'I launched the first food processor. I launched fish fingers. ... My husband used to compare me to Stanley Matthews – too early to reap the great big earnings.'

followers would tolerate. 'A Harben recipe for "Veal and Ham Rarebit" in 1957 proved to be a version of *saltimbocca alla Romana*, but with the sage leaves replaced with "anything sliceable" or even "that convenient sliced cheese you can buy in packets".' While 'Steak Stroganoff' was presented in an 'English reconstruction of the dish', with suspect soured cream replaced by a reliable domestic marinade of lemon juice and Worcester sauce.

But in Mennell's analysis this emerging interest in fancy foreign flavours happened to coincide with the rise of convenience foods and the introduction of the home freezer (in the early 1960s) into increasing numbers of British homes.[85] He quotes the magazine *Good Housekeeping* in 1963, which gave its imprimatur to 'boil-in-the-bag rice, rapid-cooking pasta, pizza in a bag complete with yeast, dehydrated Chinese and Indian dishes, bottled Melba sauce, garlic powder and frozen food in general'.[86] The result of this coincidence was that the gap between the era of standard English cooking (with much of the variety in the pudding course) and the age of quick food was so brief that it allowed little chance for more gastronomic methods to take hold – except among the same enthusiastic minority that had always appreciated fine food. The typically British compromise was that 'convenience foods, so often seen as undermining cookery skills and traditions ... also played a vital part in committing housewives to be more adventurous and varied in their cooking'. This shallow-rooted tradition is exemplified by *How to Cheat at Cooking*.

In the highly restricted schedules of the early television years, Philip Harben operated without much real competition, though Marguerite Patten, describing herself as a home economist rather than a cookery writer, offered homely ideas to the working housewife. In Bateman's

---

85 ... though not all homes. The thriller writer Len (*The Ipcress File*) Deighton, who also wrote a cookery strip for the *Observer*, told Michael Bateman that the fridge was something he could do without. 'The opening and shutting of the door causes fluctuations in the food temperature, one of the quickest ways of turning food bad. The best thing it can do is provide ice, and what is a tray of ice-cubes, compared with a large slab from your fishmonger?'

86 These are items I recognise from my university days in the late Sixties: there was nothing quite so satisfying as those packets of dehydrated curry cooked on the Baby Belling, which required less effort than it took to open a can of beer. The result of all these developments was to produce a generation which had absolutely no idea how to cook anything: if I'd ever bothered to ask my mother, she would have delighted in teaching me her favourite recipes – fish pie, rissoles, shepherd's pie, spaghetti Bolognese – but it took me twenty years to realise what I was missing.

Cooking People her sample recipes included 'Kippered Eggs', 'Kedgeree of Salmon', 'Country Pie', 'Cheese Flan' and 'Stuffed Prunes': Harben, by contrast, chose a range of foreign rice dishes – Italian Risotto, Chinese Fried Rice and 'Pilaffe'. The arrival of ITV in the mid-Fifties opened up new opportunities for the television chef: the fearsome Fanny Cradock, resplendent in ball gown, and her browbeaten husband Johnny, always in evening dress, helped to reinforce the principle of eccentricity among the fraternity of television chefs (and in her case snobbery and social pretension, too). The lugubrious Clement Freud was not far behind and the line of succession takes in such iconic figures as Graham Kerr's Galloping Gourmet and the charismatic Keith Floyd.[87]

Television's influence was making itself felt in other ways, too. Artemis Cooper quotes a piece by Elizabeth David on the subject of the TV dinner, which was launched with a fanfare at the Olympia Food Show of 1956. Exhibitors proudly demonstrated a plastic tray, pre-filled, 'so that the awful fag of transferring the frozen chop and two frozen veg from shopping basket to dish is eliminated'.[88]

None of this caused Elizabeth David to change her views on the broadcast media and, throughout her career, she shunned all but a handful of requests for interviews. It's not hard to see why. In 1960 she was persuaded by a friend to appear in a radio programme from Manchester to talk about her newly published *French Provincial Cooking*. Lisa Chaney describes the grisly results, after David's ill humour had been stoked up by a sandwich lunch in the BBC canteen, and quotes the remorseful friend: 'She was awful on the programme ... sounding like a bad-tempered school-ma'am and said she never wanted to do it again.'

'That was awful, wasn't it?' said David.

'Yes,' said the friend.

According to Chaney, 'Elizabeth's style of public performance did not improve with the increase of her reputation. With age it became worse.'

---

87 I loved Michael Bywater's verdict on Cradock in the *Independent Review*: 'People watched Fanny, not for the food – *surely* not for the food, the gastronomic equivalent of those frilly-skirted bog-roll covers – but for the cruelty. It was the perfect S & M metaphor: the snarling, whip-tongued domme lashing up complex creations not to delight, but to humiliate her Ganymedes.' Bywater reckons the attraction of Kerr was watching him get drunk. Or pretend to. And Floyd, whose successive series on *Food, Fish and France* broke much new ground, was quite capable of ticking off his producer or cameraman on air.

88 This trend started in America, obviously, and has continued remorselessly on both sides of the Atlantic. Robert Putnam's *Bowling Alone* says that the number of American families who regularly shared an evening meal dropped by a third in the last quarter of the twentieth century alone.

Even without television, Elizabeth David continued to sell huge numbers of books (she was one of those who attended a special Penguin event for million-selling writers), and to be in constant demand as a writer for newspapers and magazines: in this fashion she inspired others whose celebrity would depend largely on the written word, like Jane Grigson. The writer Paul Bailey came to know Elizabeth David through his friendship with Grigson and believes that both women fell into food writing almost by accident. 'Elizabeth was a failed actress who wanted to be a writer of some kind,' he says, 'and her subject just happened to be food.' This was Grigson's view, too. She told Bailey that Elizabeth 'was immeasurably better than other food writers because she was a writer first, and an expert on food second. Just as people have to discover whether they're writers or poets or biographers, she discovered she wanted to explore aspects of eating and cooking.' Stephen Mennell describes David and Grigson as operating at 'that ill-defined margin at which the gastronomic essay gradually shades into the cookery book'.

Paul Bailey detects this sense of her priorities in her recipes: 'Sometimes you get a recipe that you can do straight away from her writing, and other times you have to make that imaginative leap.' Tom Jaine agrees: 'Her recipes require a certain confidence – they're not always as straightforward as the American, stepped style.' It's hardly surprising that David should have drifted from conventional cookery books to more academic, scholarly tomes – on *Spices, Salts and Aromatics in the English Kitchen* and *English Bread and Yeast Cookery*, which struck a blow for freedom from the ubiquitous white sliced 'Chorleywood' loaf. (Jill Norman tells how Elizabeth David used to take her own bread to restaurants to avoid such delights as white sliced loaves dyed dark-brown to give the impression of wholesomeness. In the bad old days her bag might also contain a pepper mill and a nutmeg grater.)

It was while David was scouring libraries and archives to uncover the secret history of bread that Delia Smith made her first television appearance – in September 1973, 'dispensing easy-to-follow recipes in short, ten-minute bites', in her biographer's words. The *Daily Telegraph* thought she came across as 'a friendly, unaffected young housewife at home in the kitchen', the kitchen, in this case, being a superannuated weather studio in a dusty corner of the BBC Television Centre. Over the next few years she (and her publishers and agents) was to discover what benefits could accrue for someone who works hard at her writing, contributes to a range of newspapers and magazines, and is constantly present in the living rooms of potential book buyers.

Delia Smith's utilitarian approach, delivered in a no-nonsense way by a typical English authority figure (elder sister, matron, nanny, schoolmistress, mother superior) turned out to be exactly what we all needed – eternally reliable, sexually and professionally unthreatening and as efficient as every amateur cook aspired to be. Hers has never been a particularly original culinary mind. Alison Bowyer points out that 'over the years, the same recipes have cropped up over and over, albeit with minor changes or "updates". Her old standby, beef in beer [first sighted in her inaugural *Mirror* magazine column] has appeared time and time again, as have lamb in coriander and bread-and-butter pudding [ditto].' An unkind television producer was more brutal: 'She has an unerring touch to render metropolitan chic down a couple of notches for the suburbs. If shaved parmesan on rocket is "in" in a London restaurant one year, she will be doing it in her programme in year three: and so it will migrate from Covent Garden to Surbiton via Delia's good offices.' Her 2002 book (*Delia's Vegetarian Collection*) contained a meagre 25 new dishes among '250 favourites from previous collections'.

But it is possible to adopt a more positive view of Smith's working methods: I found a review which praised the fact that '... she quite simply takes a recipe, tests it until she has what she considers to be the best possible product, and then provides a recipe which is foolproof *if followed exactly* [my italics]. She teaches you little about the feel and sensation of food, and there is little encouragement to experiment in any of her books, but followed to the letter her recipes will always ensure that you eat well.' This helps to explain why a single mention by Delia Smith on TV of an unconventional item of food or equipment (cranberries, liquid glucose, pickled walnuts or an omelette pan, for instance) can drive the nation into a purchasing frenzy, as her disciples strive to follow her instructions to the letter. Bowyer says that the first mention of using glucose in a chocolate truffle torte was broadcast on 6 December 1990: within two weeks there was none to be had in Europe. The risk of using the *wrong ingredient* was simply too awful to contemplate. What would Delia say? And how could we be sure that the dish would not be wrecked by our sloppiness?

In the early 1980s Delia Smith published the three separate parts of her Cookery Course: these were amalgamated into the *Complete Cookery Course*, her definitive work, which has sold more than 1 million copies in hardback. For most of the second half of the 1980s she forswore her cookery writing and even gave up television, to concentrate on using her name to spread the word of God. Three devotional books sold substantial numbers of copies; how many professional clerics managed to contain a shiver of jealousy when they heard that Smith's *A Feast for Advent* and *A Feast for Lent* had sold 125,000 copies between them? And how many book buyers were slightly surprised to discover that they had bought recipes for salvation, rather than for beef in beer? (Though *A Feast for Advent* does include a discussion on food imagery in the Bible). She even became a Roman Catholic lay minister, with the right to take communion to people in their homes. It wasn't until 1990 that she returned to the secular world, bestowing benedictions on our kitchens with *Delia Smith's Christmas* and associated TV appearances. The two activities – Church and stove – were not as far removed from each other as they might seem, at least not in Delia Smith's mind. She told her biographer that God was in the 'warp and woof of everyday living':

He is just as interested in helping people with their cooking as with prayers, and I began to wonder if cookery were more spiritual than the spiritual.

Bowyer speculates that Smith came to believe that teaching people to cook was a mission from God and had no compunction in saying so:

To put it very simply, I think that in the whole of God's creation, part of his plan is to help people with their cooking and I'm just one little bit of that whole.

No wonder the *Complete Cookery Course* and its successor volumes, *Delia Smith's Christmas, Summer* and *Winter Collections*, were bought in quantities matched only by the Bible (500,000 copies of the last of these were sold in a week in 1995). If cookery was a metaphor for life, this was the new Holy Writ, the way things should be done. Delia herself now refers to her choice of career as a vocation. And so at the turn of the new millennium came the ultimate testament from the prophetess of simple, good food – Delia's *How to Cook*, addressed to a generation no longer schooled in home economics (any more than in divinity), a generation with a desperate need to go back to basics. In an article about *How to Cook – Part Three* she addresses her on-line correspondents as 'my faithful followers'. In the introduction she explains that the book is intended to offset the dangers of an age of plenty in which no thought or effort is required of the consumer. She bewails the loss of culinary innocence and decries the decadence of gastronomic pretentiousness. And she proposes two lessons for a happy life:

> One is to reintroduce people to the pleasure of basic, simple ingredients, and the second is to provide a first-time cook-book, something that will be a good grounding in the simple basics and provide a springboard for a lifetime of learning – not just in how to cook, but in how to experience the sheer joy and pleasure of eating good food every single day.

And where better to start than with the egg, that 'powerful symbol of something new happening – new life, new beginning'? Those who felt comforted at being offered a nine-point guide to the creation of perfect toast might in other times have been amenable to a nine-point guide to a better life, like the Lord's Prayer, for instance. As with many biblical injunctions, Delia's precepts might be more honoured in the breach than the observance, but the presence of her books on the kitchen shelf has proved endlessly reassuring. Smith's spiky-haired rival, Gary Rhodes, who was blisteringly rude about *How to Cook*, is quoted by Alison Bowyer as saying (when in more generous mood), 'Delia is an institution. She will always be with us. We need Delia, in the way some people reluctantly say we need the Church of England.'

When Elizabeth David died in 1992, Richard Boston wrote in the *Guardian*, 'It is no exaggeration to say that for middle-class British people of the second half of the century, she did more to change their way of life than any poet, novelist or dramatist of our time.' Those artistic comparisons are appropriate. David was one of those who helped to change the way we thought about cooking as much as the way we cooked, and she did so by the quality of her writing. Her influence spread beyond the recipes themselves. Steve Jones and Ben

Taylor (from Nottingham Trent University) published a critique of Elizabeth David and Jane Grigson in the *European Journal of Cultural Studies*. They found that both women played a vital part in the dissociation of cooking from the rest of what was traditionally regarded as 'women's work'. They quoted Grigson, writing in old age: 'Intelligent housewives feel they've a duty to be bored by domesticity. A fair reaction to dusting and bedmaking, perhaps, but not, I think, to cooking.' And then David: 'Rationing, the disappearance of servants, and the bad expensive meals served in restaurants, have led Englishwomen to take a much greater interest in food than was formerly considered polite.'

In rather more earthy terms, Julian Barnes wrote, 'The legend went like this: poor benighted Brits, mired in snoek and Spam, believing olive oil was something you bought at the chemist's to dewax ears, were hauled into culinary awareness by E. David, whereupon they all started growing their own basil and baking their own bread. In some respects, this legend is accurate.'

Despite the status she achieved Elizabeth David retained to the last a visceral suspicion of television and went to her grave regretting her one lapse – when she agreed in 1989 to take part in a film called *A Matter of Taste* on Channel 4. Lisa Chaney calls the programme 'a disaster', in which 'Elizabeth came across as a woman of most unsympathetic mien'. The authorised biography gives a more kindly interpretation of the circumstances in which the wine writer Jancis Robinson persuaded Elizabeth David to take part: yet the conclusion is much the same. Even though the interview was filmed at her favourite restaurant and under the most benign conditions, the subject proved to be prickly, anxious and uncommunicative. The last straw came when Jancis Robinson sought quite reasonably to publicise the film with an article in the *Listener* magazine: David responded with a letter full of outrage that she had been 'the subject of vulgar and insensitive journalism ... bounced around every magazine in the country. I should have known all this could only end in tears.'

By the time this small catastrophe unfolded, of course, cookery had been subsumed by television. Delia was one of the precursors of a new world which came of age in July 1982 with the first edition of the BBC's *Food and Drink*. No one could have imagined, from this awkward, stilted production, that *Food and Drink* would herald a new age of programming and would itself still be going strong two decades later. The host of the inaugural show was the disc jockey Simon Bates,

working with a middle-aged audience drawn largely from Women's
Institutes (those with husbands had made them dress in sports jackets
and ties as if they were going on to the Rotary Club). This unlikely
cast staggered through items on polyunsaturated fats, using diet to
influence the sex of your baby and cocktails. Even Jilly Goolden, later
to become a colourful personality in her own right, was forced to
cower nervously behind a row of wine bottles giving a tedious lecture
on labelling.[89]

When Peter Bazalgette took over *Food and Drink* after its first few
faltering episodes he soon found that he had alighted upon a subject of
consuming interest to many viewers. With a judicious mixture of
journalism, entertainment, information and stunts, he turned it into a
staple of the BBC output. Its style was exemplified by the idea of
sending the distinguished Swiss chef, Anton Mosimann, to cook a
meal for the family of a Sheffield council worker – his job involved
clearing drains – on a shopping budget of £10. Bazalgette says that in
such ways *Food and Drink* helped to democratise the idea of eating
and drinking well. While Elizabeth David was writing for the quality
end of the middle-class market, 'we were seen as vulgar and cheap, and
quite often we did it with a smile on our face. I call it the Tchaikovsky
first piano concerto syndrome – everybody likes it, so it can't be good.'
Huge numbers of people wrote in for recipes and, in an early example
of interactivity, Bazalgette commandeered Ceefax to spread the word.
But did people use *Food and Drink* primarily as a source of ideas for
their own kitchens? Or was this merely an excellent topic for factual
programming, like antiques, pets or home decorating?

Bazalgette acknowledges the curious fact that the rise of *Food and
Drink* coincided with 'de-skilling' of cookery at all levels of society –
'... more fast food, more prepared food, television destroying the
family meal, teenagers in the house using convenience food to make
their own eating decisions. ...' People watched others doing what they
could no longer be bothered to do for themselves and no longer needed
to do, either. Since the notion of cooking as a pleasure in its own right
had never been well-established, the mass of consumers slumped back

---

89 Jilly Goolden's publicity website includes the following information: 'She has also
appeared on innumerable television programmes across all channels featuring both as a
wine expert *and as a personality* [my italics].' In this 1982 appearance, that personality
was not much in evidence. She did provide the depressing information that the best-
selling wine in Britain was Hirondelle (white and red) telling viewers that it was a hybrid,
based on wine from 12 different countries, including Morocco and Romania. The trick
was the production of a consistent taste – it was a 'lab job, but perfectly respectable' ...

into the new comfort food and, as Philip Harben would not have been surprised to discover, they did so for the most basic of reasons – because they liked it.

The countervailing trend was typically British, too: the desire of Thatcher's new property-owning middle class to appear more sophisticated. A 'dinner party' was once again an important expression of that ambition, just as it had been in the Sixties. To begin with *Food and Drink* never used the word 'dinner' – the evening meal was always 'supper'. But towards the end of the 1980s Bazalgette lifted the prohibition and viewers were guided towards ways of 'impressing the neighbours, buying wine, and seeing food and lifestyle as a statement of "who I am and what I do".'

A sister programme, *Ready Steady Cook* launched in 1990, added the programme-makers' favourite ingredient, a single, simple format needing a minimum level of preparation and production. It was also one of the early examples of the airwaves being thrown open to a succession of ordinary people. While they enjoyed a taste of fame, the audience could share the thrill vicariously and imagine themselves on set with the celebrity presenters.

Alongside these stalwarts a string of celebrity chefs have strutted their culinary stuff on television to enduring public approval. They do it in studios, on location, at home and abroad, in their own restaurants or someone else's; they invariably write books and newspaper columns as well, and appear in television advertisements. In the early days of this phenomenon, those involved had usually served a long apprenticeship over a hot stove and had reached the pinnacle of their profession: Marco Pierre White was the star of *White Heat* in 1990, while Anton Mosimann featured in two successful series of his own. The second of these in 1991 (*Anton Mosimann – Naturally*[90]) attracted an audience of nearly 15 million. But by then he had spent 13 years at the Dorchester and achieved the first Michelin Two Star rating for a hotel restaurant outside France. In Rojek's classification, Mosimann and his ilk are certainly 'achieved celebrities'.

But frustratingly for producers, the best chefs do not always make the best television presenters (Elizabeth David and Jane Grigson, to name but two). Conversely, it turned out that a number of natural

---

90 I started taking a serious interest in cooking around this time and the spin-off book from the series was my first 'proper' cookbook. His Char-Grilled Swordfish Steak Niçoise remains one of my favourites because even a complete fool can do it.

performers and communicators, whose only drawback was youth and inexperience were working in and around kitchens. Jamie Oliver, for example, was spotted at the River Café in London. 'A documentary about the restaurant was being filmed,' Oliver explains, 'and the editors decided to show a lot of this cheeky kid who was so into the cooking that he'd answer back to the crew – telling them to get out of the way, or whatever. The day after the programme was shown, I got calls from five production companies all wanting to talk about a possible show. I couldn't believe it and thought it was my mates winding me up!' He was not yet 25 years old.

Ainsley Harriott, whose cookery interests had had to compete with a second career in a singing duo called The Calypso Twins, was finally 'discovered' catering for the Long Room at Lords. He was soon appearing on *Good Morning with Anne and Nick* as chef-in-residence, before gravitating to *Ready Steady Cook, Can't Cook, Won't Cook* and every TV quiz show/chat show in the schedules. In Chris Rojek's analysis Oliver and Harriott must be considered 'attributed celebrities': they are ' "ordinary people" ... vaulted into public consciousness as noteworthy figures, primarily at the behest of mass-media executives pursuing circulation or ratings wars'.

The proof is that viewers who have never cooked a dish recommended by Oliver, or Harriott, or Nigella Lawson, would instantly recognise them and respect them – because they cook *on television*. Their programmes are not fundamentally sources of information or even inspiration: they are popular entertainment, comparatively cheap to make, and reliable audience fodder. Many observers judge that this outpouring of expertise has made little difference to the way we eat. Rebecca Mead, in a lengthy essay for the *New Yorker*, wrote that English children were still raised on 'a range of foodstuffs that are more or less inedible', including 'the chip butty, perplexing toppings for toast like canned spaghetti and baked beans, and Marmite, a black, salty yeasty spread that causes gagging in foreign nationals'.

Nigella Lawson, in particular, has attracted a considerable amount of critical attention, because her shows represent the apogee of what has been dubbed gastro-porn – in other words they portray a 'sensual' performance, which the viewer could not hope to emulate, but which offers the opportunity for vicarious satisfaction. With much lingering finger-licking and artful mid-shots of her ample apron, we have travelled a long way from the 'pornography' of Elizabeth David's food writing. The author Paul Bailey, friend of Elizabeth David and Jane Grigson, says, 'It really is like watching a pornographic movie: you think to yourself, no one could do that in a million years.'

The Lawson formula has been carefully contrived, in Rebecca Mead's view, so that she appeals both to men (as 'posh totty') and to women (as someone gorgeous but vulnerable and prone to putting on weight). Mead quotes Lawson as supporting the thesis that her programmes are about much more than mere food: 'I think human beings have a fantasy about transformation of the self. Food is like that: you are transforming something by cooking it. And you are watching television thinking you might transform yourself into someone who might do that.' This sounds convincing and helps to explain why people watch other lifestyle shows, like the highly successful *Changing Rooms* in which strangers are invited to trash, and then transform, your home. There is no real intention on behalf of most viewers, even self-deceptively, to believe that they will ever imitate what is being done on the screen, whether it's cooking, home improvement or gardening. But watching it being done by admired performers – especially when they interact with ordinary people like themselves – is a considerable pleasure in itself.

Mead sums up, 'Learning to cook is not really the point of Lawson's show, just as MTV does not exist to show people how to play the electric guitar ... Cooking instruction is still provided on British television, however, by Delia Smith. If Lawson is the Princess Diana of the kitchen – glamorous, tragic and endlessly hungry – then Delia Smith is the Queen: strait-laced, reliable and chilly.'

Is she right? It is hard to argue with book sales of more than 10 million, but there is an air of unreality about the whole Delia phenomenon. For one thing she refuses absolutely to cook in front of a live audience, claiming that she can 'only do it with a camera'. And even Delia Smith's television performances are, in a sense, illusory. Viewers have grown used to seeing her (in Alison Bowyer's description) 'in the middle of her enviably large and bright kitchen, her immaculate English country garden tantalisingly visible through the glass, effortlessly cooking up delicious-looking festive feasts'. In reality, the 'kitchen' became an elaborate studio set, built from scratch in her conservatory at the start of each new series and dismantled at the end.[91]

---

91 'We do try and give the impression that Delia is being filmed in her own kitchen', the producer says. And for verisimilitude, a Christmas series filmed in March required the removal of all the daffodils from her garden.

The majority of the food preparation was done '... by Delia's three assistants in a large industrial unit parked alongside the cottage'. Nor will she ever taste her own food on air. 'I can't bear anyone putting anything in their mouth,' she told Rebecca Mead. 'They can't speak while they are eating; and then, if they do speak, it is always the same thing – "Oh, delicious!" "Oh, Yummy!" Yuck.' Mead's tart comment is that, in a country so ravaged by food scares, it makes perfect sense to have a cooking-show host who is disgusted by eating: 'Watching sensuous television about beating eggs with cream and butter serves as an excellent displacement activity. It's a lot safer than eating.'

It is also, apparently, more fun to watch cookery on television than to participate in the act itself. Professor David Warburton, from Reading University, is an academic researcher into the psychology of pleasure who has found that celebrity chefs, far from encouraging us to give more dinner parties, generally scare us witless. The unrealistic cooking standards set on TV and in cookbooks, he says, have produced a new social disability – Kitchen Performance Anxiety. Thanks to this syndrome, 68 per cent of us hold fewer dinner parties and, when we do take the plunge, 61 per cent find the experience 'worse than attending an interview or going on a first date'. (One remarkable piece of tangential evidence came in a survey showing that, although potato consumption has remained constant in recent years, the proportion of vegetables sold fresh and unprocessed has dropped from 80 per cent to 50 per cent. Why waste time peeling the thing, when someone else will do it for you and put it in a packet?)

Inspired by such research (in December 2001) Michael Bywater conducted a survey of 'gastro-porn' in the *Independent*, and decided that Kitchen Performance Anxiety Syndrome was just another reflection of British sexual inadequacy. His theory is that we have become terrified of cooking (as of sex) so we sublimate that fear by watching other people cook food on television. 'People who like to cook', he suggests, 'don't watch television; they are, on the whole, cooking.' Tom Jaine still finds it puzzling that sales of cookbooks and the ratings of TV cookery programmes have risen in parallel with the use of the microwave, the popularity of ready-made meals (sales up 35 per cent in the past five years) and the frequency of eating out. 'What seems to be happening is that we're cooking much less, and thinking about it much more – which is pretty bizarre.'

Matthew Fort summed it up in a *Guardian* millennium special edition, 'Our attitude to food has changed, for better or worse. Fifty years ago it was an essential, today it is a social accessory. We watch it on TV. We buy the books. We dream and drool. And then we pop out to eat the real thing prepared by someone else.' The proof of the pudding, it seems, is in the viewing.

FOUR

Arthur Scargill – A Working Man

By the time I was old enough to be aware of my father's professional activities he was a Beaver Boy, an employee of Lord Beaverbrook's newspaper empire, and remained so until his death. It had taken him an unusually long time to settle down to a permanent job, mainly because of the war, but he was never in any doubt that he wanted to be a writer. His mother had expected him to study medicine, in line with family tradition (his father was a GP who died in the Great War), but the idea did not appeal to him. Instead, he was 'put into a bank', because this was the sort of solid career to which any bright boy would want to aspire, even one who had never passed a maths exam. In the words of a jovial autobiographical note some time later, he 'liked the bank even less than it liked him, and resigned gracefully before they could do anything about it'. After a desperate search for a newspaper that would take him on, he signed up for London University's Diploma of Journalism course in 1935 when he was already 22 years old.

It was a success. There were vacation jobs (the *Cambridge Daily News* warned him sternly, 'You will of course understand that this post does not carry any remuneration'). And then, after two years, he emerged with the Harmsworth medal as the outstanding student on the course.[92] This was a passport to a job with the *Daily Express* in Manchester, where he stayed until the outbreak of war. The experience was decisive. In 1939 he wrote a letter of appreciation to Mr Burnyeat, an *Express* executive who had encouraged him:

> *I started off my newspaper life with the firm idea that I wanted to be on a paper just so long, and then to get out and do some worthwhile writing, whether it earned me money or not. Now I know newspapers have some part of my soul and that I'm not quite as I was. I still tell myself that I'm bound for more serious stuff – but each week I'm less convincing to myself than I was before. ... I and my colleagues get, or tell each other we get, fed up with our jobs, about twice a week. Unfortunately the jobs get into our blood before we know where we are, and we get into being the kind of people who would be hopeless in nearly every other kind of work. But it is enormous fun, this journalism.*

With such a strong sense of what life had in store for him, there was little likelihood that he would switch careers later, and he was still writing for newspapers until the week of his death. He never did manage to fit in much 'serious stuff', apart from four slim volumes on the England cricket tours he covered for the *Evening Standard*. I am sure that my grandmother (who lived until 1956) eventually came to terms with her son's rather racy existence, but she was a Victorian, by birth and in spirit, and must have wondered what had gone wrong with his upbringing. Her instincts were still widely shared in the early 1950s: a job was like a ladder. You started at the bottom and heaved your way to as near to the top as you could manage before the retirement clock chimed. The precariousness of ladders made job swapping unattractive for most people. A job was not something to be trifled with. The constraints of rationing and the economic strait-jacket of the Korean War were still holding back the consumer boom (and car

---

92 I still have the examination papers and they provide an interesting insight into what sort of people journalists were supposed to be. There are two English Literature papers and among the questions he chose to answer were, 'Write a critical account of any one novel by Richardson, Fielding, Smollett or Sterne' and 'The age of Queen Anne was the golden age of English journalism – discuss with particular reference to the *Tatler* and the *Spectator*'. Other papers included 'History of the Modern World from 1789' and 'Social and Economic Structure of Today'.

ownership), which would eventually encourage real labour mobility. With average wages rising quickly (by 50 per cent between 1950 and 1955) and unemployment rarely straying above 2 per cent, there was no urgent need for people to leap from job to job in search of better prospects. In June 1953 the unemployment rate fell to 1.2 per cent, well below most definitions of what constitutes full employment.

It was in these placid economic conditions that Arthur Scargill emerged from White Cross Secondary School in Worsborough in the summer of 1953, happy to let his mother, Alice, do her best to steer him away from his own family tradition: the pit – the destiny of the Scargills. He applied instead to the local engineering factories, but nobody wanted the 15-year-old who had thrown up the chance to go to the grammar school. So a miner he would be, after all, and almost certainly, therefore, a miner for life.

In the course of the next 50 years his progress would encapsulate the rapid rise and sharp downturn of trade union power, the resurgence and relapse of British manufacturing industry, the short-lived triumph and painful demise of left-wing politics and the death of traditional demagoguery in the hostile world of the modern media. And through-out these momentous decades he himself would steadfastly refuse to recognise that he had not won every battle he decided to fight. At the end of the period he would be president (more or less for life, like some Caribbean dictator) of a toothless union that mostly refused to speak to its employers, and head of a political party whose main achievement was the glorification of its own leader. Arthur Scargill's story is another parable for our times.

One of the defining features of miners everywhere is their sense of being a different breed, doing a job marked out not just by the physical dangers, but by the primacy of their position (historically) in the economic scheme of things. They have always believed their jobs to be more real – more vital in every sense – than those of other workers. Post-war British miners also bore the scars of the General Strike of 1926, when they were abandoned by the rest of the union movement and left to fight a hopeless battle alone. In that year, 162 million days were lost to the strike (more than the combined total of the next 45 years) and the mineworkers accounted for 146 million of them. Their relations with other workers have often suffered accordingly. In 1946 the TUC (Trades Union Congress) bridled at the idea that miners should be given an extra meat ration. Their policy was for a universal allowance for all workers. Despite the carping, miners retained their special ration-book status until meat rationing ended in 1954.

In coronation year the coal industry was going through a strange period.[93] The end of the war had allowed many reluctant miners to drift away in search of better-paid, less demanding jobs. Those who remained celebrated nationalisation on 1 January 1947, but the Labour government proved to be no pushover for the newly formed NUM, the National Union of Mineworkers. Even under state control managers, faced with desperate coal shortages, were constantly striving for increased production, yet still insisting on wage restraint. As Michael Crick puts it in his book about the 1984 miners' strike, 'After years of campaigning, the miners and their leaders felt the pits were finally "theirs": they felt they had a duty not to disrupt things', although they were still being managed by the same people who'd done the job for the private coal owners. By the grim winter of 1946–7, power cuts crippled the country and Polish workers were drafted in to plug the gaps at the coalface. Gradually, the depletion of the workforce improved the NUM's bargaining position and, in its dying months, Clement Attlee's government was forced to concede better pay and pensions, in return for undertakings on strikes and absenteeism.

The return of the Conservatives in 1951 might have brought confrontation and strife, but the NUM leadership had grown comfortably close to government. There was no real trouble, even when ministers vetoed a pay award agreed by arbitrators. Nor was the wider labour movement in militant mood. Between 1948 and 1952, the number of days lost to strikes in Britain ticked along at between 1 and 2 million a year – a low level that would not be reached again until the recession of the early 1990s. It was a golden period for industrial relations. There was no enthusiasm for kicking up a fuss in the workplace, any more than there was in society at large. People who had survived the war, and hunkered down during the dismal years of austerity, looked for security where they could find it.

It couldn't last.

The general placidity of the national workforce was fed by the rising prosperity of most of its members. But these stable conditions, in turn,

---

93 ... though coal was still a crucial part of Clarke family life. The 'coal-hole' lay beside the kitchen, with a hatch through which coal (and coke, for the antediluvian range) was delivered every fortnight or so. It came in thickly woven sacks, which looked as though they were constructed from coal dust.

were sowing the seeds of a new period of union militancy. Unions had established the right of their members to decent wages, and unemployment posed no obvious threat. According to Christopher Booker (in his survey of the Fifties and Sixties, *The Neophiliacs*), union leaders began to feel free to flex their industrial muscles. In the space of a few months from December 1955 dockers, Fleet Street printworkers and railwaymen all went on strike for higher pay:

> *Over the next ten years, there would be few patterns in national life more familiar than the round of threats, urgent consultations and appearances of grave-faced union leaders on television, carried away by a self-important charade that often seemed to have little connection with economic or any other kind of reality. The hunger for drama and excitement that was an end in itself would by no means be limited to the fantasy worlds of teenagers, artists and intellectuals.*

Looking back from his vantage point at the end of the 1960s, Booker suggests that unrealistic wage claims – and the inflation they helped to feed – were part of a 'great collective fantasy', characteristic of societies on a wave of material improvement. Such societies 'generate an illusion of betterment outstripping reality'. These were perfect growing conditions for what became known as the British disease, the twin epidemics of industrial action and inflation (wages chasing prices in a never-ending spiral without any corresponding improvement in productivity, or reform of working practices) that eventually came close to laying low the country's economy.

Bernard Levin took a sideways look at the same phenomenon and what he called the 'chaotic and antique state' of industrial relations:

> *At times it seemed almost as though a contest had been arranged, and substantial prizes offered, for the most prolonged and fruitless industrial dispute any competitor could organise. The competition for the first prize was keen, and the balance swung this way and that throughout the decade, likely candidates including the dispute between two sets of workers over which of them should be allowed to bore the rivet-holes in the sides of ships, which went on for some four months.*

Levin makes it sound as if many disputes were like medieval jousts –

steeped in tradition and incomprehensible to the untutored observer –
though with the real risk that someone might get hurt.

The formal posturing reflected the well-entrenched class system,
which fossilised relations between managers and workers in the
traditional 'them and us' mould. The 1959 film *I'm All Right, Jack*
parodied this state of affairs, with Peter Sellers stealing the show as the
union official chained to his rule book – his faith in Communism
inspired by resentment at 'all them cornfields and ballet in the evenings'.
A flourishing economy offered no real incentive for reform and there
were plenty ready to play the game for all it was worth.

Like Charles Saatchi, Scargill is a myth maker. But unlike Saatchi,
who chose to direct the story of his life from the wings, out of the sight
of his audience, Scargill quickly adopted a different approach. From an
early age he was ready to broadcast his story from any available platform to anyone who would listen. Nor has the story been set in stone:
it has evolved over the years, transmuted to suit the requirements of
different audiences or different times. Nobody has been able to say for
sure how far this was a conscious process. Maybe he was simply
blessed with an unreliable memory.

The story of his schooling is a case in point. The facts are that the
young Arthur did well at his primary school in Worsborough Dale, well
enough to be considered a possible candidate for the grammar school, a
few miles away in Barnsley, and to go through a year of intensive
tuition designed to prepare him for the 11-plus exam. As a child of
caring parents, both of whom Arthur respected (and, in the case of his
mother, loved dearly) he would not have lacked encouragement to
better himself. Yet for some reason he never sat the exam. Why?

In an interview with Joan Bakewell for the *Illustrated London News*
(in 1978) he explained that he had been reluctant to leave his home
village, though in retrospect he could see that he'd been wrong. When
he spoke to Hunter Davies 15 years later, the story had taken on a
different emphasis: 'I thought the grammar school was a place for snobs,
and I didn't want to go.' In 2001 Deborah Ross interviewed Scargill for
the *Independent*. Now, the grammar school seems bathed in a nostalgic
glow of lost youth. 'I'd have gone to the same school as Mike Parkinson
and Geoff Boycott,' he told her with pride. Was it homesickness, class
protest, or something that was never meant to be?

Much of Arthur Scargill's early life presents similar puzzles. It's not clear, for instance, why he rejected the idea of working in his father's pit, Wombwell Main, or any of seven others around his home village, and chose instead to make the daily ten-mile trek to Woolley Colliery north of Barnsley. This entailed two bus journeys or a long bicycle ride before dawn. His own explanation later was that he had cleverly spotted that shift times were half an hour shorter at Woolley. But as Paul Routledge points out in his 1993 biography, shift patterns were habitually the same across the South Yorkshire coalfield. And any time saved at work would have been eaten up (and more) by the time it took to get there. It seems more likely that the real reasons were too humdrum to justify inclusion in his 'back-story'. Scargill's early years are like a canvas to which the artist returns again and again, touching up, changing perspective, adding or taking away details – because he is never fully satisfied that the work is complete.

The picture that emerges from this process is of a sensitive boy, who – from the moment he witnessed the awfulness of a miner's lot – vowed to devote himself to improving it. Not that anyone would quibble with his first reactions to working conditions at Woolley: he was one of six new recruits assigned to the coal screens, where a mixture of callow youths and damaged adults stood by a conveyor belt removing stones and debris. It was like Dante's Inferno, he told Sue Lawley on *Desert Island Discs*: filthy, cloying dust reduced visibility to a few feet (or sometimes yards, in other descriptions of the same scene) and the noise was so great that the men had to communicate in sign language. When snap times (meal breaks) came round they had to wash the caked filth from their lips before they could eat.

This appalling pre-mechanisation environment would have shocked any youngster, but young Arthur's feelings were not confined to self-pity or despair. He told Joan Bakewell that, before the end of his first shift, he had begun to ask himself how such conditions could exist in 1953: 'I promised myself that one day I would try to get things changed.' And before long he apparently had the time, and intellectual maturity, to reflect on the plight of his fellow workers, 'men with one arm and one leg, men crippled and mentally retarded'. Such people, he concluded, should never have been working. In the journal *New Left Review* (in 1975) he described how these initial impressions quickly crystallised into a plan of action. 'At the age of 15, I decided that the world was wrong and I wanted to put it right, virtually overnight if possible.'

It wasn't long before the young Scargill found himself risking the wrath of the management on behalf of the trainees. They had been told that they couldn't leave early with the rest of the men at the start of a holiday – even though they had finished their work. Arthur was deputed to confront the imperious figure of the manager, Mr Steele, in his intimidating office. 'It seemed to me that his office was about 300 feet in length, it took me so long to walk across the room. He was sitting there, smoking a pipe, and he said, "What's tha want, lad?" I said, "I've come to represent all the lads in the pit-bottom." "Oh aye. About what?"' Undaunted, he explained his mission. Mr Steele replied, 'Tha knows I can't give thee that permission.' Arthur thought his first attempt at negotiation had failed. But as he made his crestfallen retreat, it dawned on him that the manager hadn't said 'no' – just that he couldn't give permission. 'When the time came for us to come out at the end of the shift, I promptly led them all out with the rest of the men and to everyone's astonishment, we all got paid our full wages. From that moment on, I was regarded as something of a champion in the pit.'

This Dickensian story, which he told (complete with Mr Steele's comic accent) on *Desert Island Discs* in 1988, was a refined and elaborated version of the one offered to Joan Bakewell 13 years earlier. It had an extra twist, too, in the manager's parting comment: 'Tha'd be better off, tha knows, training in Moscow, thee, rather than here.' In a few deft strokes the teenaged Arthur Scargill is portrayed as bold, clever, radical and ready to challenge authority. Oddly, the story does not appear in the lengthy *New Left Review* interview that amounts to the testament of Scargill's youth – 33 pages of transcribed conversation in which he describes the origins, germination and flowering of his political thinking. 'From '53 to '59 I led a whole series of battles as a young miners' leader,' he tells the *Review*. If any of those battles was lost, it does not warrant a mention.

Was this early dissatisfaction really so clearly articulated and channelled at such a tender age? Some impetus to activism must have come from his father, Harold, a strong union member and a Communist, who reportedly took his son to his first political meeting when he was 12 years old. But Scargill says his father did not try to force his political development and that he needed no external prompting to consume the classic texts of the left, like *The Ragged Trousered Philanthropists* and Jack London's *The Iron Heel*. Indeed, by his father's testimony the boy 'went through Marx and Lenin while he was still at school'. His biographer, the journalist Paul Routledge, is not at all sure about the portrait of 'the lad in shorts poring over *Das Kapital*', quoting Scargill's comrades who found his Marxism 'hesitant and superficial'. But it forms another layer of this impressionist self-portrait of the artist as a young man – who, one day, would be castigated as Britain's 'enemy within'.

The next application of colour to the portrait of the activist as a young man comes when Arthur Scargill throws in his lot with the Young Communist League. The date is 1955, the year in which coal production is reaching its post-war peak. (At the time, the experts were still predicting coal shortages in Britain and across Europe: few would have guessed that coal's fortunes were about to plunge into several decades of steady, often steep, decline.) His adoption of the Communist cause was quirky rather than emotional. The Labour Party (his first choice) lost out by failing to respond to his letters: the Young Communists, by contrast, were knocking on his door within 24 hours of his writing to the party paper, the *Daily Worker*. Routledge recalls the minutes of the Barnsley branch of the League for 31 March 1955: 'Today the comrades visited Billy Smart's Circus. Arthur Scargill and Derek Stubbings joined the party. The membership is now 11.' In this very small pool, Scargill quickly began to behave like a big fish. He was Branch Secretary within months and by the following year had been elected to the YCL National Committee. Later he boasted (to Joan Bakewell) that he had increased membership of his branch from 10 to 190: Routledge suggests that this is a Pied Piper fantasy, since the total number of members in the Yorkshire region at the time was only 120.

In parallel, Scargill joined the union and began to make waves at Woolley, though he had, inadvertently, joined one of the most right-wing pits in the entire coalfield and soon made himself as unpopular with the NUM as with the management. At his first branch meeting union officials walked out and left him talking to himself. And he had no doubt that those same officials made sure he was consigned to three years of night shifts, to limit his opportunities for rabble-rousing. Matters came to a head when he organised a strike over training, which provoked the local branch to expel him.

Like some latter-day revolutionary hero, he didn't flinch from facing down the forces of reaction: 'The right wing at that time had guards on the door of the branch meeting and wouldn't allow me to enter the room. This may seem incredible to you. This can be checked with anyone. There are people around here who were there, in fact some of them were guarding the door! So here was a young man of eighteen years of age being denied the right, *physically*,[94] even to go to his own branch meeting.'

In an article full of detailed (if self-serving) self-analysis, Scargill makes a ringing declaration about the location of real power: not with political parties, but either with the ruling classes or the working classes and – by extension – the trade union movement.[95] Hence his frustration: 'We had to struggle on two fronts: first of all struggle within the industry against the Coal Board and, far more importantly, we had to struggle within the union for democracy, bearing in mind that we had an ultra-right-wing leadership holding back not only Yorkshire and the miners, but holding back the whole of the trade union movement in Britain.' Elsewhere he describes the leadership as being 'well to the right of Genghis Khan', and 'bosom pals of the management'.

The nature of Scargill's adherence to Communism has given rise to a great deal of speculation, not helped by the man himself. To begin with he was full of youthful verve. He was not among those who quit the party when Soviet tanks rolled into Budapest to suppress the 1956 Hungarian uprising: on the contrary, he thoroughly approved, believing the revolt to have been a CIA plot. Six months later he was happy to travel to Moscow for the Sixth World Youth Festival.[96] Michael Crick records Scargill's pleasure in recalling a dinner in the Kremlin with Chairman Khrushchev (a story omitting to mention the fact that he shared this contact with several hundred others); and another version of the same event, which has him berating Soviet officials for downgrading Stalin's reputation. But within five years or

---

94 The italics are from the original NLR text. I am particularly fond of 'This can be checked with anyone': Scargill knows that it sounds like a tall story and he defies the reader to dispute the facts – a much-used technique of his oratory.

95 This may or may not have had something to do with the fact that the only time he stood for elected office (outside the union) he was soundly thrashed. At the age of 22 he was a Communist candidate in the Worsborough District Council elections of May 1960. He attracted 138 votes against 945 for the Labour Alderman, Charles Boland.

96 This Festival was held in a different Warsaw Pact capital every two years. Moscow in 1957 attracted 34,000 guests from 131 countries. If the Kremlin was taken aback by Arthur Scargill, it was more discomfited by encouraging rock 'n' roll musicians, under the mistaken impression that 'rock 'n' roll' was merely a popular song. The resulting effusion of electric guitars was a shock to the Soviet system. The writer Gabriel García Márquez, who attended the Festival, credits the event with prompting Moscow to shed its staid image. But only very slowly.

so – the dates are hazy – he had left the YCL, and the reasons are hazy, too. Sometimes he told journalists that he'd been expelled for refusing to stick to the party line, sometimes he said he'd resigned over aspects of Soviet policy – such as the Kremlin's refusal to allow dissidents to leave the Soviet Union and the insult to Stalin when the city named after him was redesignated 'Volgograd' in 1961. On yet another occasion he described a dawning realisation that Communism was 'too authoritarian and not sufficiently socialist'.

A fourth scenario reduced the matter to the most mundane level: he was deterred by the party's requirement that he sell the *Daily Worker* on a Friday evening, because it interfered with his union work.

A more likely theory than any of those is that his YCL association threatened to hinder his union ambitions: the right-wing Woolley officials, for instance, tried to persuade the NUM to cancel the membership of all Communists. By 1974 Scargill felt able to describe himself to a *Times* profiler as 'never a very active member', who fell out with the party over 'deep-seated political differences' and joined first the Co-operative Party and then, in 1966, Labour.

Paul Routledge characterises Scargill's relationship with Communism as 'a flirtation, a teenage passion that cooled as he grew to manhood and found something more worthy of his ardour: his own destiny as the revolutionary class warrior'. He left before graduating to the Communist Party proper, and headed without much enthusiasm for the Labour camp, but the main focus of his attentions remained the union. In the language of Marxist dialectic, he was caught up in a 'continuous struggle, of expulsion from the union, reinstatement, physically being barred from attending branch meetings, until finally it built up and I was elected branch delegate'. Only one strong link with the party remained – his lifetime admiration for Frank Watters, a significant figure who launched a CP recruitment drive in Yorkshire in 1953 and acted as Scargill's agent in the Worsborough council elections.

———

Over the next ten years Arthur Scargill conducted one of the most efficient and effective campaigns the modern labour movement has ever seen – designed to capture the fastnesses of the NUM for the left and for himself. From lonely left-wing delegate at right-wing Woolley in 1964, to all-powerful Yorkshire Area President in 1974 – his progress was majestic. Not even prime ministers could stand in his way. No wonder they called him (like his first pit pony) King.[97] But other forces were at work in that same decade. Between 1964 and 1968 alone, 40 per cent of the country's collieries were closed and the labour force fell equally quickly, as demand for coal plummeted, mechanisation replaced manpower and oil became the fuel of choice.

The King had his cause. What better way could there be to galvanise the political power of the mineworkers than for the protection of their own livelihoods? Other issues of pay, hours and conditions would play their part in strengthening his hand, but the destruction of jobs would eventually be the most emotive topic of all. Yet if you chart on a graph Scargill's rise against coal's fall from grace, you end up with a giant cross. By the standard he set himself – protecting his industry from the depredations of market forces – Scargill's efforts would be in vain, signifying next to nothing. His impact on the nation was real and potent, but his own members had few concrete reasons to be grateful to him.

Pit closures were not new. Even in the first optimistic decade after nationalisation in 1947 the number of mines had fallen from 980 to 822. At the time, however, forced redundancies were rare: there was always plenty of work to be had and many Scottish miners made their way south – bringing with them a strong tradition of militancy. It was after 1957 that optimism began to drain away. Over the next six years a further 264 pits closed, including some which had barely started work. Vic Allen, a sympathetic chronicler of the industry, points out that Rothes colliery in Fifeshire was opened with a fanfare by the Queen in 1957: the celebratory brochure spoke of its coal reserves lasting 100 years. Those reserves had hardly been touched when the place was mothballed five years later.

The 1960s – during which Scargill was manoeuvring his way up the union hierarchy – were a particularly difficult time. Vic Allen describes how miners were caught in a pincer movement between pit closures and mechanisation. Without mechanisation, pits were uneconomic and had to close. With mechanisation, the need for manpower dropped anyway. Allen says that miners worked 'with the

---

97 Of 'King Arthur', my encyclopaedia says: 'half-legendary king of the Britons, who is represented as uniting the British tribes against the pagan invaders and as the champion of Christianity. It is very doubtful if he is a historic figure.' Without wishing to abuse the analogy, it is tempting to substitute 'the forces of the left' for 'the British tribes' and 'capitalist exploitation' for 'pagan invaders'. Scargill always claimed to be a Christian, too. I forbear to comment on 'half-legendary' or 'doubtful historic figure'.

threat of losing their jobs hanging continually over their heads. The impact of pit closures was so unpredictable that working miners never knew which pits were next on the list.' The implications, in Allen's vivid words, descended on the men like an avalanche.

Any hope that the post-1964 Labour government would halt the slide were misplaced. Far from making miners a special case, Harold Wilson made matters worse by overseeing tough Prices and Incomes legislation which put a brake on pay increases. Labour even flirted with new trade union laws, too – though Barbara Castle's 'In Place of Strife' was finally shelved in the face of fierce opposition.[98]

The deteriorating atmosphere saw an upsurge in industrial action in unlikely places: from dustmen in Hackney to sweatshop workers in Leeds. The miners were unlikely to be left out. In 1969 unofficial strikes broke out in Yorkshire, but soon spread to South Wales and Scotland, over the issue of surface workers' hours. These strikes involved around a third of the national workforce, suffered from chronic disorganisation and produced a compromise with the Coal Board after a fortnight. Surface workers didn't get the deal they wanted, but the union's pay claim – unprecedentedly – was met in full. Vic Allen sees this as a crucial dress rehearsal for future strikes, by proving that industrial action was not – as everyone had warned – necessarily counter-productive: it did not bring the wrath of the management and/or the government down on their heads. The miners, Allen goes on,

> ... had become victims of inertia and cynicism, following their own individual solutions, believing nothing better could be done. The traditions of militant mining trade unionism had come to mean nothing to them, except as folklore. Then suddenly, without warning, with virtually no organisation, they had an experience which showed how wrong they had been. After this the future was unlikely to be as placid as the immediate past.

---

98 The numbers of trade union members grew at a steady rate through the 1960s, reaching 44 per cent of the workforce (just under 10 million people) by 1968. Then, as relations between politics and industry became more tense, the membership graph began to rise steeply. But there was a catch. More than half of the 3 million new unionists (between 1968 and 1979) were in the public services like health and education. Many more were in thriving private-sector firms. The old industrial unions – dockworkers, railwaymen and miners – were all in decline. This transformation would have profound long-term implications for revolutionary-minded union leaders.

Yorkshire was the driving force behind the strike: half the pits in the county were mobilised (and therefore immobilised) and the Coal Board Chief, Lord Robens, gloomily recognised that 'the capture of the Yorkshire coalfield by the militant Left was complete'.

In that shady half-world where fact and fiction meet, Arthur Scargill admitted that the strike failed to meet its objectives. But that wasn't the point. 'I don't care who the historian is, but if he regards '69 as anything other than a complete victory, it's time he went and did some more thinking,' he told *New Left Review*. 'Because '69 was responsible for producing all the victories to come.' Perceptions and impressions were changing. A further wave of unofficial action over pay the following year added to the psychological pressure on miners to reconsider strikes as a strategic weapon.

Arthur Scargill's motives in this period remain elusive. Was he seeking to use the power of the union(s) purely as a means of improving the miners' lot? Or did he already envision a role for them as the motive force for wider political change? Andrew Taylor is an academic whose father succeeded Scargill as Yorkshire Area President in 1981. He believes that Scargill can be seen as a latter-day syndicalist – a descendant of the French union movement which aspired to capture the means of production on behalf of the workers. 'Lobbying governments didn't work,' Taylor says. 'Getting MPs elected to Parliament didn't work. The only solution left was industrial action – in a sense a purer form of political action than becoming engaged in the inevitable compromises of party policies and elections.' Kim Howells, NUM activist turned Labour minister, agrees: 'Quite simply, he believed that if trade unionists could close down industry, they could change politics for ever.'

To the twin evils of job insecurity (through pit closures) and pay restraint, was added in October 1970 the election of a Conservative government under Edward Heath. Arthur Scargill's hour was approaching.

The immediate spur for the great strike of 1972 was pay. The NUM claim at their conference in the summer of 1971 was for increases ranging from 35 per cent to 47 per cent – more than four times the rate of inflation. And who proposed the motion? The Woolley Colliery branch. Delegates also voted to reduce the majority needed in a strike ballot from two-thirds to 55 per cent. (Just as well, since the strike vote a few months later was carried by just 58.8 per cent. Under the old rules it would have failed.)

On 8 January 1972 the mining workforce of the entire country walked out and stayed out for 58 days.[99] Routledge points out that when the strike started, no one outside his immediate circle had heard of Scargill: 'When it finished, he had become a household name for militancy, credited with the invention of flying pickets and the technique of mass picketing.' From the start, he treated the exercise like a military campaign, casting himself as the general in the field, empowered to deploy his troops without interference from headquarters. The war analogy is not fanciful. Neil Kinnock later called him 'the Labour movement's nearest equivalent to a First World War general', and this is what Scargill himself told the *New Left Review*:

> *We took the view that we were in a class war. We were not playing cricket on the village green, like they did in '26. We were out to defeat Heath and Heath's policies because we were fighting a Government. Anyone who thinks otherwise is living in cloud-cuckoo land. We had to declare war on them and the only way you could declare war was to attack the vulnerable points.*

This, then, was to be a Blitzkrieg, in which the miners not only had the benefit of surprise, but the flexibility to adapt their tactics as soon as the need arose. Against them was ranged a complacent establishment – politicians and commentators in London who couldn't see beyond the recent history of the union movement, with its narrowly focused, essentially selfish, disputes. They failed to detect the stirring of atavistic forces which had been suppressed for nearly half a century. *The Times* was typically sanguine: disruption to industry and commerce, it opined, would be minimal.

Scargill's own account of the miners' advance on East Anglia would

---

99 We now know that Edward Heath and his ministers should have been well-briefed about these developments. A BBC investigation by Peter Taylor in 2002 revealed that the NUM President, Joe Gormley, was one of two dozen union leaders signed up as informants by Special Branch, and that this intelligence was shared with MI5, including advance warning about the 1972 strike, 'because he loved his country,' according to his handler. 'He was a patriot and he was very wary about the growth of militancy within his union.' When Scargill was asked for his comments on this remarkable story, he said he wasn't at all surprised that 23 senior figures might have spied on their unions. 'I thought it would be many more than that,' he said.

sit quite happily alongside the memoirs of a military commander, starting with the despatch of scouts to spy out the region. They were billeted with friendly natives at Essex University and Scargill relished this contact with the country's youth – doubtless because it gave him the sense of initiating a great national movement. 'We showed to the university students a degree of discipline and organisation which they had probably read about in their Marxist books, but had not seen for themselves. The first thing we did was to tell them we were in charge and that we would determine what we did, because we knew how to operate. We weren't being facetious or bigoted, but we knew exactly what we were doing.' And before long tremendous things started to happen: 'Our people were becoming politically educated and aware of what the class structure and what the class war was. In a matter of days they were changing. Never mind about a thousand lectures, this was it!'

Then, when battle was joined, unwise counsel within the war cabinet (aka the strike committee) decreed that 1000 available men should be spread out thinly between every power station and fuel depot; Scargill, the audacious maverick, condemned the plan as stupid; Scargill, the brilliant tactician, persuaded his colleagues that all 1000 men should be sent to a single location – Ipswich docks; Scargill, the decisive victor, celebrated the closure of the docks within 60 minutes. A token picket was left on guard and the rest of the flying pickets flew off to the nearest power station. 'Within two days', Scargill purrs, 'we'd shut the whole of East Anglia.'

That was just the start. From his headquarters in Barnsley he masterminded the rapid movement of pickets around the nation, wherever a piece of coal or coke was on the move. This was real power with a real impact on the nation – power to the workers, which led to the imposition of power cuts for everyone else. In due course the government had to sanction intermittent supplies of electricity – every three hours your lights went off. The declaration of a State of Emergency became inevitable.

The climax of this glorious campaign came four weeks into the strike, when reports of large-scale lorry movements at a coke depot in Birmingham reached Scargill's bunker. The Saltley Works were supposed to be subject to a permit system, allowing priority customers like hospitals and schools to receive supplies. The system (according to the pickets) was being roundly abused, and hundreds of lorries were ploughing backwards and forwards with no intervention by the police. Scargill summoned his crack troops, including the battle-hardened men from East Anglia, but even they only succeeded in stemming the tide of fuel for a few hours. Physical altercations broke out on the picket line; dozens of miners ended up in jail or in hospital, and television cameras offered up pictures of this real-life drama to a transfixed populace. For many, it was the first time that they had ever witnessed such raw conflict outside the context of a genuine war. Some wondered whether Britain, four years after France, might be experiencing its own civic revolution. One scene encapsulates the Scargill approach, which was to emphasise at every turn the nobility of the working man against a brutal and callous Establishment (the police):

> *They had one lad fifteen years of age from Woolley colliery, fifteen years of age, just like a school-kid – the police dragged him and one of them hit him, smash in the face. The kid's nose burst open. I ran across and they threw me back. I shouted to the TV cameras: 'This is the sort of brutality they're displaying, why don't you film this? They won't even let me see him.' Well, of course, they knew that this had been said so they changed their tune. 'Why don't you come and look at him.' So they took me to this van and the kid was there, his face streaming with blood. 'He looks all right, doesn't he?' I said, 'He looks a right bloody mess. Let the cameras come and film him.' And one of them said, 'Well, he shouldn't be here,' closed the doors and away they went.*

Somehow ministers in London let themselves be driven into a corner where Saltley had to be kept open at all costs: and Scargill happily set up camp in the opposite corner, committed to shutting it down. The difference was that the ministers had everything to lose and Scargill had everything to gain. He had already established his hypothesis that – for working people – mobilisation and solidarity represented victory, whatever the apparent outcome of any dispute. Closure of Saltley would be a victory; a valiant failure to achieve closure would be a victory, too.

His next move was decisive: a co-ordinated day of action, scheduled for Thursday 10 February, in which local trade unionists and sympathisers of all kinds would march on Saltley. From every direction they came, in scenes of which Hollywood would have been proud –

massed ranks of engineers and car assemblers and transport workers, waving banners and cheering, thousands of extras filling the set for Arthur Scargill's big scene. The hero leaps on the back of a lorry, seizes a megaphone and begins to chant:

'Close the Gates! Close the Gates!' and it was taken up, just like a football crowd. It was booming through Saltley: 'Close the Gates!' It reverberated right across this hollow, and each time they shouted this slogan they moved and the police, who were four deep, couldn't help it, they were getting moved in. And Capper, the Chief Constable of Birmingham, took a swift decision. He said, 'Close the Gates', and they swung them to. Hats were in the air, you've never seen anything like it in your life. Absolute delirium on the part of the people who were there. Because the Birmingham working class had become involved, not as observers but as participants.

The crowning moment (in Scargill's filmic account) came when the police chief begged him to disperse the crowd. Graciously, he agreed, provided he could borrow the police public address system. The cowed forces of law and order had no choice. Standing on top of a handy urinal, Scargill delivered a victory speech, which was carried by television to every corner of the land. And afterwards he reflected:

Here was the living proof that the working class only had to flex its muscles and it could bring governments, employers, society to a total standstill. I know the fear of Birmingham on the part of the ruling class. The fear was that what happened in Birmingham could happen in every city in Britain.

The capitulation of the authorities at Saltley coincided with the collapse of the government's will to resist – especially when the number of workers laid off by power cuts passed $1\frac{1}{2}$ million. A swiftly convened Board of Inquiry recommended that the bulk of the miners' pay claim should be met and, after some last-minute bargaining at Downing Street between the Prime Minister, Edward Heath, the miners' leader, Joe Gormley, and the rest of the NUM executive, a deal was struck. Arthur Scargill refused to vote for the deal because the pay demand was not met in full. This predictable gesture did not affect the ballot: 96.5 per cent of the men accepted an arrangement which added a range of other benefits to the large pay increase. Michael Crick quotes the diaries of Douglas Hurd, then Heath's Political Secretary: 'The Government now wandering over battlefield looking for someone to surrender to – and being massacred all the time.'

In the labour movement Arthur Scargill was now officially a (class-) war hero – his celebrity both attributed and achieved. But that was partly a function of his own telling and retelling of the story, and his undoubted talent for publicity. He knew where the cameras were and what would make an impression on the evening news. Revisionist versions of the story, by NCB insiders, police or politicians, never quite managed to compete. Yet even Scargill's friends and fellow thinkers tend to confirm the exaggeration of his role.

Vic Allen's book, *The Militancy of the British Miners* (1981), is a trusted text for the left – and his account of the '72 strike offers a subtly different view of Scargill's role. Yes, he was an important figure – but his prominence in the Yorkshire area was largely due to chance: one senior figure had recently died and two others were ill. ('There is always scope during a strike for new leaders to emerge. Strikers who analyse incisively, give direction and express themselves eloquently, can gain recognition as leaders even though they may not hold official union posts. In order for this transition from relative obscurity to be possible, however, there has to be a fluid leadership position.') The references to Scargill (in this work by a Communist writer who was close to the action) make him sound more like a key supporting actor than the star, an actor who made the best of his lines, rather than writing the script.

> *The strike gave Scargill an opportunity to display his undoubted qualities and, through his work on the committee dealing with the control of pickets, he achieved a prominence which extended well beyond Yorkshire ...*
>
> *A picketing strategy began to emerge in Yorkshire through a series of ad hoc decisions arising out of practical problems as they cropped up ...*
>
> *On Tuesday, February 8th 1800 Midland car delivery workers struck in sympathy with the miners and on the following day about 200 shop stewards in the Midland engineering industry called for a solidarity stoppage by 40,000 engineering workers and a march to Saltley on Thursday, February 10th ...*

The closure of Saltley was proclaimed a victory by the trade union movement and Arthur Scargill, who had been given much publicity during the struggle, as a potential miners' leader ...

The historian Andrew Taylor, after lengthy and detailed researches, is convinced that the strike, in every meaningful sense, was heading for a conclusion before the Saltley confrontation. The arrival of the car workers, who were mainly protesting about the government's Income Policy, simply overwhelmed the police. 'There was no point in their risking more violence to defend the place,' says Taylor. 'Saltley had no effect on the outcome of the strike, because it was basically a large dump for a waste-product (coke) which couldn't be used in power stations. The Gas Board were virtually giving the stuff away to get rid of it.' If Taylor is right, it underlines the tactical errors made by government. For the sake of a heap of fuel waste, they nurtured the myth that Saltley had produced 'the purest, truest form of political conflict'.

However history finally determines the importance of Scargill's role, Saltley, like many of his previous and subsequent victories, did bring into play the law of unintended consequences. There is no doubt that the anti-union legislation introduced by the Tories in the 1980s, which helped to defeat the miners and deplete the power of the whole union movement, was a direct response to the tactics of the 1972 strike. Hugo Young's biography of Margaret Thatcher says that the name of the NUM was branded on her heart. 'The miners were where she came in ... if they hadn't humiliated the Heath government into fighting an election it had lost, she would not [have become] party leader and prime minister. But this mattered less than the memory of that bloody defeat itself, and the apprehension that it might be capable of happening again.' In this sense Arthur Scargill created the monster that would consume him.

Seumas Milne, the *Guardian* journalist who has written the definitive account of the attempts to destroy Scargill's reputation after the 1984 strike, believes that this period prepared the ground for what became a 20-year vendetta against the miners – 'a single-minded and ruthless drive to destroy the NUM, and, if necessary, the bulk of the British coal industry in the process'.

In victory lay the seeds of future defeat, then, not least because Scargill himself misunderstood the nature of the Battle of Saltley Gate. He believed his own publicity. He thought that he had unlocked the potential of the British working classes and that they would – from that day onwards – be on stand-by for the revolution. Many home-grown revolutionaries shared that optimism. A recent review of the period (*Glorious Summer: Class Struggle in Britain 1972*) places the strike at the heart of the 'international revolt against capitalism' along with the Vietnam War protests in the United States. Or as the Marxist writer Michael Pablo puts it:

> *For several years now in several European countries we have seen situations escalating into major national revolutionary crises, where the question of the 'struggle for power' has been posed (and thus also the possible victory of the 'revolution'). May 1968 in France and the situation in Britain in 1972 during the long miners' strike, are varying examples of that kind of situation.*

Ian MacGregor, the dogged Canadian industrialist who, as Coal Board Chairman, was to confront Scargill in the 1984 dispute, felt that this was a formative moment in the character of the enemy chieftain: 'Those glorious days of "revolution" gave [Scargill] his first taste of three drugs, the effects of which were to addict him forever. They were the glamour of leadership in battle, the power of the revolutionary mob and the magic of performing on television.'

Fresh from his virtuoso performance at Saltley, Arthur Scargill could hardly fail to win his next big NUM job – as Yorkshire Area Compensation Agent, handling the claims of tens of thousands of men and their families. And that was the perfect platform for him to become the NUM's Yorkshire President in 1973. His elevation, and that of strong left-wingers in other regions, served to bring the union's right-wing leadership under increasing pressure. The advance of the left, as planned, had been taking place across a broad front. At Executive meetings in London, Scargill would be the first to leave so that he could brief the press (especially the television correspondents), applying his own undercoat to the official gloss that would be disseminated later in the evening.

In the second half of 1973 history began to repeat itself: a huge pay demand, an overtime ban through the winter (to ensure that coal stocks ran low) and a strike call in the New Year. And this time fate conspired to give the miners an even easier ride. In October 1973 the Arab assault on Israel at the start of Yom Kippur was backed by

OPEC's imposition of punitive oil price rises. Overnight, safe, reliable domestically produced coal started to look like a much more attractive option and any residual fear that a strike might lead to accelerated pit closures was laid to rest. Scargill claimed at the time that Edward Heath was bent on a confrontation to sort out the miners once and for all. Rather to the contrary (though Scargill was kept in the dark) Heath held secret talks with the 'patriotic' NUM President, Joe Gormley, in a desperate effort to avoid another strike. All their negotiating skills could not damp down the head of steam behind the miners' belief in their chances of victory. More than 80 per cent voted for a strike and two days later Heath called a snap election to decide who governed Britain.

Many Conservatives were deeply dubious. The Alan Clark *Diaries* are revealing: on 25 January the would-be Tory member of parliament (and candidate for the safe seat of Plymouth Sutton) went to the dentist and spotted a stooped figure in a raincoat, reading *The Times*. It was the former Prime Minister, Harold Macmillan. The old man was in gloomy mood, reckoning that an election would be a disaster. He believed the miners should be bought off until North Sea Oil came on stream – and referred to 'the real agitator' on the union side as ... Clark couldn't quite hear what Macmillan was saying ... Scrimgeour, was it? Clark listened entranced to the doom-laden prognostications of this great figure from his party's past, but managed to comfort himself – 'I don't see how we can actually *lose* this election, or at least how I can lose it' – before wandering off in blissful self-absorption, transferring his anxieties to the performance of his sex organ.

From the other side of the Atlantic, Ian MacGregor, unaware that 'Scrimgeour' would one day be his problem, wondered at the spectacle of a government being 'brought into such disrepute' by a labour union. Two questions occurred to him: how had a group of workers achieved a position of such power and invulnerability, and why had Heath challenged the miners with no way of withstanding a long dispute?

Even with the odds on his side, Scargill heard the siren call of Saltley Gate: what he wanted was a clash that would define this new confrontation in the public imagination. He believed he'd found it in the drive to close the British Steel complex near Scunthorpe. Although Anchor had already been working below capacity because of the power cuts, Scargill decided that it was a suitable target for sustained picketing and that halting steel production would be a suitable symbol of the might of the miners: 'It was clear that if we could stop the Anchor works we could halt British industry ... historians, when they look at this, will see that the real crunch came with the steel works.[100] That's the reason Heath had to take a decision. He had no alternative. He had to have a general election or concede to the miners.'

Few later assessments support this claim: even Vic Allen, with his focus on the militancy of the miners, refers to the picketing of steelworks only in passing, and doesn't even mention Anchor by name. Myth makers pay no account to such niceties.

When the election was called, Scargill – in line with his disdain for party politics – resisted any suggestion that ending the strike might help Labour's cause. The wage claim was sacred and not a political plaything to be set aside for mere electoral advantage. No doubt he felt vindicated when Heath fell short of an overall majority and then failed to come to an accommodation with Jeremy Thorpe's Liberals. But the pressure for a conciliatory gesture became even more intense – not least from many in the NUM leadership – when Harold Wilson was invited to form a minority Labour administration. Scargill and his colleagues were having none of it, arguing that a starving man was just as hungry under Labour as under the Tories. Only by maintaining the state of crisis could miners be sure of getting their just deserts:

> The one thing that annoys me about the trade union movement is that we've got one set of standards when we've got a Tory Government and a completely different set of standards when we've got a Labour Government, even though our case may be right.

Scargill's confidence in the power of a crisis to concentrate minds paid off. The new Prime Minister had little choice but to offer the miners a record-breaking pay deal, with coalface workers receiving everything they'd asked for. Yet because some grades of workers had to settle slightly below the figures in the original demand, two members of the NUM Executive voted against acceptance. One was the Communist secretary of the Kent miners, the other was Arthur Scargill, marooned in that nether world of pure victory, where compromise is a mortal sin.

Others on the left might have been thrilled at the return of a Labour

---

100 References to history and historians are very common in Scargill's pronouncements: in the end, it was his failure to detect the movement of historical forces against him that would lead to his downfall.

government and even more so when Wilson went to the country eight months later and won a (tiny) majority. Scargill, who had helped to cast down the hated Heath, had no time to enjoy the idle pleasures of self-congratulation. Locked into the cycle of perpetual struggle, he knew that Labour's presence in Downing Street would make his task immeasurably more difficult. Unions would lose their impetus to challenge the Establishment, or worse, might be inveigled into believing that they had a duty not to rock Labour's precariously balanced boat.

There was another factor: he regarded many in the Labour leadership as Tories in disguise – including Shirley Williams and Roy Jenkins, and above all Harold Wilson. Only Tony Benn, in Scargill's eyes, had the potential to drag Labour towards a Socialist future.[101]

The next five years were a kind of hell for the militant Left – as Labour lurched from one economic crisis to another, hanging on to power by the skin of their parliamentary teeth, and then only by constant ducking and weaving. This was the worst of all worlds: a supposedly friendly government, introducing unfriendly policies (like the Social Contract, which imposed universal pay restraint) against whom no serious resistance could be mounted for fear of handing power back to the Tories.

Looking back at the period (in anger) the International Trotskyist Committee was scathing: 'It was the 1974–1979 Labour Party government which, in cooperation with the trade union bureaucrats, carried out the major attacks on the shop-floor movement, giving particular attention to the miners. Though conceding the miners' 1974 pay claim, this government proceeded with widespread closures of coal pits and introduced a productivity bonus scheme which set area against area within the NUM.' This highly partial interpretation exaggerates the level of pit closures and misses out the fact that Labour signed up for an expansionist 'Plan for Coal', later described by Ian MacGregor as 'an Alice-in-Wonderland document' based on 'a series of assumptions, nearly all of which turned out to be

---

101 Scargill's deepest disenchantment with Labour tended to coincide with that party's periods in office. In 1975 he thought it might be possible that 'a broad Left base' might use Labour as a vehicle to haul the country along the road to a Socialist Britain, but thereafter it would have served its purpose and would have to be replaced by 'a totally new socialist party', ready to carry out wholesale nationalisation. 'I can't compromise on this,' he told New Left Review. 'It's no good compromising. History is littered with abortive attempts to reform capitalism. What we need is a complete and utter change in this society.'

incorrect.[102] But the Trotskyists were right to be worried about incentive schemes, which began to create big pay differences between coalfields, undermining the solidarity of the miners. The schemes were opposed by Scargill from the start.

Paul Routledge notes that during this difficult period the atmosphere within the NUM became poisonous and the new star Scargill quickly found himself at loggerheads with established figures on the left like the union Vice-President Mick McGahey – a rivalry which suited the top man, Joe Gormley, very nicely indeed as a way of keeping his unruly forces under some sort of control.

What Scargill had on his side was a lively appreciation of what the media could do for him. He was a speed reader of the daily press and an assiduous watcher of television news programmes. One smart move was to set up his own newspaper as a counter-balance to *The Miner*, the official organ of the NUM. *The Yorkshire Miner* was a tabloid (complete with page three girls) produced in Barnsley rather than London and allowing Scargill to communicate directly with his men. Vic Allen says that this and other local organs went some way towards offsetting the strong conformist message from the national leadership, but never managed to contradict 'the images created by the mass media', which gave a bad name to 'extra-parliamentary activity by trade unions'.

There was plenty to contradict. A 1975 article by Mike Parkin in the *Guardian* ('Arthur's Legends') compared Scargill with 'the dead Alsatian dog in the refrigerator of a Chinese restaurant'. In other words he was the subject of a string of lurid personal anecdotes purporting to be solid fact:

1   The NUM was secretly building him a £20,000 bungalow (around £100,000 today) as a reward for his strike leadership.
2   The Czechoslovak government had offered him a new Skoda car every year for service to the revolutionary cause.
3   Scargill had decided to protect his home with an electrified fence with guard dogs roaming the grounds.

---

102 Production had fallen by nearly 50 per cent from its peak in the 1950s to a mere 120 million tonnes. The number of miners over the same period dropped from 700,000 to 270,000. No wonder the Plan for Coal was as popular as a Lewis Carroll Caucus race ('EVERYBODY has won, and all must have prizes.') It promised an extra 42 million tonnes production, by extending the life of older pits and sinking new ones. Obviously, lots more miners would be needed.

Many of the stories were constructed on the victim's known weak-nesses – for smart cars, for instance. But the alleged gifts became ever more exotic: the Skoda became a Jensen and, as for his homes, hardly a pretty village in South Yorkshire and the surrounding counties was excluded from the list of his potential homes. The *Guardian* consulted a Mr Tony Green, a lecturer at the Institute of Dialect and Folk Life Studies, who described these stories as 'folklore in the horizontal tradition' – stories that spread rapidly and widely, but would quickly perish (unlike the Chinese predilection for dogmeat). 'I suppose it is an accolade for Mr Scargill in a way,' Mr Green said.

Undaunted, Scargill continued to court (and was courted by) the media, lunched at *The Times* and was probably the first union leader to warrant a two-page feature by the glamorous Joan Bakewell in the *Illustrated London News*.[103] He was certainly the only workers' repre-sentative to appear in a Penguin collection of John Mortimer's newspaper profiles, 'Interviews with Some of the Most Influential and Remarkable Men and Women of Our Time', according to the book's cover. Here Scargill sits comfortably alongside politicians, actors, writers, judges, priests, artists and even Mick Jagger.

One of the most prescient pieces appeared in an unlikely quarter: *Harpers and Queen*. The fashionable monthly decided to draw up a list of rising young leaders – partly as a protest against a portentous article in *Time* magazine naming 150 people likely to fulfil the world's need for strong leadership. The *Time* list, with a distinct lack of imagination, included (in its British section) Prince Charles, Roy Hattersley, Shirley Williams and Peter Jay. *Harpers and Queen* thought it could do better, and its front cover for October 1974 featured six men and women destined to end up running the country. 'It is a measure of the change from the Swinging Sixties to the Earnest Seventies that we are all now more interested in people with a solid base of power and influence than in the "glamorosi".'

---

103 Bakewell told me about two sequels to the *ILN* interview: Scargill invited her, along with the newly installed MP for Grimsby, Austin Mitchell, to open the Durham Miners' Gala. (Much against her better judgement, she also had to judge a baby contest.) She was surprised when a plush limousine collected her from the station, but Scargill was blasé. 'If it's good enough for the toffs it's good enough for the workers,' he told her. Yet this disregard for the conventions of the class war had distinct (if perplexing) limits. Some time after the Gala, when Scargill was visiting London, Bakewell invited him to the first night of a play by the Socialist dramatist John McGrath and he refused. 'People in Yorkshire wouldn't like it,' he explained, 'me being seen out in the West End with another woman.'

Arthur Scargill was one of the six.[104]

The choice was easily justified: 'Now that the miners are once again the vanguard of the working-class movement, their bargaining power underlined by the Energy Crisis' (the capital letters are telling), 'the miners' leaders are significant figures.' The youngest, Arthur Scargill, was 'the most militant and yet, paradoxically, the most flexible. The miners' leader, I would hazard, who will go furthest.' The magazine, highlighting his role in Heath's downfall, notes that he must be a considerable irritant to his senior NUM colleagues with his 'barrack-room lawyer habit of saying "I told you so"'. The writer, Peter York, is struck by other ways in which this new breed of unionist differs from his traditional forebears – with his large, comfortable office, massive desk, an electronic calculator to hand: '[He] projects the style of young management, and looks like someone who properly belongs in the *Sunday Times* Business News, selling a great many buses to Cuba.' In passing, York also describes Scargill as 'a shorter, plumper David Frost'. Of whom, more later.

It was hardly surprising that the Barnsley headquarters of 'King' Arthur should become known as Camelot. The King was quite capable of reinforcing his perceived status with airy claims about ambitious future projects, as well as tales of lucrative offers already rejected. He told *Harpers and Queen* that he could have had a five-fold increase in salary – to £20,000 – by taking a (carefully unspecified) 'senior industrial relations job in industry'; and that he was working on a plan for a million-member National Energy Union. Neither claim could be substantiated, but that didn't matter because they gave the portrait greater depth of field. Charles Saatchi would have recognised the technique. Much later Scargill pushed this process to its logical conclusion when he informed the *Independent* that, in 1977, he could have become chairman of the National Coal Board. This unlikely scenario leaves Paul Routledge unconvinced – even though Tony Benn, a Scargill ally, was Energy Secretary at the time. Routledge thinks it more likely that Arthur was simply tantalising his critics yet again with unprovable intimations of greatness.

---

104 The others were Edward Heath's Private Secretary, William Waldegrave; a young political adviser named Jack Straw; the 25-year-old woman running the National Council for Civil Liberties – Patricia Hewitt; a dashing entrepreneur, Dennis Stevenson; and a Scottish banker, Angus Grossart. To pick three future Cabinet ministers, a life peer with a string of directorships and a battery of public appointments, and a knight of the realm with a similar c.v. in Scotland, wasn't a bad strike rate. But it's always nice to see how such articles might return to haunt the subjects: Jack Straw, for instance, recommending the abolition of the public schools.

With Heath out of the picture, and in the temporary absence of any home-grown crusades, Scargill was quick to associate himself with other campaigns against capitalist exploitation – most notably the Grunwick dispute. Asian workers at a mail-order film-processing company in North London went on strike over their conditions and demanded union recognition. The company refused, and bussed in an alternative 'scab' workforce. Mass picketing drew the miners like a honeypot and before long the scenes outside the north London works, according to one Yorkshire miner, made Saltley look like a children's Sunday picnic. Scargill himself was arrested for obstruction, which may have suited him quite well, especially when he was acquitted with the help of photographs taken by the *Morning Star*.

Kim Howells remembers vividly his first visit to Scargill's office in Barnsley (on an NUM publicity mission from South Wales): 'He showed me this huge painting, grey with startling reds in classic Socialist-Realism style, with Arthur, like Lenin, addressing the crowds at Grunwick from the back of a lorry. He was inordinately proud of it.' Howells thought it betrayed delusions of grandeur, but he was even more surprised to hear Scargill speaking about himself in the third person – as the embodiment of the workers' struggle. 'It disturbed me that the hopes of the Left were pinned on someone who was so ignorant of reality.'

———

For all his self-importance and self-promotion, Arthur Scargill never neglected the laborious process of building his power base, brick by brick. And on the other side of the hill the Conservative politicians who returned to Downing Street in 1979 had been just as busy, assiduously preparing the conditions in which the NUM could be defeated. Scargill had made sure that his union would be identified as one of the most dangerous units in the entire labour movement when the great fight came. This might be a source of pride for him, but it also meant that special attention would be paid to ways of weakening his position. At a time when the unions were close to the pinnacle of their post-war strength, and with unemployment becoming a serious social problem, who knows what might not have been achieved with a less determinedly confrontational approach?

A general in the field does not like to hear the language of parley. The war had been interrupted five years earlier and now had to be fought to a finish. On that, at least, the new government agreed. Margaret Thatcher came to power determined to ensure that mineworkers – to recall one of the great clichés of that age – could never hold the country to ransom again. The equation was simple: 80 per cent of the country's electricity was generated by domestic coal. The absolute priority was to provide as many different energy sources as quickly as possible and nuclear power was the first favourite. Nigel Lawson, Mrs Thatcher's first Energy Secretary, admitted later that the policy of 'energy-diversification', which he deployed to justify controversial new nuclear technology, was the code for 'freedom from NUM blackmail'. On this principle, gas-fired power stations would later be given exceptionally generous encouragement and docks were developed for the expansion of coal imports. It took more than a decade for all these developments to reach fruition, but the long-term, terminal decline of the coal industry had begun.

Writing just after the election, Vic Allen ended his book on militancy in the industry with an assessment of the miners' state of mind. He believed that 1972 and 1974 had shown what could be achieved by united action, but in both cases pay was uppermost in the men's minds: a good settlement sent them quickly back to work. As a Marxist commentator, Allen regretted that 'the miners' consciousness did not rise to a consistently higher permanent political plane'. What gave him hope was the way the Left had organised itself at area and branch level, in such a way that 'miners were no longer taken for granted'.

The early Thatcher years saw miners and ministers sparring – an unofficial strike here, a plan for pit closures there. Each was weighing up the other's strength. The most dramatic skirmish came in the first few months of 1981: under a new act, the industry was supposed to become self-supporting within three years, something that couldn't possibly be achieved without axing dozens of pits and sending miners onto the dole. Arthur Scargill held a ballot in Yorkshire and won 86 per cent support for a strike – but the Coal Board's plan was so radical that even the national leadership under Joe Gormley leapt to the barricades. Rather too quickly for Scargill's taste, the government capitulated. The closure programme was cancelled and Scargill was left with a strike threat, which had to be withdrawn without anyone being able to conclude that he had sullied his hands in the murky pool marked 'compromise'.

In the spring of the same year he was interviewed by *Marxism Today*, and tried to explain why talk of victory was misleading and dangerous: 'It's got to be recognised that the Government merely avoided an actual confrontation ... to concede the claim within 36 hours [of the first unofficial walkouts] appears to me to be a very premature decision on the part of the ruling class.' If the battle had not been so rudely curtailed, other workers might have become involved and 'that could possibly have brought the Government down'. He needed to convince his members that ministers had only backed down in order to dull the cutting edge of the miners' rage. A victorious miner is a calm, contented miner: what he wanted was to tap into the 'enormous reservoir of working-class anger and frustration'.

His attitude discomfited his fellow left-wingers, especially the Communists. Andrew Taylor points out that the Communist Party had always been tactical in its thinking – take what you've got and keep your powder dry, or 'three steps forward, two steps back'. For Scargill, compromise, lack of principle and betrayal were synonymous. 'I will never prostitute my principles,' was a frequently repeated theme of his speeches. 'You knew that what he was demanding was not a bargaining tactic,' Taylor says. 'It was a simple statement of his intentions.' This made Scargill an extremely effective orator, but hobbled him as a negotiator. In the increasingly subtle world of the modern media, honesty was a mixed blessing.

Not that Scargill was averse to seeking ways of using the media to his advantage. Like Princess Margaret, he believed that the national press was against him, in principle and in practice. 'One of the things that saddens me', he told *Marxism Today*, 'is that in spite of the barrage of filth, smear and distortion by the capitalist media, the working class ... still has not come to terms with the need for a mass circulation daily newspaper.' Even he realised that the Communist *Morning Star*, with its tiny, totally committed readership, was unlikely to make much difference. His dream was of a trade union daily, read by 10 million members, to combat the 'filth and vile smears' peddled by everyone else. That was one reason why Scargill never blamed working people for putting Mrs Thatcher into power. It was the capitalist press barons, and their lackeys in the failed Labour government, who shared the blame. Consequently, simply electing MPs would never bring Socialism to Britain.

Within a few months Scargill's campaign for the NUM presidency was in full swing. He published a manifesto that ranged far beyond the job he was supposed to be seeking: he railed against Tory economic policies 'accelerating the decline and destruction' of British industry; warned that Mrs Thatcher was 'hell-bent on protecting private enterprise, even if it entails the sacrifice of the human race' (through nuclear war); and told miners that they were at the centre of 'this political maelstrom'.

The longest section, however, concerned pit closures. This was the would-be president's secret weapon. If the NUM failed to take a determined stand, he argued, the future of the industry would be jeopardised. His policy would be to agree to closures only when a pit was exhausted, and in the meantime to campaign for 30 or 40 new pits to restore production to 1960s levels: 'We are not just talking about our own jobs but the future jobs of miners' sons and grandsons.' He also proposed a four-day working week for five days' pay, raising coalface wages on a par with management, retirement at 55 – and, in passing, an egalitarian Utopia:

The NUM must always have at the centre of its perspective one of the basic aims of its constitution: that of bringing to reality the dream of Keir Hardie and the Labour pioneers – the establishment of a socialist society in Britain.

The right-wingers in the union hierarchy had no answer and couldn't even agree on a single candidate. When the ballot was held, Scargill romped home with more than 70 per cent of the vote. Which did nothing for his stunted sense of modesty and realism.

One of the last acts of the outgoing President, Joe Gormley, was to try to dent his successor's rampant self-confidence. The elections (in 1981) coincided with the latest pay negotiations and Scargill – as a matter of course – poured scorn on the Coal Board's 9 per cent offer. A strike ballot was called and he found himself campaigning frantically for a 'yes' vote before he was really ready to send his troops into action. Gormley, as unhelpfully as possible, broke all the usual conventions by writing a signed piece in the *Daily Express*, advising the men that the best they could hope to achieve was a few extra pounds: 'I have no false hopes that Maggie Thatcher will cough up for us.' And then, with cool calculation, he proceeded to decry the agenda of the man who was about to take over the union: 'Some people are trying to turn it into a political argument. That creates dangers that I don't think any trade union should be involved in. If we want to change the Government, we should do it through the ballot box.'

The miners appeared to listen. In any case they voted 'no'. Downing

Street uttered a private cheer. Even Scargill had difficulty dredging a claim of victory from this setback, the first of three he was to suffer before he was finally able to lead his men over the top in 1984.[105]

In the meantime he set up court in the union's London headquarters, where staff greeted him with some trepidation. Most had voted for him, but it was understood that he might want to shake things up and even, one day, to move the offices to a coalfield location. They didn't know the half of it. Within days, stories began to emerge of what was characterised as Scargill's despotic behaviour: the cancellation (without consultation) of a £50 Christmas bonus; the vetting of all invitations to members of staff; the requirement that the President personally should check all incoming mail. This was behaviour verging on the paranoid. Perhaps he regarded all those who had worked with Joe Gormley as inherently untrustworthy, bent on forming some sort of fifth column dedicated to undermining his regime. In the light of Gormley's newly uncovered Special Branch connections, perhaps he was right. Gormley, by contrast, heading for comfortable retirement in the home counties, was rather generous to Scargill, believing that he would mellow in high office, provided he learned his lessons as he went along.

What Scargill never bothered to do was to waste time trying to persuade people to love him. Many of the old-style union leaders, whom I came to know as an industrial correspondent in the 1970s, were outgoing by nature: they regarded cajoling and charming – often in a social setting (a bar) – as an important part of their armoury. Scargill lived his life privately, didn't smoke and rarely drank or socialised. In their book on the miners' strike Martin Adeney and John Lloyd wrote, 'He could be tremendously amiable and charming, but the very power of his charm made it difficult to accept as other than a carefully produced front. He did not offer, socially or publicly, any of the usual weaknesses or habits or dependencies which allow others to feel comfortable, or a little superior.' Instead, he demanded and received 'either adulation or detestation'. Vic Allen, also writing after the 1984 strike, went further: 'He is an intensely shy person, and tends to project himself as a form of protection.'

---

105 Ian MacGregor thought the miners were 'beginning to be unhappy at the prospect of being used as revolutionary cannon fodder in Arthur's army and were perhaps sensing that the Prime Minister's economic policies were, in the long run, the best for the country'. The second half of this contention seems to me almost as unreal as some of Scargill's aspirations. Middle-class, share-owning miners were still some way off.

A year and ten days after his arrival at 222 Euston Road, Arthur Scargill proudly announced that the NUM would be moving to Sheffield. 'London is a place where you can easily get sucked into the system,' he said. 'I have no intention of allowing that to happen.' Most of the staff declined to follow him northwards. *The Times* commented tartly, 'The miners will not miss London. The feeling is probably reciprocated.' The move took place on 16 April.

So it was from his new Yorkshire fastness, two months later, that he watched Margaret Thatcher crushing Michael Foot in the general election with a 141-seat majority. Three months after that she was ready to appoint her champion for the battle ahead – the fearsome Ian MacGregor, invigorated by three years of swingeing rationalisation in the steel industry. Under his chairmanship, the British Steel Corporation workforce had fallen by almost half, from 150,000 to 85,000. Few miners were deflected from their bad opinion by the fact that MacGregor had also managed to stem the precipitate slump in the industry's capacity and had begun to put BSC's long-term finances in order. 'I had had a warm-up at Steel,' he wrote in his autobiography. 'Now, at Coal, if I was to do the job asked of me, I was really going to be running on the ragged edge of acceptability. Or even into the area of unacceptability.' Scargill wrote in *The Miner*, 'Waiting in the wings, waiting to chop us to pieces, is the Yankee steel butcher, MacGregor.'

Was Ian MacGregor responsible for provoking the final showdown in the spring of 1984? Conspiracy theorists were quick to see the announcement that Cortonwood colliery in Yorkshire was to close as a deliberate ploy to force Arthur Scargill's hand. The theory was simple: a threat to a pit in his own backyard was a calculated snub that the NUM President would not feel able to ignore. He would have to call a strike ballot, would probably be defeated for the fourth time and would end up fatally weakened like a wasp that has used its sting. MacGregor himself makes no reference to such a tactic in his self-congratulatory autobiography, but he was writing in 1986, when the issues were still highly sensitive. If it was his clever idea, it must have been galling not to be able to say so.

What MacGregor did was to designate the Coal Board's area directors as 'field commanders', giving them the task of cutting capacity as a top priority. It was the field commander in South Yorkshire, George

Hayes, who identified Cortonwood as a way of achieving his target with a single closure. 'We both felt he should get on with it,' MacGregor said. 'After all, what he was planning was in the best interests of the men.' Hayes claimed later that his main motive was to make sure that men could be found alternative jobs in nearby pits. At the time, this argument sank without trace. As befits the start of an epic struggle, the occasion was marked by the local branch secretary, Jack Wake, with a dramatic speech to the men: he told them that the body of Cortonwood was on the operating table, the area director had the scalpel in his hand and the morgue was beckoning. It wasn't until a decade later that commentators like Seumas Milne could write with confidence about the underlying plan: the key was to choose a pit that was not exhausted, merely uneconomic, a crucial distinction for most miners. If it hadn't been Cortonwood, it would have been some other pit in a militant area. And the miners' leaders were happy to seize this first opportunity to launch their long-laid battle plan.

Scargill knew the risks of another failed national ballot, so he took the simple expedient of not holding one. A few days after the Cortonwood announcement the Yorkshire area was called out on strike: the NUM leaders used the 1981 vote (never implemented), when 86 per cent of the men had agreed not to accept any pit closure except on grounds of exhaustion, to justify their decision. The Scottish coalfield was already seething over another closure plan and by the beginning of the following week the final piece of the jigsaw had fallen into place: MacGregor and his NCB team met the unions, and conceded that the new rationalisation plan would mean scrapping 21 collieries and 21,000 jobs (some 10 per cent of the workforce). Since UK unemployment had just peaked at 15 per cent, this was a suitably frightening prospect.

The lack of a national ballot was still one of the defining features of the confrontation that followed. The journalist Donald McIntyre, a labour correspondent at the time, believes that other unions, like those in the traditional Triple Alliance, which included workers in the steel and transport industries, could have been much more effective allies without this democratic deficit in the NUM. 'Many people thought Scargill might have won a ballot,' he says. 'But even if they had lost, he would have lived to fight another day.'

The few anti-strike voices within the union were swiftly silenced. Kim Howells remembers how Scargill swept aside one particular concern: 'We sent our boys up from South Wales, and they reported that power-station stocks were at record levels. Arthur gave a speech to explain that it was a trick – that the Coal Board had bulldozed out the centre of each pile to make it look higher. As usual, nobody could prove (in time) whether he was making this up.

Scargill had already signalled his willingness to exploit the union rule book to achieve a national strike without the tiresome business of balloting the members. If, under Rule 41, an individual area chose to call a strike under its own constitution, it could do so. Naturally, if all areas followed that course, Scargill would have his strike.

The plan worked immaculately. Both sides were well prepared. Scargill had

(a) circumvented the need for a full-scale ballot;
(b) softened up the industry with the usual winter overtime ban;
(c) established the primacy of the Left in all but a handful of coalfields;
(d) devised a picketing strategy to ensure that the strike would be solid;
(e) put the bulk of the union's funds (in theory) out of the reach of the courts.

Under Mrs Thatcher's tutelage, the government had

(a) begun to drive a wedge between miners through incentive schemes;
(b) allowed coal stocks to build up at power stations and made more of them dual-use, able to burn oil as well as coal;
(c) promoted nuclear power;
(d) introduced fierce new laws to restrict both secondary and mass picketing, and to sequestrate the funds of unions who broke the law;
(e) appointed Ian MacGregor as a guest general.

Paul Routledge observes:

Scargill's dream of a rolling, all-out strike was being realised: a strike that would put all others in the shade, costing some £6 billion, lasting almost one year, leading to 10,000 arrests of miners, 1,000 injuries, three dead, a hundred pits closed and 100,000 jobs lost, the splitting of the once mighty NUM, and deep social unease.

And naturally, Arthur Scargill would declare himself the winner.

It was the nearest that post-war Britain had come to the sort of social revolution seen in France and the United States, but it came too late to have any real chance of changing things. The idea of mass action struggled to achieve credibility: Mrs Thatcher's message of individual opportunity and responsibility had already begun to work its way under Britain's collective skin. After all, many working people had voted for her less than a year earlier. The Labour Party, split, despondent and confused, was in no position to give the affair a wider political focus, even if it had wanted to do so: the breakaway SDP, led by those Labour rebels once described by Scargill as Conservatives, was confidently predicting that it could take over the mantle of the Left.[106] Neil Kinnock, who had succeeded Michael Foot as leader, even argued against using his allotted parliamentary time to debate the strike: he thought it would be a suicidal gesture to ally himself with union leaders who had treated his own party with contempt and whose adherence to democratic rules was questionable.

At the start it was by no means clear that the NUM would be defeated. The strike developed swiftly and by the time the union's Executive Committee met to discuss calls for a ballot, many of the men had been out for a month. Scargill vetoed the ballot, anyway.

The war that followed was fought on many fronts, from the physical battles on the picket lines to emotional blackmail over working miners (and miners' families) but also – as a running theme – bitter competition for the dominant media images. Inevitably Scargill had his eye open for a new Saltley, an iconic television victory for the fledgling strike, and in late May he thought he'd found the perfect location. The Orgreave works near his headquarters in Sheffield supplied coke to the Anchor steelworks. When train drivers refused to cross picket lines, British Steel organised convoys of lorries. On Bank Holiday Monday, Scargill visited Orgreave (realising, perhaps, how grateful the media would be for stories to enliven a holiday weekend) and appealed for help in stemming the flow of fuel.

When thousands of men answered the call, they were confronted by matching numbers of police, and the resulting violence caused dozens of injuries and arrests over a period of three weeks. One part of the

---

106 In alliance with the Liberals, the SDP came just 2 per cent behind Labour in the 1983 election – even if the breakdown of seats was a rather more decisive: 209–23. Such is the reality of the first-past-the-post system in British politics.

script required the NUM President himself to be arrested by the ruthless agents of capitalism. It duly happened as he marched at the head of a band of 50 men towards a favoured picketing position. After a vigorous verbal exchange, Scargill was hustled off, crying in anguish '1984 – Great Britain!' – which was possibly a nod to George Orwell's vision of a police state, but also described the simple facts of the matter. It was an invaluable aid to his publicity drive.

As the days wore on, and convoys of coke lorries continued to plough their way through the picket lines under police protection, it became clear that Orgreave, unlike Saltley, would not provide Scargill with the hoped-for grand finale. Instead, on the climactic day, there was mayhem. The Labour MP Stan Orme, who was trying to keep lines of communication open between Scargill and MacGregor, watched a video of the fighting and was reminded of the English and French armies slugging it out at Agincourt. The President himself fell down a bank and was carried away by ambulance to Rotherham Hospital. In the confusion, it was impossible to tell whether he had indeed been struck by a police shield, or whether he had simply lost his balance.

The King's departure from the field left his troops even more enraged. But for all the violence on both sides, and despite the presence of 10,000 pickets on the final day, 18 June, Orgreave remained open. Michael Crick, writing a few months later, judged that the miners had been too disorganised and ill-disciplined to compete with an army of police officers determined to stand their ground. In addition, a demoralised trade union movement was unwilling or unable to provide the same level of support on which Scargill had relied at Saltley.

The miners were convinced that the media contributed to their setback, by repeatedly broadcasting pictures of pickets on the attack – one famous scene showed them using a telegraph pole as a battering-ram – and suppressing pictures of police assaults on their lines. But most viewers were not in a position to make refined judgements about the rights and wrongs of Orgeave, or anywhere else where mass picketing took place. What they saw on their screens was a level of violence that was alarming and – to most – unacceptable.

It falls to the victors to write the history of the wars they have won. In 1972, Scargill had forced the authorities to engage in a fight they were likely to lose at Saltley Gate. This time the tables were turned. Ian MacGregor was able to look back with some satisfaction at the way in which Scargill committed himself to closing the coking plant:

'We were quite encouraged that he thought it so important and did everything we could to help him continue to think so, but the truth was that it hardly mattered a jot to us – beyond the fact that it kept him out of Nottingham.' And Nottingham was turning out to be the key to the whole dispute.

Of all the coalfields, Nottingham, the second-largest in the land, was the least willing to accept Scargill's law. The rivalry with the neighbouring Yorkshire area dated back to the 1926 strike, when George Spencer set up a breakaway union to protect working miners. The union only survived for a decade, but its act of betrayal was never forgotten across the border in Yorkshire: Spencerism was regarded as a mortal sin. By the 1980s Nottinghamshire boasted many of the most high-productivity pits in the land and the men, as a consequence, were among the highest-paid in the industry. Since both history and economics suggested that their solidarity could not be relied upon, Yorkshire activists began picketing Nottinghamshire pits immediately – often mob-handed and without official sanction. A series of bitter and bruising encounters followed, which did immense damage to the prospects of union solidarity. Mick McGahey, Scargill's Communist Vice-President, admitted later (to Martin Adeney and John Lloyd) that this action alienated the Nottinghamshire men. 'I think if, as an executive, we had approached Notts without pickets, it might have been different,' he said. As it was, Nottinghamshire's ballot produced a 73 per cent vote against the strike.

Thousands of pickets from striking coalfields tried to bring Nottinghamshire to heel. And the police devoted extraordinary levels of manpower to the task of keeping pits open. Andrew Taylor was working for Channel 4 at the time, and when he realised that 8000 officers were being concentrated on this one area, it dawned on him that the miners were going to lose. 'I remember telling my father [the Yorkshire NUM President, Jack Taylor], "I think it's over. They're not going to back down."' That was on 16 March, one week into the strike. Ian MacGregor explained why the Nottinghamshire struggle was so vital: 'While the men there were working, their presence would act as a beacon to encourage those elsewhere to come back, too. It would show it was possible to defy the NUM and live.' The union claimed that it managed to get 12,000 of the area's 30,000 miners out on strike by the end of April – though the Coal Board put the figure at nearer 5000. (This statistical skirmishing was a regular feature of the strike – with

each side offering an alternative version of what was really happening.)
Whatever the numbers, the NUM were unable to defeat the men they
called the scabs.

The damage done by this complete breakdown of union solidarity
would prove to be irreparable. A year later, when the strike was over,
Nottinghamshire and South Derbyshire, along with another group of
'scabs' from Durham, left the NUM to form the Union of Democratic
Mineworkers (UDM). The hatred generated between coalfields thrives
to this day and will take longer to die away than the lives of those
involved.

It seems strangely appropriate, in the world of absolutes where Arthur
Scargill has always dwelt, that the best chances of resolving the strike,
during July 1984, foundered on a piece of wordplay – indeed, on a single
word: 'beneficially'. Arthur Scargill was prepared to accept an under-
taking whereby pits could be closed when they had no coal reserves
that were workable, or that could be developed. Ian MacGregor insisted
that the word 'beneficially' be inserted before 'developed'. This simple
addition – in Scargill's judgement – would allow the Coal Board to do
what it had always wanted to do: to close any pit that was losing
money. And he was right about MacGregor's intentions. 'My belief',
MacGregor wrote in his autobiography, 'was that we had to have the
right, however it was couched, to close pits for sound economic reasons.'
But in being right, Scargill also revealed how wrong his underlying
strategy had been. As Paul Routledge puts it,

> For twenty years he had hammered away on his one-club policy
> that 'there is no such thing as an uneconomic pit', and many of his
> members believed him. By sheer force of personality, he had
> persuaded a large and dedicated group of working people that he
> had the answer to their problems, and by extension to those of all
> working people. He had mesmerised a generation of miners, and a
> significant tract of public opinion. It was only when his assertive-
> ness and sense of mission came rudely up against a more powerful
> force – the state, in all its ramifications – that its weakness and
> sheer wrong-headedness became clear.

In the absence of a deal that might satisfy Scargill's search for total victory, the strike dragged on for a further eight months. But the numbers of strikers continued to dwindle through the late summer and autumn, and so too did the support of other unions. Saatchi & Saatchi played their part with a newspaper advertisement headlined 'Come Off It, Arthur!' which helped to rally opponents of the strike. Margaret Thatcher and her ministers managed, for the most part, to stay in the background, thus avoiding Edward Heath's mistakes. In Arthur Scargill they had found the perfect enemy.[107]

When the end came, the obsequies were painful for the NUM leadership and Scargill, as usual, seemed to be operating in his own special sphere: 'This union has put up the greatest fight in the history of the trade union movement'; 'The greatest achievement is the struggle itself, because we have already shown that – provided that we are prepared to fight against their policies – we can prevent their implementation'; 'Our members' achievements, I submit, have changed the course of history'; 'Comrades, it is upon struggles such as this that democracy itself depends!'

Kim Howells, having helped to keep the strike solid in South Wales, saw things very differently. 'Nobody down our way believed it was a victory. Nobody thought we'd won. Yet people were immensely proud of what they'd done. I never heard a miner say, "I lost a year's wages." When pits started to close, people just said, "Arthur was right all along." '

Those miners who stuck it out for the whole year certainly achieved one of the most remarkable acts of defiance and self-abnegation in recent history. But the sacked miners who failed to get their jobs back, the union officials ejected from warm offices and sent back down the pit and the working miners traumatised by the loathing of their colleagues might have quibbled with Scargill's assessment. Ian MacGregor, for whom the men of the UDM – and all those who resisted Scargill – were de facto heroes of the revolution, put the matter crudely: 'It simply does not bear thinking about what might have been were it not for those brave fighters. Imagine if the bullies

---

107 A small industry has grown up around the theory that, behind the scenes, Mrs Thatcher gave the security services free rein to undermine the miners' cause. Matters came to a head in 1991 when the *Daily Mirror* published an exposé alleging that Scargill had used Libyan contributions to the NUM fighting fund to pay off his own mortgage. The accusation, one of many, was disproved in due course. But Seumas Milne's investigation called *The Enemy Within* claimed that the *Mirror* story was part of an elaborate dirty tricks campaign – amounting to a 'secret war against the miners'. And eventually, a decade after the event, the *Mirror* editor at the time, Roy Greenslade, offered a public apology for his part in disseminating false accusations against Scargill, though the reporters involved insisted that they had not been duped.

had won. Imagine if the thugs now had the industry to themselves. How much mercy would they have shown to those who dared to disagree? Sadly, many of them are still there, even now skulking in corners, waiting for the chance to put razor-blades in a man's pit-bath, or urinate in his snap tin.'

Cortonwood Colliery closed a few months later, to be followed by two dozen more pits over the following year. By that time the size of the colliery workforce had collapsed to 133,000, a drop of 25 per cent. And still Scargill did not give up. At the NUM's 1986 conference he demanded action to prevent more pit closures. 'We can either surrender or fight back,' he cried. 'There is no middle ground.' An audience that had so often cheered him to the rafters listened to him in silence.

Looking back from his position as a Labour minister, Kim Howells reflects on what might have been: 'Without the strike, I do believe the pits would have closed more slowly. The unwritten story for people like me is that it helped to destroy the concept of public ownership.'

The impact of the strike certainly spread far beyond the coalfields. In the analysis by Martin Adeney and John Lloyd, Arthur Scargill succeeded in politicising the entire union movement, but hardly in the way he intended. Many union leaders and activists were turned away once and for all from policies that were explicitly, or implicitly, revolutionary; they learned to accept instead that their kind of Socialism 'came only through electoral gain, and if that could not be achieved, they had to make the best of the world as they and their members found it'. The notion that the unions could act as the vanguard for an uprising of the proletariat – the technical term is vanguardism – was discredited, probably for ever. The Communist Party itself – according to documents obtained by Paul Routledge – gave Scargill's performance short shrift. 'The "total victory" argument is a cover-up for politics or strategy that did not succeed, nor could they have done,' in the words of Pete Carter, a CP organiser. 'It stems from a philosophy that is unable to understand the politics of Thatcher's Britain.'

From the employers' side of the industrial fence, many watched what happened and drew their own conclusions. Within two years Rupert Murdoch was setting out to break the power of the print unions by transferring his operations to Wapping.

The industrial unrest of this period, along with high levels of un-employment, confirmed the steep decline in union membership from its peak (in 1979) of 13.2 million to 11.1 million in 1984 and 9.8 million in

1990. The following decade saw a further drop of 1.5 million men and women. The figures stabilised at around 8 million, especially when new super-unions began to offer personal and business services to their members. The old reasons for joining a union – solidarity, comradeship, political clout, duty – have more or less disappeared. (In 2001 a mere 37 per cent of mineworkers bothered to join the NUM or any of its rivals.) As Anne McElvoy has suggested in the *Independent*, 'Trade union leaders and members of the Royal Family ... are reminders of a society which is receding – one in which there were automatic loyalties expected of workers towards a particular union and of the general citizenry towards the monarchy.' The miners' strike helped to hasten and confirm this disjunction between working people and their traditional representatives. Which was the opposite of what Arthur Scargill had intended.

Did Arthur Scargill notice the ironic overtones of what happened in October 1992? Unlike Mrs Thatcher – driven from office by her own, once loyal, supporters – he was at least still in his post. But in the years following the strike he had watched powerlessly as his industry was dismembered: 100,000 more miners had lost their jobs; 140 pits had closed. And now Michael Heseltine, self-anointed President of the Board of Trade, with blithe disregard for that other President far away in the north, announced that 31 of the remaining 50 collieries would be closed, many with immediate effect.

An outpouring of anger greeted this plan – and not just from Arthur Scargill. To the government's dismay, Middle England rose up in all its quiet might to protest against the humiliation of a noble band of men – men who had sustained the nation at its times of trouble. From all over the Home Counties they came, to join the mineworkers on the streets of London; the smiling Scargill joined them, was cheered by the businessmen on the Yorkshire Pullman Express, received bouquets from twin-setted ladies and blithely ignored the fact that many of his new friends were pillars of the very Establishment to whose overthrow he had dedicated his life.[108] More importantly, enough Conservative

---

108 This was another black mark in Scargill's black record among other far Left groups. The 'Save Our Pits' movement, according to the Marxist organisation Social Equality, 'suppressed any independent political movement of the working class' at precisely the moment when the 'entire financial and political strategy of the bourgeoisie was threatened' by Britain's ejection from the European Exchange Rate Mechanism. Damn, another revolutionary opportunity slips by.

MPs rallied to the cause to threaten the government's small majority. The plans were duly deferred. At last Scargill had a victory of a sort to celebrate.

But this victory, like so much that had gone before, turned to coal dust. The protests withered, the restless media moved on and the MPs, more or less sheepishly, returned to the fold. Scargill fed this process (especially the desertion of the Tory MPs) by calling for strikes whenever it looked likely that elements of the plan might be reintroduced. The tide was running hard against him. His employers, now called British Coal, lured away more and more men with enticing redundancy terms; the newly privatised electricity companies showed no interest in buying more coal and thus falling again into Scargill's embrace. Nine months after Heseltine's first statement, even pits he'd originally reprieved started to close.

Arthur Scargill had been proved right again. Every prediction he ever made about the decline of coal came true. The only question he never seemed willing to answer was: would the story have been different if one of those engineering firms in Barnsley had looked more kindly on the 15-year-old Arthur back in 1953 and saved him from a miner's lot?

By 2002 the number of surviving pits had fallen to 13 – all in the hands of the capitalists. The ranks of the mineworkers had been decimated. Fewer than 5000 now worked in the industry, a reduction of 97 per cent since 1984. Consequently, the National Union of Mineworkers had been cut to a core of around 3000 and its conferences, once a byword for passion and commitment, were reduced to a single day every two years. Because it refused to sit at the same table as the treacherous UDM, the NUM was even excluded from negotiations with its main employer. Sheffield City Council was threatening to issue a compulsory purchase order on the grandiose headquarters that Scargill built in 1989, but abandoned five years later.

Also in 2002, the year in which he finally retired as President of the NUM, Arthur Scargill persuaded his colleagues to retain him as a consultant to the union for a salary of £12,000 a year, and honorary president – presumably for life.

As for politics, Scargill's ambivalence to Labour never waned, even though (by his own account) he was offered several opportunities to become a Labour MP: he told Joan Bakewell in 1978 that he'd turned down three seats; when he spoke to John Mortimer in 1983 the number had risen to four; and by 1988, in his *Desert Island Discs* interview, he was telling Sue Lawley that six safe parliamentary seats had been open to him. He was never tempted: 'If you ask who is the MP for so-and-so constituency they'll have very great difficulty telling you. On the other hand, if you ask them who is the president of the NUM, or the general secretary of Transport Workers, I've no doubt they'll tell you instantly.' That name recognition for union leaders has largely evaporated in the few short years since then.

What turned his deep-seated disappointment with Labour into outright rejection was Tony Blair's success in scrapping Clause 4 of the party's constitution. On May Day of 1996 he announced the creation of the Socialist Labour Party as 'the only real alternative to the multifarious marionettes of capitalism' and 'the political heir' to the miners' strike. Here, at last, was his chance to prove that the labour movement could be mobilised purely to create political change, with the unions providing a counterbalance to Labour's lurch to the right.

Twelve months later he faced his first public election since his inauspicious attempt to become a Worsborough councillor in 1960. Standing in Newport East against Alan Howarth, who should have been an easy target because he had defected to Labour from the Tories, Scargill scored a respectable 1951 votes, came fourth and saved his deposit. He even persuaded Ken Loach to make an election broadcast for him. But this turned out to be the high-water mark of his fortunes. After bitter wrangling before the 2001 general election, the SLP declined to join the left-wing grouping known as the Socialist Alliance. Just in case there was any confusion in voters' minds, SLP candidates went under the banner: 'Socialist Labour Party – Leader Arthur Scargill'. He mustered 116 candidates, but their average vote was just 500 and even the leader only persuaded 912 people to vote for him in Hartlepool, standing against the symbol of everything he hated about the Labour Party, Peter Mandelson. Many were surprised that he'd made so little impact. Would there ever be a better chance for the Left to make a statement about Tony Blair's New Model Party?

The rival Socialist Alliance fared only marginally better across the country. Nonetheless, the magazine *Red Pepper* concluded that the Left had done enough to build solid foundations for future elections –

'foundations which could be dramatically strengthened if the two groups [Scargill's SLP and the Alliance] can work out a way of not splitting hairs and splitting their vote'. That did not seem particularly likely. The factions of the far Left are capable of deep mutual dislike, and find both forgiveness and compromise distasteful. 'Given the burning necessity of constructing a genuine Socialist party in opposition to the Labour Party,' runs one commentary on the World Socialist website, 'Scargill's attempt to advance the SLP as such a formation can only engender confusion, political disorientation and even antipathy.' And in case readers missed the point, it goes on:

Six years after its formation, the SLP is home to a small group of ageing NUM bureaucrats and the political detritus from the extreme fringes of the old Stalinist and Maoist parties.

Hence, the web writer deduces, Scargill's efforts to maintain his position as NUM President – 'unelected head of an all-but defunct organisation, in order to bolster the fortunes of a party that is similarly dead on its feet'.

Scargill didn't like the Socialist Alliance much, either: he called them 'splitters' and 'a conglomeration of Trotskyist parties'. Rather than kowtow to criticism from that quarter, Arthur Scargill will surely prefer to stay among those who share his belief in Arthur Scargill. And it's hard not to admire his refusal to take no for an answer. In February 2003, he declared his intention to run for a Welsh Assembly seat on a platform of renationalising and reopening the mines. He never wanted to be an MP, anyway. Donald McIntyre sees his indefatigable self-belief as both a strength and a fatal weakness.[109] Paul Routledge is convinced that he would want his epitaph to be 'I was right'.

Many of those who have met him over the years have attested to his personal charm and charisma. Tony Benn reckoned that 'history will treat Arthur much more generously than any of his contemporaries'. The man himself believes that he always suffered from the public's mistaken image of the Scargill they saw on television: but he never seemed to mind too much. And in many ways what people saw was exactly what there was. The columnist Deborah Ross allowed herself

---

109 McIntyre told me that the only political figures who had ever figured in his infrequent dreams were Margaret Thatcher and Arthur Scargill: 'He was a very vivid figure in the national consciousness. And in mine too, I suppose.'

a flight of fancy when she interviewed him: 'The thing about Arthur is that ever since he refused to sit the 11-plus he's been fighting, fighting, fighting. And it makes you wonder: doesn't he ever get fed up? Doesn't he ever tire of it? Doesn't he ever wake up and think – no, not today. Today the proletariat can look after themselves. Today the bourgeoisie can have it all their own way.' But she knew the answer to her own question.

FIVE

David Frost –
Television Man

In 1967 David Frost – already a media superstar at the age of 28 – wrote a humorous survey of contemporary life and culture, *To England with Love*. His co-author was Antony Jay, future creator of the television series *Yes, Minister*. Their aim was to distil the essence of Englishness at a time of flux. Had our traditional hypocrisy, frigidity and snobbery really given way to honesty, warmth and equality? Or to put it another way, did the liberating atmosphere of the Sixties signify new life, or the last fling of a declining Empire (a word which often still qualified for a respectful capital in more traditional circles than those occupied by the authors)? The book is an affectionate snapshot capturing a moment of extreme self-doubt, the beginning of the end of certainty.

Ruin and misery the pundit sees as he gazes upon his England. Huge debts, inefficient industries, antiquated unions, uncompetitive managements, inadequate exports, depleted reserves, severely restrained wages, congested roads, decaying cities, irresponsible adolescents, irreligious clerics, escaped convicts, television addicts,

short-sighted bureaucrats and myopic politicians. All trying to
support the crumbling ruins of a derelict empire with an inadequate
army, a doubtful currency and a Royal Mint with a hole in the
middle [This last refers to the building of the new Mint at Llantrisant
in South Wales].

The authors come to no firm conclusion on the questions they set
themselves, but in their wry commentary on such subjects as
class, religion and politics, they are struck by the disjunction
between the conservative instincts of the Fifties and the apparent
attractions of the liberated Sixties. The rapid onset of new freedoms,
they decide, was unsettling for all but the young, who were too busy
enjoying them to worry. But many others thought it wasn't fair.
Those whose own youth had coincided with periods of depression
or war had grown up expecting to enjoy the good times in later life –
a reward for tireless endeavour and financial caution. The new
generation wanted everything immediately, and didn't feel the need
to say thank you.

England's youth are all living with each other; they ignore or insult
their parents and teachers; they break into houses and beat up old
ladies; they have no respect, no discipline, no morals. They are out
taking drugs while their parents are safely tucked up in bed with
eight whiskies and three sleeping pills inside them; they have sex
orgies when respectable people are reading the News of the World,
listening to pop groups while their parents are seeing The Sound of
Music *for the 133rd time.*

For Frost and Jay (at 28 and 37, somewhere near the generational
cusp), this hypocritical resentment was the stuff of satire. But it
also pointed to the harsh fact that many people felt diminished, not
liberated, by the Sixties. And Frost himself, as one of the leading
debunkers of the age, had made his own contribution to the undermining of those social institutions which the young had come to
despise or ridicule – not just Church, family, democratic politics
and the monarchy, but respect for authority, deference, self-
restraint and a belief in shared (traditional) values. All that was
left of the old ways, the writers decided, was the deeply ingrained
class-consciousness of a nation 'suffused with the essence of

snobbery'.[110] They painted a picture of an elite – an Establishment – constantly renewing itself, giving ground where necessary, dealing with revolution by inviting the revolutionaries to join its ranks, but always, ultimately, in control.

The book relies heavily on scripts from one of Frost's television projects of that period, the *Frost Report*. The theme of the first edition – in March 1966 – was 'authority' itself and the list of targets is revealing: local council staff (local *authorities*), the Civil Service, the police, teachers, private education, the Bible, unprincipled industrialists, park keepers, soldiers, politicians and all those who blindly do as they are told. Frost's own verdict – 'so much of authority is a confidence trick'.

There is one interesting omission from this list: television itself. Apart from a piece of technical trickery that gave the plummy-voiced newsreader Robert Dougall a broad Birmingham accent, this programme set TV (and certainly its satirical storm troops) apart from the fray, wittily portraying the action from the sidelines. David Frost is always the master of ceremonies, guiding his audience through the sketches and quick to underline the serious points behind the fun. His is the new authority figure, a figure practically immune to challenge (except occasionally in the libel courts): you laughed with him, or you were – by definition – judged to be an accomplice of the butts of his humour, guilty by association of hypocrisy, abuse of power or cant.

No wonder the satirical outpouring of the early Sixties was so popular. It was refreshing, dangerous and funny. It released a safety valve that had been screwed down tightly since before the war. It was fiercer and more pointed than anywhere else because it needed to be: the Establishment's grip on the way society worked had been so complete. It was brave. The BBC, and to some extent its commercial cousins, were embedded in the Establishment, hamstrung by the

---

110 By definition a class system is shaped like a pyramid, and it relies on the understanding that there's always somebody on whom you can look down – as in the classic television sketch with John Cleese (6'5"), Ronnie Barker(5'8") and Ronnie Corbett (5'1"), which ends:

Barker: We all know our place, but what do we get out of it?
Cleese: I get a feeling of superiority over them.
Barker: I get a feeling of inferiority from him [Cleese] *but a feeling of superiority over him* [Corbett].
Corbett: I get a pain in the back of my neck.
This appeared in the *Frost Report* in 1967.

authority which gave them the licence to operate. And it all began with an ill-defined sense of grievance and dissatisfaction among those 'untainted with the brush of the Fifties'. 'Increasingly, as a country,' Frost wrote in his autobiography, 'we no longer trusted the people whose business was leadership, who were born to rule, and who were older and knew better than us.'

Gradually, as the assault developed through the decade, authority realised that it had little choice. As it has always done at times of social change, it simply waited for the storm to pass, knowing that the best way to neuter the perpetrators was to swallow them up and regurgitate them as grateful members of the club. Few underwent the process so swiftly and painlessly as David Frost: the osmosis was complete when he became a knight of the realm and was able to call on Princess Diana as godmother to his youngest child. As the comedian Frankie Howerd once remarked, 'David started by attacking the Establishment, and ended up owning it.' Yet – in the words of one television critic – 'how much more secure he might feel up there at the top of the tree, but for the satirical excesses of his youth'. There is no doubt that the old Frost would have been one of the young Frost's prime targets.

———

Not many men have their epitaphs written so early in a long career. The remark in question was made by Kitty Muggeridge, at a lunch with her husband, Malcolm, and Christopher Booker, early in 1968. The two men had been chatting about Frost and, in a pause, she suddenly said, 'I suppose you could say that Frost was somebody who rose without trace.' Thanks to her journalist husband, the description soon appeared in print and has stuck to Frost like the mark of Cain, ready to be recycled in every unkind profile. There have been plenty of those. For a man of such moderate and urbane behaviour, David Frost has attracted curiously fierce feelings – from bewildered admiration of his talents, through irritation and incomprehension at his success, to blind jealousy and simple scorn.

Christopher Booker, a fellow Cambridge undergraduate and TV writer, became a leading Frost sceptic. 'Did the "Frost phenomenon" ever have any reality?' he wondered in 1977. 'Or was it always something of an illusion? The answers to these questions, I believe, tell us a great deal about the curious nature of this freakish medium which in the past twenty years has passed into the centre of our public and private lives.'

Bernard Levin, (ten years older than Frost, but a performer with him on *That Was the Week That Was*) was inclined to be more generous. He, too, suspected – even at the height of Frost's fame – that there was less to him than met the eye. Levin thought he lacked 'what the decade most needed: weight. ... His talent, though often denied, was undeniable, his wit sharp and ready, his judgement shrewd ... yet by the end of the Sixties he had said no memorable thing, left no imprint on the age. Rather had the memorable things been said to him, or about him, or beside him, while the age left its mark on him.' David Frost as a hollow vessel, a blank sheet of paper, an index to an interesting book? Faint praise rings out on all sides. And this for a man who

> *fronted ground-breaking television shows before he was 25;*
> *won an ITV franchise before he was 30;*
> *was, by then, the third most famous person in Britain after the Queen and the Prime Minister;*
> *introduced the TV chat show to Britain;*
> *became the first transatlantic TV commuter;*
> *starred as Richard Nixon's TV confessor;*
> *had presidents, princes and potentates queuing up to confide in him.*

All that, together with the awards, the books, the films, the deals, the public speaking, earned him the title of 'One-Man Conglomerate'.[111] There were setbacks along the way – cancelled shows and failed business projects – but he never (or never publicly) lost his serene belief in himself. That sense of certainty has proved infectious: he has always found others ready to believe in him, too.

Christopher Booker looks at the list of Frost's achievements with the telescope inverted and great deeds become small and insignificant. Frost's, he thinks, has been the quintessential television career, that of

---

111 David Frost's *Who's Who* entry is one of the longest in the book – 66 lines of it: the word 'Frost' appears 37 times, largely because so many of his programmes have been eponymous. Flicking through the rest of the letter 'F' I find that he is only matched by Professor Christopher Frayling, the cultural historian. In his entry the word 'Frayling' appears twice – once in reference to his father and once to his wife. Norman Foster, even after listing many of his most celebrated buildings, only manages 57 lines.

a man lacking any particular talents, but driven by an all-consuming ambition to be famous: 'With most people it is possible to localise their ambition – they want to be Prime Minister, or write a great novel, or make a million pounds. But David's ambition had a kind of distilled purity. He simply wanted to be famous for being David Frost.' In this jaundiced view, Frost's career is like an ice-sculpture, surviving only by constant attention to the ambient temperature: it is magnificent, it can be awe-inspiring, but left to its own devices it will end up as a damp patch on the carpet. As the young Frost put it, so much of authority is a confidence trick.

The first volume of David Frost's autobiography covers his life until 1970. It was published in 1993, and so far – despite its last line, 'But that's another story ...' – there is no sign of the promised sequel. I rang the publishers, HarperCollins, who told me that they had no information about Part Two, let alone a projected Part Three.

Why did he stop? There is plenty of ground still to cover, since Part One only takes us to the age of 31. It bears the cumbersome title *From Congregations to Audiences*, which positions Frost as a performer, but lacks the pithiness that made its author famous. Critical reaction was mixed. His old friend Ned Sherrin highlighted the coyness with which Frost treated both his professional and romantic triumphs, and would clearly like to have heard more about 'the Feydeau-esque complications in which the latter landed him'. The newsreader Alistair Burnett, also well-inclined to his subject, thought that 150 pages of old television scripts could have been edited out of the text. My own impression is that Frost produced a one-dimensional portrait on a monumental scale, almost devoid of human insights, (the pain, the anxiety, the self-doubt, the mistakes – or was he spared such symptoms of weakness?) and reading like a 530-page curriculum vitae.

What had stirred the boy's passions? What might have driven the young man into the vanguard of Sixties social protest? The autobiography offers lean pickings. Everyone is pleasant and decent. David's schooldays are carefree. He is blessed in the schoolteachers he encounters. His parents' love for each other is strong and constant. He chooses the right school subjects. Teaching in a gap year before university, he is instrumental in developing the talents of an ill-disciplined youth. He finds himself 'intellectually engaged' in religion after listening to Billy Graham on his evangelical mission to Britain in 1954 (and being seriously tempted to go forward to be saved).[112]

The worst he can find to say about himself is a passing reference to a watershed in his life when he was getting in with 'bad company'. No clue is offered about what this might have entailed, but luckily the Billy Graham experience at the Harringay Arena, when he was 15, saved him in the nick of time: 'I remained happy to be a mischief-maker when it looked like being fun, but there was never any danger of my going off the rails.' No.

So from this benign and contented background, with two (much) older sisters to reinforce the child's sense of security, what made Frost so keen to expose the essential shabbiness of the world around him? The strongest social commentary in a skimpy opening chapter (15 pages take him to the age of 19, compared with 512 paperback pages covering the next 12 years) follows the story of how he diverted two secondary school pupils away from the local boot and shoe factories where an elitist educational system seemed determined to send them: 'At the time this seemed to me to be an inequity in the English school system that was in urgent need of reform: but quite soon, as my perspectives widened, I started to see that it was symptomatic of a wider need for reform across society – of attitudes as much as structures.'

His first attempt to put the world to rights was on the local Methodist church circuit in Northamptonshire, where his father was a minister. The 19-year-old preacher obviously found the pulpit very much to his liking, which may help to explain why so many of his later television programmes included snippets of advice or admonition delivered with all the authority of a Sunday-morning sermon. His mother told his early (and so far only) biographer, Willi Frischauer, 'At one time, Daddy thought David might like to follow in his footsteps, but the boy seemed anxious to go out into the world.'

Perhaps it is not surprising that a boy self-confident enough to attend to the spiritual welfare of his elders should slide so effortlessly

---

112 This struck a chord with me, having written elsewhere about another son of Methodism and his very different experience of a Graham mission in the 1950s. Alistair Cooke had little sympathy for those who answered Graham's call to Christ – 'The halt and the lame in spirit, surely, but also the pasty-faced, the careworn, a hangdog sailor, "teenagers" in desperation, a mountainous mother and her huge, sullen daughter, regiments of the awkward and the unloved.' But then Alistair Cooke was a died-in-the-wool agnostic. In a television interview in 1969, Graham himself tells Frost that he regrets not having followed up his 1954 mission to Britain – because, had he done so, the country could have enjoyed 'a great spiritual revival' under his leadership. Frost is quite happy to accept this display of arrogance at face value.

into any new environment with so little evident anxiety. Thus he arrived at Cambridge University at five in the afternoon and by six felt as if he had 'lived there for years.'[113] Over the next nine terms (and by neglecting his studies, much to his father's chagrin) he found himself a niche in the prestigious Footlights revue club, beavered away at his writing until he became editor of the arts magazine, *Granta*, and along the way, succeeded in placing articles with national newspapers and inveigling himself on to Anglia Television. Willi Frischauer ascribes these successes to Frost's inexhaustible willingness to put himself about: 'Societies, committees, organisations, functions – he loved becoming involved ... Armed with a bag of coins, he occupied the telephone as if he were linked to it by an umbilical cord. Friends, editors, television executives, were at the receiving end of his incessant calls.'

Cambridge theatre was enjoying a golden period. Peter Cook, John Bird, John Cleese, John Fortune and Trevor Nunn trip through the pages of this episode in Frost's life; Graham Chapman, Tim Brooke-Taylor, Bill Oddie and Eric Idle were not far behind; Ian McKellen and Corin Redgrave loaned him essays to help him scrape through his exams.

What caught Frost's imagination above all was the Footlights experience. The club, with Peter Cook as its guiding star, had attracted a group of (mainly) public school boys, some of whom had also undergone two years of National Service. Both experiences tended to nurture anti-authoritarian tendencies and much of the (schoolboy–squaddie–undergraduate) humour grew from a sense of disgruntlement at the unreasonable – or sometimes plain irrational – rules that governed daily life. Frost was a grammar school boy who just missed National Service, which set him apart from his peers and perhaps helps to explain his tireless desire to be recognised as an insider.[114] In

---

113 When I read this statement it made me blink. Admittedly, he was delivered by his father to the medieval solidity of Caius College, while I arrived by train, destined for modernistic Fitzwilliam and then found my digs were three miles and a steep hill (Cambridge's only hill) away from the college. Additionally my father had died the year before. Even so, one hour for acclimatisation is a startling achievement. By this time the family home was not far away, at Beccles in Suffolk. Somehow his mother contrived to supply him with regular deliveries of cakes – one friend remembers puffed wheat constructions covered with pouring chocolate: they arrived each weekend in a biscuit tin, and may have helped to ward off any incipient homesickness.

114 The National Service call-up ended on 31 December 1960, though the last man was not demobbed until May 1963. Both Cook and Booker were exempted (because of asthma and poor eyesight respectively). Frost would have been caught, but the rules had recently been waived to allow young men to graduate before their call-up. Abolition came before he'd finished his course.

his recent book *That Was Satire That Was*, Humphrey Carpenter provides plenty of evidence of snobbery and retails the story of the old Etonian actor, Jonathan Cecil, congratulating Frost on the 'wonderfully silly voice' he used in his act, only to discover that it was his real one.

One of Frost's secret weapons was his absolute refusal to be deflected from a chosen course. A fellow Footlights player told me that he was 'hopeless' to begin with, making little impression as actor, writer or in any other capacity. Yet by his second year Frost was the Club's Registrar, as well as being named as a member of the scriptwriting team and the company. The following year he had been elevated to Secretary and his name headed the list of writers. He simply never gave up. Frost himself treats his achievements in a workaday manner, implying that anyone could have done the same if they'd had a mind to. ('It was the Lent term before I really got going with the writing. *Granta* and *Varsity*, the undergraduate newspaper, each accepted a piece, and as it turned out they were published on the same day.' Easy as that.)

He certainly benefited from an intense and (most agree) genuine curiosity about everything and everybody. This made him easy to tease. One contemporary recalled a conversation with Frost about an enigmatic Antonioni movie showing at the Arts Cinema (probably *La Notte*, because he thinks it involved lingering shots of Milan cathedral):

Frost: What did you think of that?
Friend: Wonderful, wonderful.
Frost: Yes, it was wonderful, wasn't it.
Friend: But not without its flaws.
Frost: Yes ... what did you think the flaws were?
Friend: I thought it was overly studied, almost pseudo-intellectual.
Frost: Yes, absolutely. It was a bit pseudo-intellectual.

And so on. Eventually (and I accept that my storyteller was exaggerating for satirical effect ...)

Friend: In fact, by the end, I thought it was an appalling film.
Frost: Yes, it was appalling, wasn't it. Awful.

So the undergraduate Frost worked overtime to win the approval of his friends and acquaintances, and even – reportedly – wrote off to a mail-order company at Keynsham near Bristol which was offering three jokes on a chosen topic for 7s 6d. There is no record of whether this source of humour proved fruitful. But untrammelled by any vestige of self-doubt, Frost never missed the chance of a public appearance on more or less whatever terms. The future Tory Education Minister George Walden was the drummer in a jazz band,which hired him to perform in the intervals. 'He strummed a guitar rather tunelessly, and he wasn't very good. We paid him thirty shillings a session,' Walden says, 'and I cannot remember what he did to earn so much for a half-hour performance. But then after seeing him on TV today I still ask myself the same question.'

Gradually, however, his endeavours paid off: he became a part of everything. John Fortune says, 'He behaved in literary and theatrical circles the way you would expect a future prime minister to behave at the Cambridge Union. I felt certain that he would go a long way.' And if doors remained closed to him, like those of an exclusive dining club (whose members dressed up in eighteenth-century costume, complete with periwigs), he didn't mope: he formed his own club, the Cabal. It met at the Garden House Hotel, offering 'right royal dinners by our standards'. His fellow thespians enjoyed the occasional hospitality, but found it a very odd thing for a Footlights man to do – akin to consorting with the enemy.

From an early stage, talk of imitation was often heard. Peter Cook produced a highly rated sketch based on a party political broadcast by Harold Macmillan, and soon Frost was doing one, too. Cook's friends say that he came to resent the way his material was recycled, but was 'too much of a gentleman to complain'. One particular cause of aggravation was the Royal Barge sketch – that first televised dig at the monarchy – which became one of Frost's staples. The undergraduate who wrote the sketch was Ian Lang, a future Tory Cabinet minister, and in his autobiography *Blue Remembered Years* he describes his discomfiture at being caught in the middle of a blazing row between Frost and Cook over the performance rights to his work. Lang tells the story tactfully, offering first some helpful background detail. 'Frost relied on others for much of his material,' he explains, 'whilst Cook almost always wrote his own, though much of it never reached the written page.' Lang remembers Frost being on the lookout for new gags: 'He particularly fancied my Royal Barge sketch, which he duly broadcast on the show [*That Was the Week That Was*], and after protracted negotiations, he bought the UK rights to perform the sketch in his nightclub and cabaret acts.'

That wasn't the end of the affair. In due course, Lang sold the non-UK rights to Peter Cook, who wanted to give the Royal Barge an airing in New York. 'A few months later,' Lang says, 'a furious row broke out between them over who ... should or shouldn't use, on which continent, a modest little sketch that I had knocked up in an hour at Cambridge a couple of years earlier. It became quite vicious, with Cook describing Frost in *Private Eye* as "the Bubonic Plagiarist"'. (Lang is sure that Cook coined the epithet, though Christopher Booker – to whom it is also sometimes attributed – believes it emanated from Jonathan Miller.) Booker later wrote, 'Although [Frost] never produced anything very remarkable, he worked at it all so hard – at his sketches and little bits of journalism, at being everywhere and knowing everyone – that in that highly competitive world he soon became a kind of affectionately regarded joke.'

There is, however, a more generous interpretation of Frost's time at Cambridge: that his real skills were not recognised (or recognisable) at the time. As Antony Jay puts it, 'His generation at Cambridge had people of amazing talent as writers and performers: David's talent was being an editor, an impresario, and I think they felt that was vaguely parasitic.' And if some of his undergraduate friends laughed at him behind his back, they were soon forced to take him seriously after he left.

The humour of this period made such a huge impact partly because its creators were willing to abandon the deference that had sustained the status quo in Britain since the war. One crucial turning-point – at the start of Frost's second year – was Kennedy's presidential success. Harold Macmillan, who had himself enjoyed a stunning election victory only 18 months earlier, immediately began to look every one of his 65 years next to the 35-year-old in the White House. He was the most obvious authority figure of all: tall, aristocratic and – quoting Booker – a 'fuddy-duddy Edwardian father-figure'. He had become Supermac in honour of his miraculous political achievements, but in the hands of the tyro satirists the sobriquet became a running joke. Television's caped crusader exemplified all the youthful vigour ('man of steel', 'faster than a speeding bullet') that Macmillan lacked.[115]

Not that the topics chosen for Footlights revues were predominantly political: Cook, in particular, drew much of his inspiration from the surreal humour of the Goons. It was just that the complacent, class-based politics of the Tories under Harold Macmillan turned out to be a gold mine of material. (Who could resist a topic like the Blue Streak ballistic missile system, on which hundreds of millions of pounds of public money was wasted, because it took so long to load with fuel that Russia could have obliterated Britain before a single rocket left the ground?)

Some of the group embraced left-wing ideologies, though in the case of John Fortune the motive was more romantic than political. 'If you lived in a house with an outside lav,' he says, 'you seemed to be irresistible to girls.' Fortune says that it was unusual to see any of their number reading newspapers or watching television news. (Only a few – Christopher Booker was one – were genuinely fascinated by politics and for him America was where all the interesting developments were taking place.) In this sense Frost fitted in comfortably: no strong opinions were required, just the ability to spot the gaps between the superficial image of British society and the underlying reality. Twenty years later, in his autobiography, he gives this process a gloss to which few of his fellow performers would have laid claim at the time: 'It was not that we expected our generation to take over the world and suddenly turn it into paradise. It was just that we were being forced to the conclusion that we could scarcely make a worse job of things than the current crew.'

In Peter Cook's Cambridge heyday Frost himself was still a relatively minor player, but then they were all in awe of Cook's genius. In the late spring of 1961, Fortune and Frost were in the cast of a Footlights revue in Cambridge: Cook, along with Dudley Moore, Alan Bennett and Jonathan Miller, was causing a sensation in *Beyond the Fringe*, which had just opened in London. Humphrey Carpenter points out that this was the first occasion on which the word 'satire' was used

115 *The Adventures of Superman*, which ran on American television from 1953 to 1957, became the first science fiction programme to be shown on the ITV network and was hugely popular. It was the cartoonist Vicky, who gave Macmillan the Superman cape – an unmistakable image, which television quickly borrowed. The Prime Minister was therefore one of the first British politicians to have his public persona reconstructed by television. This process reached its apogee with *Spitting Image* (1984–92) which helped to define perceptions of people like Roy Hattersley and David Steel, and not always for the best.

to describe the work of these young actors. An ecstatic Bernard Levin (in the *Daily Express*) praised 'a revue so brilliant, adult, hard-boiled, accurate, merciless, witty, unexpected, alive, exhilarating, cleansing, right, true, and good that my first conscious thought as I stumbled, weak and sick with laughter, up the stairs at the end was one of gratitude'.

Before long, Cook – riding on the crest of a wave of critical approval – had taken over a Soho strip club and turned it into The Establishment, what the *Daily Mail* called the first ever satirical nightclub. John Bird and John Fortune from the Footlights crew soon became regular performers. While Christopher Booker, another Cambridge man, had spotted a market niche for a magazine to celebrate the new humour: *Private Eye* was born.

Frost had no intention of being left behind. One woman who knew him at the time describes him as 'thin, pasty, spotty, with greasy hair – and deeply jealous of Peter Cook and the others he'd been at Cambridge with', though she still found him 'sweet and funny'. His career started modestly enough. He was taken on as a trainee by the ITV company Associated Rediffusion and Christopher Booker notes: 'It seemed he might easily vanish into complete obscurity.' A survey of the comedy of the period (Roger Wilmut's *From Fringe to Flying Circus*) says Frost 'was attached as a very junior assistant to the magazine programme *This Week*'. Subsequently, he 'presented a dreadful series called *Let's Twist*, featuring the current dance craze'. Frost himself remembers the show with rather more affection – 'an instant ratings success', which had him touring Paris clubs inviting pretty girls to appear on television.

At the same time, having acquired an agent, he was given some cabaret spots in the West End. In his own words, 'I had also been keeping up with old friends from Cambridge by guest appearances at Peter Cook's new nightclub, The Establishment, in Greek Street, often on my way to a gig at the Blue Angel or the Royal Court Theatre Club.' Or, in Wilmut's version, 'He made a few odd appearances at the Establishment Club, as a stand-in for members of the cast who were indisposed, before doing the two-month stand at the Blue Angel that led to his discovery.' Humphrey Carpenter's *That Was Satire That Was* doesn't mention Frost's name at all in his coverage of those seminal Cambridge years: his first sighting is as a stand-in for John Bird at a London club: 'totally unknown' and 'terrified – or so it seemed – as he was so unrelaxed and stiff as a board that he fell off his chair'. None-theless, it was his performance at the Blue Angel of a Macmillan press conference that caught the eye of a BBC producer, Ned Sherrin, who was seeking talent for a new late-night television show.

It was an important moment for both men, but each remembers it differently (though I suppose it was late at night: Sherrin only reached the club at 1 a.m.) Sherrin recalls seeing a tousled figure, sitting despondently in a corner because his act had gone so badly that he'd been dropped from the bill. Frost disputes this. He refuses to accept that the tight-fisted club owner would have 'rested' a performer who would then have had to be paid for nothing. The upshot was the same. Sherrin liked the Macmillan impersonation, even if it 'lacked the charm of Peter Cook's interpretation, which had been created earlier'. He was impressed by Frost's improvisation skills, too, and his ability to 'bang home a prepared joke as an apparently spontaneous answer', and thought he might have discovered 'a valuable member of the supporting cast'.[116]

Frost duly became one of the team and joined exploratory meetings for the project. The idea was to bring to television screens the fashion-able anarchic humour featured in *Private Eye* and on stage in *Beyond the Fringe*. Critics like Levin and Kenneth Tynan had hailed the return of English satire. As Sherrin put it, 'The old West End targets, inbred and cliquish, were replaced by politicians, royals and other public figures.' Now TV was ready to join the party.

The honour of launching the age of TV satire fell to *That Was the Week That Was (TW3)*, but things might have been different if Peter Cook had not decided to export his comic genius to the United States. The success of *Beyond the Fringe* in New York encouraged him to open an American version of The Establishment – employing the talents of such budding stars as John Fortune, Eleanor Bron and John Bird. This venture meant putting into abeyance the idea that The Establishment might form the basis of a British TV revue. Ironically, it was Bird who had accidentally dreamed up the *TW3* title and he

---

116 Preparation was an important part of Frost's armoury. Willie Rushton used to tell a story about a trip he'd taken with Frost to Dublin to take part in a debate: shortly before they landed, Frost pulled a notebook from his bag and proceeded to run through a series of jokes suitable for the Irish reporters he was about to meet. Attention to detail became his stock-in-trade. Acquaintances were often astonished and impressed by the way he remembered not just their names, but those of their wives/husbands, children and – for all I know – their dogs.

remained Sherrin's first choice as a presenter, only dropping out a fortnight before the pilot. When the BBC scored such a hit with *That Was the Week That Was*, Bird and Cook, far away in the United States, felt rather as if they'd been robbed of their birthright. The man who benefited from this serendipity – the man chosen by Sherrin to step into the breach – was David Frost.

Frost had found his vocation. His feeling for television, fleshed out by the lessons he'd learned from Cook, Bird and the rest, set him on a course to be the first superstar of the new era, rather than a bit-part player – a superstar partly because he *was* first.

And that was typical of the sort of thing that happened to Frost throughout his working life: by dint of perpetual professional motion he was – by definition – in the right place at the right time more often than anyone else. Associated Rediffusion protested at the poaching of their 23-year-old trainee and, according to Frost, offered him a four-year deal worth £18,000, equivalent to more than £50,000 a year at current prices. It was an astonishing figure (and certainly more than my father was earning at the time – aged 49) for a company which, until then, had confined Frost to comparatively menial tasks. He must have been tempted, but agreed to accept the BBC's 13-week contract at £135 a week. His autobiography makes it sound like an act of cavalier madness, but although it was a gamble, he stood to make £1755 (more than £20,000 today) in just three months.

Once he'd signed he became – in his own words – 'de facto joint editor' of *TW3* with Ned Sherrin. Sherrin's autobiography doesn't mention this, though he does speak warmly about the work of the new recruit. 'He was tirelessly inventive and energetic in helping to shape and colour the programme,' he says, noting that Frost was one of the first graduates to know no other job than television. Other colleagues paid tribute to his 'intellectual versatility' and quick mastery of the new medium.

The first edition of *TW3* went out live on 24 November 1962. The targets included the Conservative Party, which had just lost a by-election; the Army; the public relations industry; the nuclear bomb; and the record producer Norrie Paramor, who thereby laid claim to the dubious distinction of being the subject of the first TV exposé. (The team accused him of using his position to promote his own arrangements on the flip side of hit records.) Frost was an immediate hit. Sherrin called his debut 'extraordinary' – 'a triumph, not over adversity, but of diversity'. And he summed up, 'His curious classless accent, sloppy charcoal suit and over-ambitious haircut concealed a man who had come into his kingdom at a bound.' While Christopher Booker watched a remarkable transformation: 'He even looked physically broader.'

No one could define exactly what it was that he contributed, only that he did it brilliantly. The BBC executive Donald Baverstock called him 'the most remarkable man to emerge since television began'. One critic christened Frost 'the first anti-personality on TV'. This was an interesting observation. Personalities traditionally sprang from the light entertainment side of the business: *TW3* was a current affairs programme, which blurred the boundaries between fact and fun. As audiences built up swiftly, far beyond the 3 million originally expected, Frost bathed in the reflected glory of a range of brilliant writers and performers.[117]

There was considerable artistry behind the art. Not just the reading and research that he undertook so assiduously, but also in his personal appearance. Willi Frischauer reports that many of Frost's free mornings, and much of his money, were being spent at the dentist: 'He underwent irritating and extremely painful treatment to straighten out his teeth ... the result did credit to the dentist – the teeth are among the best that flash on television – and to David's determination to allow nothing to stand in the way of success.' Being a star seemed to come naturally to him. Booker remembers sitting in Frost's dressing room during a rehearsal, discussing scripts, when a call came over the tannoy: 'Cue David.' Frost moved to the door, still chatting, until a second, more impatient 'Cue David' rang out. Again, he waited, allowing the sense of expectancy to build up, until finally Ned Sherrin's voice took on a real edge: 'CUE DAVID!' Only then did he make his entrance. And that was just the rehearsal.

As the series developed, some of the writers, like Booker and Levin, were evidently fired with a sense of mission. But society's short-comings did not seem to make Frost particularly cross. In his judgement those who broke the TV mould with *TW3* had no political agenda: it was as if they had inherited the mantle of the 'Angry Young

---

117 Early writing credits included Levin and Booker as well as a string of young men who were making names for themselves as part of the new cultural Establishment: Keith Waterhouse, Dennis Potter, Michael Frayn, Gerald Kaufman, Herbert Kretzmer, Andrew Roth, Willie Rushton, Kenneth Tynan, John Braine – and occasionally my own unofficial godfather, Quentin Crewe.

Men' of the late 1950s without the anger.[118] Frost did claim to be exasperated by 'Britain's recurring failures, by hypocrisy and complacency and by the shabbiness of its politics', but in truth those failures represented above all a source of material for comedy.

It was not just politics. Royalty started to come in for some gentle ribbing, and the Church suffered more serious satirical damage. The Consumer Guide to Religion, framed like a *Which* report on washing machines, brought a gratifyingly shrill response. The writers were encouraged to produce a condensed version of the Bible, à la *Readers Digest*: the Resurrection was characterised with a catchphrase – 'You can't keep a good man down'. Frost's religious faith, a recurring theme in the story of his life, was obviously in abeyance on this particular night.

But political tomfoolery was the company's meat and drink: identifying the silent MPs – those whose appearances in the House of Commons were as rare as daffodils in December – gave rise to much hilarity, while the Profumo affair was like manna from heaven. The minister's liaison with the call-girl Christine Keeler, who counted a Russian spy among her clients, was denied and covered up for three glorious, hypocritical months. When the truth could be hidden no longer, it seemed to justify the programme's assault on the bastions of privilege, and answering the critics who regarded them as teenaged sneerers intent on eroding all that was fine and pleasant in the land. 'The Establishment had been caught with its pants down,' Frost reckoned, 'and unable to hide, was standing red-faced as everyone else fell about laughing. Game, set and match to satire!'

Profumo's career would have gone up in smoke without *TW3*, but Frost believes that the programme played a considerable part in dismantling the reputation of Henry Brooke, whose tenure as Home Secretary was marked by a series of highly questionable decisions – including the extradition of a Nigerian opposition leader to face the possibility of death in his home country.[119] In his autobiography, Frost commented that they saw Brooke as the embodiment of the Old Order:

---

118 In his history of Britain Peter Clarke recalls the impassioned cry of Jimmy Porter, the leading character in John Osborne's *Look Back in Anger*, that there were 'no good, brave causes left' on which to expend the new generation's moral indignation – no Spanish Civil War or Jarrow Marches – and too much affluence and complacency. It was in that atmosphere that satire blossomed. By the mid-Sixties, plenty of new causes had reared their heads, notably Vietnam.

119 Enahoro, as he feared, faced trial for his life without the benefit of a British legal team to help him (as he had been promised). TW3 pointed out that Brooke knew that foreign lawyers would not be allowed into Nigeria. Luckily, the Chief survived, and was

We had always been led to believe that there was a decent ruling class who wisely guided our destinies. But were they decent? Were they wise? Forget about being wise, did they have the remotest idea what was happening under their noses? Didn't they understand that Fifties discipline, order and authority were, in the England of the Sixties, not only stifling but discredited as well? And getting more discredited every week that TW3 was on the air, because you cannot easily refute a laugh with an argument – even with a good argument, and certainly not a spurious one.

In one sense he was right. Politicians had no real defence against this new weapon. Laughter engulfed the guilty (or gullible) like Sarin gas, invisible but deadly, and many reputations never recovered. *Private Eye* was even more brutal, (and less squeamish) but its readership was comparatively narrow. *TW3*, whose audience reached a peak of 12 million, was capable of wreaking much more serious havoc. Everyone was a satirist now. The attacks were not party political, but in a country where power had resided within the same small coterie for more than a decade, the great majority of the political targets were Tories. Edward Heath was heard to growl that *TW3* marked the end of respect in Britain.[120]

Only once, in October 1963, does Frost suggest that he and his colleagues were moved to a real sense of political outrage, when the Conservatives (with the Queen's active participation, as it later emerged) chose a genial aristocrat, Lord Home, to succeed Macmillan as Prime Minister. The decision, behind closed doors, suggested that none of the lessons so generously supplied by *TW3* had been absorbed. Christopher Booker wrote a coruscating piece for Frost to read, thinly disguised as a homily by Benjamin Disraeli to his latest successor. (Frost appeared in a fetchingly wispy false beard.) The piece portrayed Alec Douglas-Home as a hapless sacrifice to forces beyond his control

---

still a significant political figure forty years later.

120 The sense that the programme was somehow an honorary member of Her Majesty's Opposition was not helped when Harold Wilson, the Labour leader, protested at the decision to axe *TW3*. 'We would very much deplore it if a popular programme were taken off as a result of political pressure,' he said. The relationship between a critical media and the governing party was beginning to undergo a profound change, a change whose impact is still being felt today. My own programme, *The World at One*, was banished from interviewing Tony Blair after 1997 because we had apparently shown, in covering the election campaign, an undue tendency to pursue an adversarial approach to Labour. This made us 'Tories' and therefore not deserving of any co-operation from Downing Street.

– a hereditary peer and now, in effect, hereditary leader: 'Your bleak, deathly smile is the smile today not of a victor – but a victim. You are the dupe and unwitting tool of a conspiracy: the conspiracy of a tiny band of desperate men who have seen in you their last desperate chance of keeping the ladders of power and influence within their privileged circle.' There was plenty more in the same vein and the item produced a record 909 calls and letters of complaint.

Three weeks later – just long enough for the voices of privilege to make themselves heard in the corridors of power? – the news broke that *TW3* would not be allowed to finish its second run: the last programme would be on 28 December, three months earlier than planned. The BBC's explanation was that 1964 was an election year, but then it had been an election year when the series was commissioned in the first place. Frost certainly believed that the decision was evidence of an Establishment fight-back – and that for them, the Douglas-Home essay had been the last straw. With admirable honesty Sherrin draws a rather different conclusion: that the love affair between programme and public could not have been sustained at such a level of intensity. When the programme-makers tried to rekindle the passion for the second series, they too often produced stilted and self-conscious material.

At the time, viewers were outraged at the loss of their favourite programme (909 complaints about the Home monologue notwithstanding) and the move was much criticised in the press. One Tory MP, however, said, 'I'm damned pleased. It wasn't English at all. There are some things that English men and women hold as sacred, and they are against these Clever Dicks and their filth.'

The writers and performers – the Clever Dicks – were briefly distracted from their dismay by Kennedy's assassination, which gave rise to an edition both more emotional, and far longer, than usual. (*TW3* had no fixed end time – an indulgence granted to few programmes before or since. The Kennedy tribute was twenty-two minutes over length.) Frost closed the proceedings with one of his quasi-religious declarations: 'The tragedy of John Kennedy's death is not that the liberal movements of history that he led will cease: it is that their gathering momentum may be lost. That is the aftermath of Dallas, 22 November. It is a time for private thoughts. Good night.' The critic Jack Tinker, in a book about *The Television Barons*, described it two decades later as a programme 'which has probably never been

surpassed for its spontaneous response to the emotions of the moment
… it was television at its most immediate and its most impressive'.
The journalist Paul Foot, a school colleague of Richard Ingrams, Willie
Rushton and Christopher Booker, found the result 'sickeningly
sycophantic'.[121]

Five more weeks remained before *TW3* came to its own untimely
end. This was no tragedy – indeed, the final show was more like
a celebration of the 37 editions – but the valedictory programme
shared something with Kennedy's epitaph: nobody thought that the
new vogue for English satire would grind to a halt, yet in television
terms, it had almost shot its bolt. Humphrey Carpenter, historian of
the satire boom, pronounces it dead during the following year, 1964.
English humour (on television at least) was about to set off on a
new track, with programmes like *I'm Sorry I'll Read That Again*,
The Goodies and, of course, *Monty Python*: a humour sometimes
straying into the zany or anarchic, but mostly gentle, ironic and self-
deprecating.

Even over such a short period, *TW3*'s creators, luxuriating in a new
kind of intellectual detachment, had been able to demonstrate to a huge
audience (as opposed to the mainly metropolitan readers of *Private
Eye*) that public men were the same as private men. Once their 'cloak
of sanctimony' (Frost's phrase) was ripped away, they could be seen for
what they were and measured against the same standards as the rest of
the population. The shock of *TW3* came from the fact that no one had
ever used television to attack British institutions before: they turned
out to be sitting targets waiting to be slaughtered, like overweight grouse
on an unexploited piece of moorland. And, in Frost's view, the programme was not so very far in advance of public opinion: two or three
steps at most, 'not seventeen'. As Antony Jay put it, 'No TV
programme could destroy the moral fabric of the nation, but if that
fabric was worn pretty thin, television might deliver the tug that could
rip it apart.'

---

121 The Americans were on Tinker's side. Decca released a record of the show, with
a gushing sleeve note: 'The famous live broadcast of this BBC series, where the satire
turned serious and, with little time for rehearsal, the regular program was scrapped for
a wonderfully unique tribute to the former President from the other side of the
Atlantic.' The following year the cast actually performed it at Madison Square Garden
in front of an assembly of Jewish women. Booker remembers sitting on stage, head in
hands with embarrassment, as sample *TW3* sketches were performed for an uncompre-
hending audience. Frost's Royal Barge commentary left them particularly baffled.

David Frost had now attained the great age of 24 and was enjoying his celebrity: as one newspaper put it, 'He is so rich he keeps a taxi waiting while he has his hair cut.' (Hairdressers grew accustomed to being asked to provide a DF cut by young admirers who presumably thought some of the satire might rub off on them.) A torrent of opportunities poured into his lap – from newspaper columns to cabaret spots and village fêtes. John Fortune remembers being told that the Liberal Party invited Frost to become a parliamentary candidate, but there is no mention of this in Frost's autobiography. The most enticing opportunity of all came when he met his adolescent film star heroine, Janette Scott: she was taking part in the pop programme *Juke Box Jury* at the BBC Lime Grove Studios where *TW3* was in production. David and Janette were an 'item' by suppertime.

As far as everyone outside the studio was concerned, *TW3* was Frost's show. As Frischauer says, 'Even if he had not been the anchorman who pulled it all together, and to whom the camera always returned, the show would still have become totally identified with him. To viewers it was immaterial whether offending lines had actually been spoken by him. Frost was responsible.'

Christopher Booker, who wrote much of the linking material (and some sketches) with Frost found the collaboration 'uncanny': 'Most of the jokes came from me, but where Frostie's skill came was that at a certain point, he'd say, "Right, I think we've got enough now." ... I would go to a typewriter and sit down, and he would virtually dictate a script – he had an amazing gift for putting a sketch together in such a way that it would work on the air.'[122] But although he admired Frost's facility with a script, nothing could convince him that there was much more to it: 'Everything to do with television brought out the hidden shallows in Frost – he had a gift for telly: as soon as he came into a television studio, something happened, he just was at home. It was the one place where he could really be fully himself.'

Others had noticed the Frost phenomenon. Work was under way for his first programme as an independent producer, *A Degree of Frost*. (He

---

122 The temptation to tease never left Booker: once he inserted an introductory paragraph which read, 'Wasn't it Goethe who described architecture as frozen music?' and waited with high anticipation to see what Frost would make of this when it appeared on his autocue in the live broadcast. Blithely unconcerned, Frost eyed the offending sentence and ad-libbed – 'wasn't it some German who said ... ?' Afterwards, almost apologetically, he explained to Booker that it wouldn't have been right for him to sound so literary.

decided to use his given names for his new company, David Paradine Productions. Why? 'It sounded more low-key, less of an ego-trip.' It had never occurred to him, presumably, to try something unconnected with the Frost persona.) More important, within a few weeks of the final *TW3*, agreement had been reached for an American version of the show and by May, soon after his 25th birthday, David Frost had become the first truly transatlantic television personality.

The United States made a deep impression on him. He was enraptured by the big-name celebrity chat shows, in which hosts like Johnny Carson and Ed Sullivan were household names. Booker, who was travelling with him, described his 'unusual state of excitement', and suggested that he spotted 'the Everest of his universe', which would have to be conquered in due course. He could see that the chat show was the 'furnace in which fame was created'.

But, like other British visitors before him, he also felt comfortable in a country oblivious to the niceties of class. He could enjoy the benefits of American anglophilia, knowing that nobody cared about his background. Better still, he had found a place that would applaud his special talent – for being David Frost. 'In Britain,' he wrote in his autobiography, 'ambition could be, and frequently was, used in a pejorative sense. In America it was not only regarded as a compliment, but a deficiency of ambition was seen as being as serious as a deficiency of red blood cells; you were enfeebled without it.' Here, surely, is Frost's riposte to those who, over the years, have turned up their noses at his dogged pursuit of fame and fortune. With a pitying nod to his critics, he goes on, 'While the class system in Britain may have prevented people from feeling that the sky was the limit, it also protected them from the worst of the rat race, and gave them something of an emotional safety net.' He apparently felt no need for such a net and his bravado still takes the breath away. When established programmes like *Panorama* approached the White House to request the first BBC interview with Lyndon Johnson as President, they found that Frost had been there before them (even if, for once, he had failed to bag his man).

Was there an unspoken, unadmitted need lurking beneath that self-confident exterior? Ned Sherrin gives a wicked insight into his collaborator's character with his account of Frost's first appearance on the *Johnny Carson Show* in New York. He and a friend joined David and Janette in a luxury hotel suite to watch the pre-recorded programme go out.

> *Just before his entrance, David became concerned and interested. 'I wonder how they announced me? It was so hectic and noisy back-stage that I didn't hear.' We very soon did. 'Would you welcome the star, producer, writer and originator of* That Was the Week That Was,*' said the genial voice-over. 'Oh,' said David superfluously, 'I hadn't heard that.'*

The producer and originator of *TW3* allowed himself a wry, private smile.

Despite the unthinking snub, Frost started work on a new Sherrin series scheduled by the BBC for the autumn of 1964 (after the election). The plan was to broadcast *Not So Much a Programme, More a Way of Life* three days a week, Friday, Saturday and Sunday, leaving Frost to fly back to New York for the American *TW3* on Tuesday evening. On Wednesday or Thursday he returned to Britain for the following weekend's output. Sherrin called it 'an awe-inspiring schedule', but awe-inspiring was not the way most people felt about the resulting BBC shows – and the star's jet lag was not the main problem.

Why was everyone dissatisfied? *TW3* fans, Sherrin decided, felt cheated by the new format, while the old show's enemies found plenty of reasons to revive old grievances. The situation was exacerbated by a scratchy, bad-tempered production team: Frost claims he was privately unhappy about sharing presentation with Willie Rushton and the writer P. J. Kavanagh, but was too reticent to say so. For a man prepared to go through intense pain for the sake of his grin, this has an unlikely ring. Then Sherrin and Frost managed to fall out over an item on the assassination of the black power leader, Malcolm X, which Frost's finely tuned American antennae deemed worthy of a special edition. Sherrin disagreed.

Nonetheless, from a 'soggy start', the series had just about found its feet – in Frost's description – when it suddenly undertook 'a Gaddarene rush to self-destruction'. The groundwork for this suicidal tendency was laid in an attack on Catholic attitudes to contraception: a priest ticks off a Liverpudlian mother-of-25 when he notices that she is, unusually, unpregnant. He gives her ten shillings, and advises her not to spend it on shoes for baby Michael, but on beer for her husband because he can only perform his marital duties when drunk. An outcry followed, partly because of the offence to Catholic sensitivities, but partly over the implied slight to the Merseyside lifestyle. In the midst of the rumpus the BBC chose to apologise profusely, which severely weakened the team's standing and reduced their ability to resist the crisis ahead.

A few weeks later came a discussion on door-to-door political canvassing, in which Bernard Levin described Alec Douglas-Home as a cretin and, when challenged to withdraw the word, substituted imbecile.[123] (When the Prime Minister was door-stepped at the airport and asked about the programme, he told journalists, 'I did not see or hear it, but I have read about it. This sort of thing is said these days, apparently, but I do think it is an undesirable development.')

Ned Sherrin accepts responsibility for the last straw (and, just in case, Frost points the finger at Sherrin, too: 'Ned was keener to use it than I was not to use it'). And what was the killer item? A gentle mock-operatic treatment of the Abdication, which had already been postponed once because its subject, the Duke of Windsor, happened to be in hospital at the time. It finally went out in the last programme of the series (in March 1965) but, unfortunately, Buckingham Palace had announced the death of the Princess Royal four hours earlier. It didn't occur to anyone that it might be in dubious taste to lampoon the Duke on the day of his sister's death, so nobody had the gumption to withdraw the sketch, which was transmitted before the body was cold. NSMAP (as it was catchily known) was axed forthwith, with no possibility of a reprieve.

Having enjoyed the benefits of being so closely associated with the success of the programmes he fronted, David Frost now paid the price: it was he who would carry the can when things went wrong. As Sherrin put it,

There was one point on which all were agreed: Frost must go. Officials in broadcasting always associate the screen face with the success of the programme – their wives want to meet it, they themselves want to hobnob with it.

---

123 Those involved were, not surprisingly, striving both to match the innovative appeal of *TW3*, but also to demonstrate the originality of the new show. One solution was to be more and more radical, which in turn provoked the critics. One of the most entertaining commentaries came in the *Sunday Telegraph*, whose leader writer wasn't being ironic (was he?) when he decried Bernard Levin's description of the Leader of the Opposition as a cretin, but was more offended by Frost's decision to address a Bishop as 'John' (which was his name) rather than 'Bishop': 'Defying that convention is a more insidious, though less shocking, threat to the amenities of life than hurling puerile abuse at ex-Prime Ministers.' Truly, nothing was sacred.

But as soon as the bottom fell out of the satire market, what did those same officials do?

They polarised their fear of the late-night monster around a determination to behead it by sacking David.

A face-saving deal was struck: Frost would be allowed to present the story as if he had voluntarily declined to commit himself to a third series the following autumn. The terms of this deal can be detected in Willi Frischauer's biography written just six years later. He makes no reference to the nature of the offensive Abdication joke, nor to the way Frost himself became the scapegoat when disaster struck. Frischauer goes so far as to suggest that the BBC was left dithering over what to do next, but that 'the decision on whether or not to engage him for another series was not left to them. Disappointed as [Frost] was about the show's sorry fate, he was too shrewd and too sensitive to the public mood to cling to a worn-out formula.'

Writing 20 years later, Frost himself still treads carefully through this hazardous ground: 'The ending of the programme was quite a shock for Ned and me ...' He analyses the problem as the emergence of a dangerous gap between 'what the raised voices of the self-styled defenders of the moral fabric of the nation found acceptable, and what the wider, quieter public found acceptable'. He quotes (at length) from a defence of their work by John Osborne and ends, 'Ned and I agreed that I would "resign" from the as yet non-existent programme – "making way for an older man" – before there could be any suggestion that I had been sacked. In retrospect it was a blessing in disguise.'[124]

When the American *TW3* also came to an end a month later, the

---

124 I may have missed it, but as far as I can see, Frost's autobiography makes no mention whatsoever of *BBC3*, the show that he had 'unilaterally' decided not to join. Even Frost-less, Sherrin regarded it as one of his most satisfying projects: one of its stars was John Bird, but its most notable contribution to the satirical pantheon was Kenneth Tynan's use of the word 'fuck' on television. It is often said that this single imprecation opened the floodgates to a sea of profanities, but the British media (especially the broadcast media) has remained remarkably resistant to the tide. Even today, I would risk dismissal if I followed Tynan's course – unless a carefully constructed context demanded it. As for the c*** word, I found myself gaping with surprise to read it on the front page of the *Guardian*, when it was attributed to the fulminating Irish football captain, Roy Keane. Obviously I don't read that paper carefully enough. When I put the word into its official website search engine, it came up with 145 hits. Even the rudest words have lost their bite. I never heard my father use a word worse than 'bloody', though I'm sure he did in private. Nowadays there is nothing left if you want to express extreme emotions: dirty words have been eviscerated.

Frost bubble seemed comprehensively to have burst. At about the same time he split up with Janette Scott and heard that one of his American sketches had provoked a $5 million lawsuit. Most 26-year-olds might have permitted themselves a smidgen of self-pity or self-doubt at this sequence of setbacks. Not Frost. He faced the cold wind of reality as if it were just a slightly chilly summer's day. He merely turned up his collar and, in the depths of January 1966, struck a bizarre and brilliant blow for (his own) celebrity.

This is how David Frost describes the genesis of the 1966 event:

> On Monday 3 January I had a simple (as I saw it), private (as I organised it), little (as I planned it) idea. The early days of January are often the dog days of the year. The weather is usually pretty depressing, and the bills coming in from Christmas make it even more so. Wouldn't it be a good time to give a party, mixing up some of the friends I had got to know from varying walks of life? Right now, this week? I settled on breakfast as the time for the party, most of all because of the short notice.

This reads like a masterpiece of understatement and false modesty. The 'friends I had got to know' – more than 20 of them – included Fleet Street proprietors, BBC executives, a bishop, the writer Len Deighton, the head of EMI records, the radical peer Lord Longford, the philosopher Professor Freddie Ayer and a publisher called Robert Maxwell. Despite being given less than five days' notice, only one luminary declined his invitation: Paul McCartney. Another of the friends the 26-year-old Frost 'had got to know' was only too glad to make space in his diary: Harold Wilson. The Prime Minister 'entered a few minutes after the first arrivals, and was in sparkling form throughout. He left for Downing Street at about ten-thirty, champagne was served a little later, and a very enjoyable party came to an end just before eleven.'

And that, Frost says, might have been that, if Downing Street had not inadvertently briefed the parliamentary press about Wilson's appointment, thereby causing 'quite remarkable coverage in the newspapers' – to the host's evident astonishment. There is no evidence that anyone has ever believed this version of events. Patrick Campbell, a journalist with a trademark stutter who had frequently appeared on

TW3, described his perplexity in a newspaper column a few days later, through a supposed conversation with a friend:

> *Campbell's friend: And what in the name of Providence were you supposed to be doing?*
> *Campbell: I haven't the faintest idea. Just having breakfast, I suppose. We finished up with champagne, but Harold left before that. I asked him if he was off to do a bit of governing, and he said he was. That's really all.*
> *Campbell's friend: Didn't you ask Frost what it was all about?*
> *Campbell: I'm sorry, I didn't. I was too shy.*

The breakfast with Frost, of course, was an archetypal PR coup, of a kind much practised these days – an event with no purpose except the pursuit of celebrity by all concerned.[125] Newspapers obediently leapt on the story: 'When Mr Wilson Passed The Marmalade To David Frost And Ate Bacon And Egg With Patrick Campbell,' reported the *Daily Mail*. Self-deprecatingly, Frost told the paper that it really had been intended to be a private party ...

Christopher Booker (in *The Neophiliacs*) pointed out that it would have been inconceivable – even two years earlier – for any media figure to have attracted such 'an assemblage of notables'. 'What gave Frost the knowledge that his gamble would come off was his intuitive sense of television's power to recreate the world on its own unreal terms – to reduce everything and everyone, politicians and pop singers, philosophers and journalists, bishops and entertainers, to the same level, as bit players in a universal dreamworld.' From then on, Frost was the man who 'invited the Prime Minister to breakfast'. Or as Bernard Levin put it, 'At the beginning of the Sixties he was unknown; at its end he was better known than anyone in the country except the royal family, and the Prime Minister himself would fain wait upon him at breakfast, in the hope that some of the publicity might rub off.'

Frost's career was about to take off like a rocket: he succeeded in

---

125 There is a fine historical precedent for the exploitation of breakfast for publicity purposes. Edward Bernays, always billed as the father of PR, arranged a breakfast to improve the image of the morose and monosyllabic Calvin Coolidge, where he was photographed with a batch of Broadway stars, including Al Jolson. It was tough going for the entertainers, but Bernays was gratified by one headline – 'Actor Eats Cake with the Coolidges ... President Nearly Laughs ... Guests Crack Dignified Jokes, Sing Song and Pledge To Support Coolidge'. Three weeks later the remodelled candidate won the 1924 election by a landslide.

bursting open two doors which had so far remained closed to him – BBC Light Entertainment and Associated Rediffusion. Six months later both had confirmed new programmes for the perpetuation of the Frost brand by other means.

The BBC bought the first of two series of the *Frost Report*, with its weekly theme (Elections, Class, Crime, Sex) and its strong anti-authoritarian message: viewers were invited to write in with their 'peeves' and Frost interviewed children for their naïve reflections on the vagaries of the adult world. 'The show was about our illusions and pretensions, and our widespread assumptions,' Frost wrote. 'Our contention was that British society was not changing that much, either for better or for worse, and that the changes were in most cases superficial rather than fundamental, and merely added to or reinforced the long-established contradictions and paradoxes of British life.'

The idea of the format came from Antony Jay and with his linking scripts – as well as cabaret turns by performers like John Cleese – the programmes were played for laughs. The heightist class sketch between Cleese and the two Ronnies was a classic example. Large numbers of writers contributed material – including the future *Monty Python* stars, Michael Palin and Terry Jones. John Cleese is quoted as saying, 'At the end of the show, before this huge list of names, the credits always used to say "Written by David Frost", which was really a bit naughty. *Chosen* by David Frost, fair enough.' Cleese adds gracefully, 'I still acknowledge that without David Frost I would have taken a very long time to get off the ground.' A specially made edition of the *Frost Report* won the Golden Rose of Montreux – the premier television prize in Europe. Just on the off-chance, Frost had taken the trouble to learn how to say thank you in all the 20-plus languages represented at the festival.

Associated Rediffusion, by contrast, settled on something in the current affairs tradition: in-depth interviews in front of live audiences, sometimes interspersed with provocative confrontations between interest groups (teachers or churchmen) and sceptical questioners. It was the debute of David Frost, chat show host, though to begin with it looked as if it might suffer from a shortage of high-quality guests. Willi Frischauer reckoned that 'the stigma of satire still clung to the star of *TW3*' and that 'public personalities seemed afraid to expose themselves in public to what they feared might be the acid wit that had been *TW3*'s stock in trade and had now turned into a double-edged sword'. Which makes it even more remarkable that, by the end of the series, Frost (and his team) had coaxed into the hot seat, among several big names, Gore Vidal, the controversial mercenary, Major Mike Hoare, the rebellious Prime Minister of Rhodesia Ian Smith, the Foreign Secretary George Brown and the Archbishop of Canterbury. Why did they all agree to run the risk?

Sometimes the answer was straightforward. Ian Smith's Unilateral Declaration of Independence (UDI) had detached him from the world community: with his defiant self-confidence and under diplomatic siege in the Rhodesian capital, Salisbury (Harare), he probably couldn't resist the opportunity to press his case with the British public, even if the main effect was to convince most viewers that he was an impossible man to do business with. But for the rest, the only obvious common cause was that they were bewitched by the new medium – that they were in thrall to the man who had had the Prime Minister to breakfast – and that nobody before had ever had the gall to ask, over and over again. In a way, they were only doing what everyone was beginning to do: to divine – dimly at first – that television alone had the power to exalt them to a new plane of reality.

Take the case of the Archbishop, Michael Ramsey. The *Frost Programme* had thrown up a number of stories with religious or moral themes. As the first series drew to a close, the team began to wonder whether they should devote a whole programme to discussing the basic question, 'What must I believe to be a Christian?' Especially if the Archbishop could be persuaded to participate. Frost writes in his autobiography, 'I visited him in Lambeth Palace, and explained what we wanted to do. Much to my delight, he agreed.' Frost crooks his finger and the spiritual head of the Church of England feels compelled to pay homage. Part of the reason for the invitation, and its acceptance, was that the Church had been invaded by its own brand of Sixties liberalism: most strikingly, a report by the Bishop of Woolwich, 'Honest to God', which recommended a relaxed attitude to dogma and morality. He interpreted the Bible's ban on fornication, for instance, as referring only to 'irresponsible sex without any concern for the other'. Nice, thoughtful sex, presumably, was fine, even on a first date. As the Bishop (one of the Connaught breakfast guests) told Frost, 'Sex is the only field in which some churchmen have always said there are absolutes. This report is just bringing this field of morality into line with every other.' When he writes about this 30 years later Frost, the one-time Methodist preacher, adds his own commentary: 'It was the disappearance of the old simple absolutes that many people found so threatening.'

At Lambeth Palace this debate was a matter of critical importance. The Archbishop's biographer, Owen Chadwick, notes that some of Ramsey's advisers feared that an encounter with Frost would 'lower the sacredness of his office'. But the majority view was that the challenge could not be ducked, even though Ramsey was no television natural. His televised address at the consecration of Coventry Cathedral four years earlier had been described as 'a sonic version of the Alps in silhouette', while a BBC memo of the same period begged him to use less homiletic language ('homiletics' – the art of preaching), to avoid lapsing into Latin and to watch out for intellectual condescension. Ramsey had the added handicap of a sing-song voice, hardly suitable for the intimacy of a close-up camera.

The Frost interview took place in December 1966. Under polite – mostly sympathetic – cross-examination, Ramsey conceded that a Christian did not necessarily have to believe in the literal truth of the Creation story, or of the virgin birth, but that the resurrection of Christ remained at the heart of what it meant to be a Christian. It was hardly the Inquisition, but Frost forced the Archbishop to do something that none of his predecessors would have dreamed of doing: debating theological intricacies with a professional scribe in front of a live audience (though the Bible says that Christ did it as a matter of routine).

None of the statements disseminated that evening to millions of viewers would have surprised a regular visitor to Canterbury Cathedral, but Ramsey (instinctively?) realised the added power his words might have when uttered in a television studio, the new *sanctum sanctorum*, the holy of holies. His biographer judges that 'his answers could not have been better' and that 'the interview evidently helped a lot of people'. Ramsey received Frost's benediction, too, for having 'walked his personal tightrope superbly', and for trying to 'soothe the distress and untangle the confusion in the hearts and minds of the faithful'. Some time afterwards ('rather late', his biographer comments) the Archbishop took a crash course in television techniques. It was the same year in which the Queen sanctioned the making of a film about the royal family. But the Archbishop also admitted on another occasion that he recognised the dangers of the television interview, because 'it put a premium on quick and clever and easy answers'.

Then there was the even more remarkable appearance in Frost's lair of the unpredictable Labour Foreign Secretary, George Brown. Brown had contested the party leadership after the death of Hugh Gaitskell in 1963 and, as Gaitskell's deputy, regarded himself as the natural successor. But his wayward behaviour (he had a justified reputation for over-indulgence, and was 'prone to tender his resignation when he felt thwarted', in Peter Clarke's description) provoked James Callaghan to stand against him. The contest ended with the election of neither, and the general assumption was that Brown had never really forgiven Harold Wilson for robbing him of his just deserts. And that, given the chance, he would wrench the crown back for himself.

After Wilson's second election victory in March 1966, Brown was moved to the Foreign Office, where the diplomatic arts failed to rub off on him: soon he was attracting a torrent of press criticism. Frost started to think that he might be angry enough, or desperate enough, to be tempted by an invitation to address a mass audience. He stalked Brown for weeks and eventually called on him at the Foreign Office 'to put his mind at ease'. The nature of the conversation is not recorded, but Frost's description gives a flavour: 'The more he was attacked, the more he wanted a forum to express himself'; 'However much under siege, he was at the peak of his political life'; 'I was intrigued by the prospect of trying to explore this paradoxical man'; and 'I wanted to try and show the three-dimensional George Brown on television'. In today's terminology, he schmoozed his victim.

No Cabinet minister had ever made such an appearance. Perhaps Brown reflected that Wilson himself had been quite ready to consort with the enemy in a flagrant photo opportunity at the Connaught. Yet right up until the last moment Brown havered, and he reached the studio in a tense and agitated state. Special measures were called for: if he fell apart or walked out (he was quite capable of both) the show would be wrecked. There was no fall-back available. As the signature tune faded away, Frost reached for the technique that would become his secret weapon: he would seek to soothe and charm his subject into a state of garrulous relaxation. Instead of a pointed question, then, a boyish smile and a jovial interchange about Brown's favourite football team, West Ham. And the first question? Frost wondered how the Foreign Secretary had spent his past 24 hours.

This is how Frost describes the reward for his gentle approach: as George Brown expounded his work schedule, 'the professional enthusiasm for his job took over, and the unease evaporated to be replaced by a growing candour'. It's hard to contradict him, reading Frost's account of how he edged crabwise towards the crucial issues of the moment.

Frost: I can see how attractive the Foreign Office was. [Subtext: we understand that your principles didn't allow you to stay at Economic Affairs and we rather admire you for it.] *And if the opportunity were to present itself, do you want to be Prime Minister, too?* [We completely understand that you are loyal to Harold and this is a purely hypothetical question, honestly.]
Brown: No. No. I tell you – I don't think I've ever said this before publicly – I ran very reluctantly in the race after Gaitskell died.

Brown insisted, at length, that all those close to him would confirm his story and Frost knew that something important was happening.

Frost: You'd resist the opportunity that presented itself? [That's right, George. Get it off your chest. You're among friends here.]
Brown: I'm not interested. I'm not interested. I think one of the things that one must do is never to make the same mistake twice. I don't believe I have what you need to be Prime Minister.
Frost: Why do you feel the Prime Minister wouldn't be ideal for you? [Speaking personally, I think you could be a natural.]

Brown replied that he was too aggressive, too assertive, for a job that needed team-building skills and patience.

Frost: And do you think the Labour Party today would be different if the late Hugh Gaitskell was still with us? [Yes, I realise this subject is taboo, but perhaps you'd like to pay public tribute to your old friend, Hugh, just for the record?]
Brown: Very different. Now here I'm really letting my hair down with you. He was a much closer friend to me than Harold Wilson, friendly as we are now, will ever be. I was very close to Hugh Gaitskell indeed ...

To imagine the impact of this exchange, you only have to replace the cast of characters with their modern-day successors: Gordon Brown, sitting on Frost's sofa and comparing Tony Blair unfavourably with the late John Smith, before issuing a categorical abnegation of his own leadership ambitions. The parallels become even more uncanny as Brown goes on:

> *It is absolutely true that Harold can get the party to do things that Hugh would have wished them to do, but could never have got.*

One newspaper, back in 1967, called it 'the frankest interview ever given by a Government minister' – another, 'a remarkable public confessional'.[126] All agreed that it was a huge story. In a way that was to become increasingly familiar, the *Frost Programme* had apparently offered a glimpse of the *real* George Brown, by allowing him to communicate directly with the public through the medium of the modest interviewer. Television had provided an instant new image for a familiar political figure. This redefinition seemed more authentic, even to some cynical commentators, than the George Brown they had known for years.[127] It was probably the first time that the public had been prepared to accept his protestations that he didn't harbour dark designs to occupy Number Ten. An Emmwood cartoon in the *Daily Mail* summed up the mood: Wilson, in trademark Gannex mackintosh, has come through a door marked 'D. Frost, Knock and Genuflect'. Pipe in hand, he asks Frost, 'How would you like me to arrange for you to interview Callaghan, Jenkins, Crossman, Healey ... [and any other possible challengers for his job]?'

Brown himself does not mention the interview in his memoirs and

---

126 Though Frost omits one part of the exchange, on the subject of privacy. Brown complained that one of his latest problems had arisen from a remark he'd made during a supposedly confidential discussion.
Frost: Nowhere's private any more, is it?
Brown: Well people have to be decent enough, sensible enough to know. And he went on, *You were once kind enough to invite me to a little dinner party. You had a very pretty French actress if I remember.*
Frost: Did I? My turn to say, no comment.
Brown: In a very revealing dress.
Both of them understood, said Brown, that such events were off the record. But if a 'newshound' had been present ... Just the sort of story, in fact, that Ned Sherrin thought would have enlivened the Frost biography.
127 Brown himself can hardly be accused of having used the medium for his own advantage. All the available evidence is that he had no clear idea what to expect from the interview: at one point he says, 'It really is odd to be discussing things as frankly as this with you in front of an audience and cameras. It really is odd.'

it did not succeed in converting him to the wonders of television. In the penultimate paragraph of his book, *In My Way*, he inveighs, in a way very familiar today, against the 'dreadful influences' represented by the mass media.

> *If I were asked to put a date on when the rot in our society set in, I'd say without hesitation that it began with the introduction of commercial television. And the BBC, which is supposed to be immune to commercial pressures, is as bad as the rest, because if it doesn't reduce its own standards to the level of the others it won't get its precious audience-ratings. All this helps to promote a society which genuinely prefers mediocrity.*

But Frost comments, 'The portrait that had emerged from the programme may not have been the whole truth about George Brown, but it was certainly the aspect of the truth *needed at that particular moment* [my italics] when he was monotonously under fire.' Or, as he might have added, it was a temporary version of the truth created by the chemistry between two men on that particular day, but one that fixed in the minds of many viewers at home a permanently altered image of an important public figure.

It was also a version of the truth that served David Frost very well. His collaborator Antony Jay regards the Brown encounter as a landmark in Frost's career. 'We knew there was a standard George Brown interview, with standard George Brown answers to standard George Brown questions, and we decided to do something different. We said, "let's do a friendly, exploratory interview" and see what happens. And he gave far more of himself away than usual.' It was a lesson for life, reaching its ultimate expression on the comfy sofa of the modern *Frost on Sunday* set. His detractors might call him a soft touch, but Jay puts the counter-argument: 'Sometimes things have come out with Frost that wouldn't have come out otherwise, either because his guests wouldn't have said them, or because they wouldn't have gone on the programme in the first place.'

It wasn't that Frost was incapable of asking hard questions. The final show of the series featured the on-air destruction of a notorious financier, whose insurance company had collapsed leaving thousands of claims unmet. Unwisely, Dr Emil Savundra volunteered to sit in a live studio, facing not just Frost, but an audience full of the victims of his frauds. Perhaps he had witnessed some of Frost's cosier chats and assumed that he could make himself lovable, too. It was a mistake. Savundra had been the subject of detailed work by the *Sunday Times* 'Insight' team, who were pioneering a new kind of investigative journalism. Armed with their files and his own ability to distil the crucial facts of a case in a televisual way, Frost was merciless and the blustering Savundra duly condemned himself out of his own mouth. At the end of the programme Frost took the unusual step of walking off the set before the credits had rolled, but not before delivering a finger-stabbing judgement over the slumped form of his wretched victim, as an Old Testament prophet might have done: 'You have a moral responsibility for all these people!'

Soon afterwards the authorities finally got round to prosecuting Emil Savundra and he was duly sentenced to eight years in prison. When the case went to appeal – partly on the grounds that 'trial by television' had made a fair trial impossible – the sentence was upheld, but the judge issued a stern warning that the makers of such programmes risked being charged with contempt of court. Lord Justice Salmon said, 'This court hopes that no interview of this kind will ever be broadcast again. It was deplorable.' Frost dashed off a letter to *The Times*, a letter bristling with righteous indignation. Its gist was that if anyone had been guilty of contempt, it was the judge, for launching such a tirade against the gallant crusader for justice, television:

> *Television has shown that it has a real part to play in seeking the truth about matters of public concern, and to remove television from this role seems to be doing both public and individual a positive disservice.*

The Savundra edition of the *Frost Programme* did not steer its presenter in the direction of investigative reporting, as it might have done. Consciously or not, he was one of the first to discover the power of the interview *itself* as an art form for the television age. And like a barrister, he was learning that the subject under discussion was often of secondary importance, a platform on which to build a performance. It would be for others to develop television's role in challenging the law, for instance, over miscarriages of justice. Frost had moved on.

If he did take sides in any argument between tradition and modernity, he was just as likely to weigh in as a defender of tradition, alarmed and even repelled by aspects of the libertarian agenda. (Satire, anyway, has a strong conservative streak: it would often prefer to see the status quo restored to health, than stir up sedition.) On drugs, for instance, Frost opposed decriminalisation, which he regarded as a piece of trendy nonsense peddled by 'the so-called intelligentsia'. Looking back, he tried to draw a distinction between the principle of allowing free and open discussion of all subjects, with no taboos (on his programmes, for example), and the 'anything goes' philosophy that might logically follow – the removal of moral restrictions and the elevation of personal choice into a code for living. Ordinary people, he reckoned, were happy to hear issues like drugs debated openly, but they did not necessarily want to be part of the counter-culture themselves: 'It was a reminder that people could have views imposed upon them not just by Government or authority, but also by "opinion-formers" who were all too often able to monopolise the media. In a sense, we had identified a fault in the liberalism of the Sixties – its debates tended to be conducted by elites.' Frost saw his studio audiences as one way of redressing the balance.

However accurate those observations might be (and they still have the ring of truth 35 years on) Frost neglected to acknowledge that he himself was a fully signed-up member of the elite brotherhood of media opinion formers. His main job may have been to facilitate discussion and to pose questions that the public wished to have answered, but his underlying purpose was to make the programmes that bore his name as popular as possible. The smashing of taboos made great television and it was not in Frost's mind (or in his gift) to wander around picking up the pieces after the show. Members of the audience looked like representatives of the silent majority, but Frost gave the game away in the caption to a picture in his autobiography, in which he is working a crowd with a roving microphone: 'The use of a studio audience not simply as a responsive backdrop, but as a key ingredient in the actual programme mix – *to be brought into the proceedings according to need* [my italics].'

The *Frost Programme* exemplifies the age in which television began to establish its primacy in national life. It could call to account national leaders, Church leaders and crooks; it was the intimate of politicians and celebrities; it was entitled to expatiate on international crises and make moral judgements on anything it chose; and because it purported to be the true voice of the people, it brooked no argument. Its practitioners might be journalists, or campaigners, or entertainers, with all their flaws, but the medium was more important than the messenger. It would be some time before television started to become the *only* purveyor of credible reality, but the trend had been set.

Did David Frost discern all this? Malcolm Muggeridge ('a television rival whose technique is to smother his guests with his own talk and his own personality', in Frischauer's pro-Frost analysis) wrote in the *New Statesman*, 'His very lack of talent makes him king of the telly. In Frost the viewer sees himself, glorified but recognisable.' While Christopher Booker saw him as someone with an instinctive, rather than a theoretical, understanding of what was going on: 'Perhaps David Frost grasped earlier than most the quality of the Sixties. Always one jump further on than where he was expected, ever exploiting a new medium, a new technique, a new hairstyle, Frost divined by a remarkable instinct what the age demanded, and gave it.'

———

He was much too busy divining what the new age demanded to do much theorising anyway. In the course of 1967, the year of his 28th birthday, the country's most recognised television host became a television magnate, too. Modestly, he describes how the idea came to him as he handed out raffle prizes at an Associated Rediffusion party and cracked a joke about a special extra prize, the plum contract for a new TV company serving Yorkshire. This was one of the boundary changes proposed by the Independent Television Authority. Another reform would be a new licence to broadcast to London at weekends, and later that evening he fell to thinking. 'I suddenly had the very simple idea: why not go for London? Why follow the pack and set your sights only on Yorkshire? London at the weekends could be vulnerable, and the talent needed for a winning bid might respond more readily to the idea of London. I knew I would.'

Showing the same sort of bravado that had taken him to the top as a TV entertainer, he proved to be a wily entrepreneur, quite ready to make what Christopher Booker calls 'self-introductory telephone calls to prospective backers': cold-calling for cash. As Willi Frischauer puts it, 'At the top level of public life, David's natural habitat, names are so familiar that formal introductions are unnecessary.' A quick call to the head of GEC, Sir Arnold Weinstock, a man he had never met, was one of a number that led to a promise of substantial financial support. Five months later he was celebrating the award of the London Weekend Television franchise. He had borrowed £75,000 (more than £750,000 today), which was secured on his own 5 per cent stake in the company, and although he acted as a 'consultant to the board', his main role would continue to be as a front-line performer – one of the key selling points of the new station. Many others were involved, of course, but in Frost's uncomplicated world-view, it had indeed turned out to be a simple idea: 'Obviously it had not been a long-held ambition to found a network company before the age of thirty. The opportunity was there, so I decided to take it. Was that audacious? With the benefit of hind-sight, maybe. But at the time it just seemed like the logical thing to do.'

This precocious achievement made him plenty more enemies. LWT's early struggles to win an audience caused a severe outbreak of *Schadenfreude* in independent television circles. At one meeting Lew (later Lord) Grade took delight in lambasting the new station and demoting the Frost programmes from prime time on his own ATV network. 'I've succeeded in business by knowing exactly what I hate,' he told an ITV committee meeting. With his eyes fixed on Frost he went on, 'and I know I hate David Frost.' Jack Tinker relates that the victim was, for once, lost for words: 'There was no bluster. No heated exchange. No counter-attack. And, more importantly, no defence. The arch-exponent of cut-and-thrust, on-camera debate, the man that critics accused of waging trials by TV, sat there meekly and took it.'

Confrontation, on someone else's terms at least, was not Frost's style, but LWT survived Grade's fury and so did he. He was similarly unscathed after an investigation carried out by Granada's *World in Action*. This was inspired by a stream of stories about how the one-time satirist had sold out to big business. It was originally planned as a fly-on-the-wall documentary and Frost willingly agreed to co-operate. But as work progressed, the producers (who included the programme's youthful editor, John Birt) were fed a more serious storyline to pursue – based on allegations that Frost had improperly used his influence at LWT to win commissions for his own production company. Frost was upset, but eventually opened his books and allowed the Granada team to do an audit trail. When they found nothing wrong, the film was dropped, to the embarrassment of the *World in Action* team: their subject was not so much relieved as disappointed at the loss of this further chance for television exposure.

By now David Frost lived in a tall, elegant house in Knightsbridge, just down the road from Harrods, a fitting base for one of London's most thrusting entrepreneurs (and eligible bachelors). His old acquaintances could only watch and wonder at his dizzy progress. One night Peter Cook, after a long and unsuccessful session at a nearby casino, found himself wandering the streets, puzzling over where he could find the money for a taxi back to Hampstead at three in the morning. A sudden brainwave led him to 'Frostie's' front door in Egerton Crescent. After much ringing of the bell, a tousled head finally appeared at a window three floors up. Frost peered up and down the street, and finally caught sight of the dishevelled figure below. There was a time when the correct response to this intrusion would have been a chamber pot emptied over the head of the offending party. David Frost, however, merely beamed. 'Peter, super to see you!'

That was a good example of the vexed (and often vexing) relationship between Frost and his contemporaries.[128] They found his success hard to cope with: more or less privately, many resented the fact that they were cleverer, funnier, more creative than he was – but that he was richer and more widely recognised than they would ever be. But he always made it hard for them to hate him. He took part in an appeal concert to raise money for *Private Eye*'s first failed libel suit, even as the magazine routinely laughed at him.[129] He was assiduous in promoting the careers of performers like Cleese, Barker and Corbett, and Marty Feldman. He happily gave Peter Cook the money for a cab fare home. And as far as it's possible to judge, he did these things with no other motive than that it was 'the logical thing to do'.

Whether the same rules applied to his love life it is hard to say. In the phraseology of the time, he was enjoying a 'playboy lifestyle'. Willi Frischauer, writing in 1971, enthusiastically recorded Frost's conquests:

---

128 A friend of both Cook and Frost told me that whenever he met Cook, 'we would have a ritual half-hour of Frost abuse'. Cook himself dined out for years on the story of how he had saved Frost from drowning in his Connecticut swimming pool in 1963. Frost quotes his rescuer as saying, 'Thank God I did. With all those stories at the time about our rivalry, no one would have believed I didn't do it on purpose.' An alternative version, which Alan Bennett recalled at Cook's memorial service in 1995, was that saving Frost had been the greatest regret of his life.

129 He features on the *Eye*'s cover of 24 November 1967 as 'Minister of Propaganda' in an imaginary coalition government; and is invited a few weeks later (as part of Robert Maxwell's 'I'm Backing Britain' campaign) to help his country by 1 pulling out his sock drawer, 2 extracting sock, and 3 placing sock in mouth.

130 One of Carol Lynley's websites lays out the distinguished company Frost was keeping: 'Carol was romantically linked with singers Frank Sinatra, Lee Hazelwood, and Gram Parsons, directors John Avildsen and Roman Polanski, actors Red Buttons, James Earl Jones, Oliver Reed, Stuart Whitman, and Bud Cort, producers Yoram Globus and Jack Haley, Jr., Monte Kay [who was the ex-husband of Diahann Carroll], L. A. Rams' football executive Don Klosterman, comedian Dick Martin, and most notably British talk-show host David Frost, with whom she had an eighteen-year on-and-off relationship.'

Janette Scott, of course, but many others besides – Carol Lynley,[130] singers like Jenny Logan and Julie Felix, and later Diahann Carroll ('beautiful star of nightclubs, film and television'). They were some of the most alluring female celebrities of the moment, though all had to fit in with his perpetual-motion lifestyle. One of his girlfriends, Anne de Vigier, told Frischauer, 'When I have a date with David, I always take a book.' On his transatlantic travels he found 'no shortage of American girls who took an interest in the young visitor from London'.[131] He 'did the town untiringly', almost always with a girl on his arm. On one occasion, he was seen in company with Tony Armstrong-Jones who was visiting New York on a television assignment.

Just sometimes, the planning went awry. Frost's biographer has an unnamed lover storming into the Egerton Crescent house and smashing a picture when she found a rival on the premises: 'Because the pictures were abstract images of a certain shape, friends read a Freudian motive into the girl's violence.' Or perhaps she was plain jealous. This is evidently the type of 'Feydeau-esque complication' that Ned Sherrin would have liked to read about in Frost's autobiography. Instead, the reader is offered an anodyne distillation of potentially interesting moments, with the TV host dictating terms:

> On Tuesday night I took Jenny to the Mirabelle to celebrate. I thought something special was called for, so we had a bottle of 1890 Château Lafite. I was in a mood to celebrate, Jenny slightly less so. 'You've been a great source of strength during this weekend,' I said.
> 'Yes,' she said, with a touch of melancholy. 'I'm helping you towards something that is going to take you away from me.'
> I could not argue very convincingly. I feared that might be true.

Even though many of his girlfriends were taken back to Beccles to meet his mother, only rarely, during his playboy phase, did things get really serious. He became engaged to Diahann Carroll and in 1981 he was briefly married to Lynne Frederick, Peter Sellers's widow – a fact that does not appear in his Who's Who entry. Frost told the Daily Mail much later that the marriage had been a mistake: 'It was a smashing affair, and that's the way it should have ended, really.'

---

131 After a time, Frost set up his operation in the opulent surroundings of the Plaza Hotel and one friend remembers seeing him setting off for a date in a stretch limousine. He was wearing a pink tweed suit.

In 1968 David Frost smoked his first cigar, when he was trying to cut down on desserts. This was a love affair which would never fade and it suited his image nicely. He began to pursue his vocation as television interviewer/chat show host with unbelievable energy. He gave a speech to 150 American TV executives in London (he was billed as 'Britain's Number One TV Personality') and, as a result, won a lucrative contract to make a series of profiles of all the main candidates for the 1968 presidential campaign, including Robert Kennedy, Ronald Reagan and Richard Nixon – thus raising his US profile higher than ever.

His three programmes for the newly launched London Weekend Television (*Frost on Friday*, billed as 'Actuality Frost'; *Frost on Saturday*, 'The People's Frost'; and *Frost on Sunday*, 'Funny Frost') attracted everyone from a recently released Nazi, Baldur von Schirach, to the Israeli Defence Minister, Moshe Dayan, from Mick Jagger to Cardinal Heenan, from Mohammed Ali to Noël Coward, from John Lennon to Enoch Powell. (The Powell interview was unusually argumentative and Frost devotes 12 pages of his autobiography to the exchanges – to prove, perhaps, that his reputation as a 'soft' interviewer has been undeserved.) At the end of the LWT run, Frost did what was beginning to come naturally – he threw a party.[132] Having arranged for a huge funfair to be set up inside Alexandra Palace, the great impresario made merry with some of the celebrities who had shared the limelight with him. The Bishop of Southwark and the radical peer, Lord Longford, shared a dodgem.

By the end of 1968 Frost had scooped for himself the biggest plum of his 29 years – a syndicated American chat show of his own, in which he would replace the popular Merv Griffin. This news was greeted with disbelief at LWT, especially when it emerged that he intended to work what sounded like an eight-day week – five shows in New York on weekdays and back in London in time for *Frost on Friday*.

---

132 Willi Frischauer, clearly captivated by his subject, includes this priceless story of Frost, the perfect host. 'For Christmas Eve he invited a few personal friends, Jenny Logan, the Forbeses, and the Maudlings [Reginald Maudling, the current Tory Home Secretary, and his wife] among them. They were sitting down for dinner when David appeared with a tray of expensive trinkets from Asprey's, on Bond Street, a present for each of his guests. "He is the most generous of men," Nanette Forbes said. "Mine was a golden thimble – lovely, except that I cannot sew."' Incidentally, he had become friendly with the film producer Bryan Forbes after introducing himself in a branch of Cecil Gee and handing him a box of chocolates. Frischauer does not say if Frost carried sweets everywhere on the off-chance that he might bump into someone important.

Admittedly the five American programmes were to be recorded in three days, but his LWT boss, Michael Peacock, did not believe that he would be getting the best out of a performer whose schedule included two transatlantic flights a week. Frost seemed bewildered that anyone should doubt his capabilities, rang all those who had helped put together the LWT bid and finally wore down Peacock's resistance, though he did concede that *Frost on Sunday* might be moved to another part of the year. (And he never seemed to be tired, anyway. Friends said his stamina came from a voracious appetite: every meal he ate was 'fantastic'.)

Frischauer records that after the deal had been struck, Frost asked his driver to take him to Westminster Abbey so that he could indulge in a few moments of private meditation. The chapel he'd had in mind was closed and when he tried the Scottish Presbyterian Church near his home, he found it full of cleaners. The story continues,

*Nonetheless he achieved his meditation. 'You can think anywhere,'
he said. And pray. The prayer settled David's destiny for years
ahead. He committed half his professional life to the United States
of America, and turned himself into a complete transatlantic man.*

In an effort to establish his US credentials, the first *David Frost Show* included one of those keynote moments in media-monarchy relations, the filmed interview with Prince Charles, who was about to be invested as Prince of Wales. It was an uneasy encounter, mainly memorable because it allowed people to hear the diffident Prince speak in his own words. Frost treated his subject with kid gloves, proving that for him, at least, the age of deference was certainly not dead. His first question was, 'Your Royal Highness, what would you like your first act as Prince of Wales to be?' which turned out to be extremely difficult to answer. Charles bumbled through a response, ending with a vague thought that it might be a good idea to take a real interest in Wales. For the wags at *Private Eye* this encounter was almost too good to be true. The magazine added a photo bubble to the picture of Frost with Charles: 'Any chance of getting Mum on the Show?' Frost is asking. And it prints its own bowdlerised version of the interview transcript:

*Charles: Good evening, hullo, welcome and super to be here. And a
big hand for my old friend David Frost. Dave, tell me, it must be*

very difficult being someone in your position, with millions of
people watching everything you do. Don't you find this a great
responsibility?
Frost (getting up off knees): Well, Your Majesty, obviously I do. But
I think society needs figureheads, and particularly someone like
myself, to go round the country opening fêtes and making speeches
and that sort of thing. And one feels that since one has been called
to this kind of thing, one must just do it as best one can.

The exchange ends,

Charles (bowing out of the room backwards): Super to have you on
the show, Dave, bless you and keep in touch.

Frost described the real royal filming session as a delight and ended the
interview with the words, 'I couldn't have enjoyed it more,' but
critical reaction to the first edition of the *David Frost Show* was
mixed. The *New York Times* reviewer suggested that the host was like
'a visitor in search of a format', who was 'seldom very amusing and
deferential enough to be assistant to a television vice-president'.
David, says Frischauer, reacted to such comments 'more in sorrow
than anger'. And the Frost style soon began to grow on the American
audience – so much so that the series went on to win an Emmy, a
television Oscar. By the end of two seasons 1500 celebrities from every
corner of the cultural firmament had passed through his studio and in
December 1970 he was invited to put together the White House
Christmas Show for President Nixon. Billy Graham was in the audience,
and afterwards asked if he could have a copy of Frost's musings on the
history of Christmas.[133]

In many ways 1970 marked the pinnacle of Frost's career – which

---

133 By now, Frost and Graham were firm friends: among a number of encounters,
Frost had recorded two 90-minute interviews with the evangelist, which were published
– unexpurgated – in 1971. As he says in his introduction in this booklet, the interviews
read like 'two good friends engaged in an ambling conversation'. Rambling might have
been a better word. And I question whether they are also – as Frost claims – 'deeply
revealing'. My own impression is that they are conducted wholly on Graham's terms,
since he is allowed to get away with assertions which ought to have made any satirist
worth his salt leap out of his chair. Graham, for instance, had always refused to go to
South Africa: when asked whether the Archbishop of Canterbury had been right to meet
the apartheid government, he replies, 'I've looked on his trip as sort of a John the Baptist
thing for me – that some day, if he gets along well and gets through all the pitfalls, I
might consider an invitation.' What Archbishop Ramsey made of the idea of playing
John to Billy Graham's Jesus is not recorded.

may explain why his own autobiography stops there. In a single week he was awarded an OBE, made a Doctor of Laws at Emerson College, Boston and honoured by the 'Religious Heritage of America' for communicating the relevance of Judaeo-Christian ethics to twentieth-century America.[134] American showbiz honoured him with an appearance on Lucille Ball's sitcom *Here's Lucy*. The episode was called *Lucy Helps David Frost Go Night-Night*.

He was so famous that he was often able to bypass the rest of the world's press. When the Bangladeshi leader, Sheikh Mujibur Rahman, visited Britain immediately after being released from a Pakistani jail, he was besieged by reporters at his London hotel. Frost was the only media figure to penetrate the Sheikh's security and persuaded him to agree to an interview as soon as he returned home.

Over the next two years, however, his programmes on both sides of the Atlantic began to lose their edge. In May 1972 the *David Frost Show* in New York was axed. Frost let it be known that the decision was at his request, because he felt it was time to move on to something new. Sharply reduced ratings may also have had something to do with the matter. Then the regular LWT slots also began to dry up.

When Booker published his analysis of the 'Frostie' phenomenon in May 1977, he decided that in the intervening few years the whole fragile structure had come close to disintegration. He compared Frost with Richard Nixon and Harold Wilson, suggesting that all three were men without a centre, 'as if they had become so completely absorbed and submerged by the demands of their public image, and by the whole shadowy realm of receding mirrors they inhabited, that in any other terms they had virtually ceased to exist'. Certainly, the mid-Seventies represented (comparatively) a trough in Frost's career. After the demise of his American chat show, his voluminous *Who's Who* entry resorts to such items as *David Frost Presents the Guinness Book of Records* and *Frost over New Zealand*. Booker's article, however, was written to coincide with the first of the Nixon-Frost interviews and he conceded

---

134 Papers released by the Public Records Office in 2002 showed that 1970 almost brought Frost a drugs charge, too. A 'psychedelic revolutionary' called Jerry Rubin was invited to discuss his book, *Do It*, which urged children to leave home, burn down their schools and create a new society. In the course of a lively interview, Rubin's supporters invaded the stage and passed round what looked suspiciously like a joint. Frost declined to take a puff. Police records show that vanloads of officers poured into the studios after the show searching for evidence. When he was questioned, Frost seemed 'visibly shaken' that traces of cannabis were found in the dustbins and categorically denied that the whole thing had been a publicity stunt.

that this extraordinary project might breathe new life into the fading phenomenon.

Over 12 days, Frost conducted more than 28 hours of conversation with the disgraced former President. John (now Lord) Birt worked with him on the interviews: they prepared themselves by total immersion over many months in the detail of the Watergate scandal and in the legal niceties Nixon had always used to justify his actions. 'We focused on the allegations we thought we could pin him down on,' Birt says. 'We knew the law backwards and David beat him in argument. Nixon came the nearest he ever came to an admission of guilt. It was drawn out of him very dramatically by David and came to be seen as an act of contrition by the American people.' Birt claims that no other interviewer at the time could have handled such a difficult assignment. Nixon's words – 'I have let the American people down and I will have to carry that burden with me for the rest of my life' – became part of the historical record. For many people, the 'real' Nixon, in as much as anyone ever discovered what that was, is substantially the Nixon revealed in Frost's television portrayal.[135]

Was it more than Nixon meant to say? It took hours of gentle coaxing to eke out those few words of apology and regret. No 'normal' interview, carried out in a conventional time-frame, could have achieved it. Frost's techniques were the familiar ones – discursive questions, solid research (by a high-powered team of journalists), the constant reinforcing of the bond between the two protagonists. His patience, persistence and polite pressure had never been more necessary: the performance had to have a finale that would justify his own considerable expenditure.

The Nixon interviews were a commercial, as well as a professional, risk for Frost. He first contacted Nixon's staff within weeks of the resignation statement in August 1974; tortuous negotiations lasted a year and depended on an act of considerable faith by his backers. The deal he struck involved an outlay of more than $2 million, including a payment to the former President of $600,000 (well over $2 million today), which may still hold the record for the largest sum ever paid to a potential interviewee. He knew that this would lay him open to accusations of chequebook journalism and constructed an elaborate defence:

---

135 Christopher Booker may see parallels between Frost and Nixon, but there was one obvious difference. Frost, the master of social intercourse, found himself dealing with a man who had no small talk: once, as they sat down to start a new session on a Monday morning, Nixon made an inept stab at a bit of friendly banter with his interviewer: 'Did you do any fornicating this weekend?' he enquired.

1 *Precedent: President Johnson had accepted money (after leaving office) to be interviewed on CBS.*

2 *Human Rights: if our concept of privacy means anything, then a man's life has to be his own to dispose of in any way he wishes – after he leaves public life.*

3 *Logic: no one complained that Nixon was to be paid for writing his memoirs, so why should speaking them be any different?*

In the event, the quibbling was overshadowed by the success of the enterprise and the investment paid off handsomely. The broadcasts won the biggest audience for factual programming in American television history; stations wanting to show the interviews had to barter for the right to do so; and the shows were eventually sold to 70 countries. (In 2002, the Discovery Channel was still happy to pay for the privilege of replaying the tapes and including some of the unbroadcast material.) This was the exercise that had brought together all Frost's roles – as entrepreneur, fixer, impresario, interviewer, editor and friend of the famous. His own fame, not to mention his fortune, received a tremendous boost. He had become a worldwide celebrity and (if Christopher Booker is right) had thus fulfilled his destiny – to be famous for being David Frost.

The achievements that have followed this triumph tend to support Booker's view that Frost's real skill has been to play himself, with an acute awareness of any financial benefits that might accrue from the performance. Jack Tinker's book, *The Television Barons*, lists the range of his interests at the start of the 1980s, a business empire based on the company called David Paradine Ltd:

David Paradine Productions supplied television films for the United Kingdom and the United States. David Paradine Films made feature films for the cinema. David Paradine Plays had interests in West End productions. David Frost Enterprises handled his television appearances ... The list of Frost's financial investments spread on into property and into publishing until it rivalled Lord Grade's. In one publishing agreement alone, he is paid a yearly sum of £150,000. His homes are in the two continents to suit his much-publicized Concorde-hopping across the Atlantic.

As Ned Sherrin once remarked, nobody knew better than Frost how many boardroom doors could be unlocked by television. It was always likely that he would be involved in the contract for the first commercial Breakfast TV show in 1983: the project quickly imploded, but unlike his fellow stars who scurried away from the sinking ship, Frost stuck with it to the bitter end.[136] Over the following ten years he joined the board and established *Frost on Sunday* as one of the reconstituted station's most popular programmes. In legend, TV-AM may have been rescued by Roland Rat, but Roland had strong support at breakfast time on Sundays. Why did Frost stick it out through the dark days? My guess is that it was his only regular TV outlet at the time and he couldn't bear to let it go.

Frost's publications offer further evidence of his complete lack of interest in whether he was regarded as a serious commentator or not. The list includes such makeweight titles as *How to Survive Under Labour*,[137] *Who Wants To Be a Millionaire?*, *I Could Have Kicked Myself – David Frost's Book of the World's Worst Decisions*, *David Frost's Book of Millionaires, Multimillionaires and Really Rich People*, *The Mid-Atlantic Companion* (or How to Misunderstand Americans as Much as They Misunderstand Us). Often these books were collaborations with other writers, which has inevitably raised the suspicion that Frost's most important contribution to a project was his name, but that theory is challenged by Michael Shea, a writer who used to be Press Secretary to the Queen. The two men co-authored two books about the Anglo-American relationship, one humorous (*The Mid-Atlantic Companion*) and the other a piece of popular history called *The Rich Tide*. Shea assumed that he might have to do most of the work, but he found Frost to be anything but a sleeping partner. In the case of *The Rich Tide*, which required a great deal of research, Frost was 'hard-working and precise', as chapters were exchanged, refined and edited. 'There is no question about it,' he says. 'The effort was shared 50–50.'

Some of the other books, by contrast, are shamelessly superficial projects at which more self-important journalists would turn up their

---

136 David Frost teamed up with Angela Rippon, Michael Parkinson, Anna Ford and Robert Kee – collectively, the Famous Five. All left within months, as did TV-AM's Chief Executive, Peter Jay.

137 This is full of the sort of humour that Frost loves, and still peddles on programmes like *Through the Keyhole*. An example: 'Songs of the New Era – A Harold Day's Night, Ramsay Macdonald Had a Farm, Hark the Herald Wilson Sings'. I think he should have demanded his money back from the Keynsham joke factory.

noses. Frost has never drawn distinctions between the lofty heights of broadcast journalism and the rest of the entertainment business. To him they are all one, their common thread being an ability to offer him a platform and win an audience. Take his long association with the *Guinness Book of Records*: an edition of *Frost on Saturday* in 1968 featured the world champion sausage eater and a man who claimed to have the strongest head in the world (the organisation's co-founder, Ross McWhirter, used a sledgehammer to break a slab of concrete on Albert Cornelius's head). Other presenters might have betrayed a hint of condescension at such fairground stunts, but not Frost. Instead, he was filled with genuine enthusiasm for the whole concept and immediately spotted its television potential.

'There was always the fascination', he wrote 25 years later, 'of somebody trying to be the best in the world at what they did – even if it happened to be something that scarcely anybody else would wish to do.' Sausage swallowers and the rest of the record breakers eventually joined the Frost stable of entertainment products, alongside Nixon, Henry Kissinger, Harold Wilson, George Bush (Senior) and the Shah of Iran – and so many others who entrusted him with their reputations.

This process – known in the dairy industry as homogenisation – reached its natural outcome with *Through the Keyhole*, which first featured as a small segment on TV-AM. In its mature (long) version, 20 years on, the unsurpassed master of ceremonies oversees a show in which he and a gaggle of celebrities in the studios are invited to nose around the homes of other celebrities and to guess their identities from a video of the decor, and the belongings they have left artlessly lying about. Frost knows that it's an easy show to despise. 'There's a cynicism among the chattering classes towards this sort of TV,' he has said, 'in part because it appeals so much to ordinary people.' And that, of course, is the point. It is one more way in which 'ordinary people' can participate in a little vicarious celebrity.

1 *Because they appear on a programme hosted by David Frost, the celebrity of the celebrities concerned is confirmed and celebrated.*

2 *Because he has (remote) access to the underwear drawers and kitchen cupboards of celebrities, Frost's pivotal position in the celebrity superstructure is reinforced.*

3 *Because of his reputation and contacts, Frost is able to attract unlikely (sometimes serious) people to appear on the programme,*

*possibly because they are flattered to have been considered, even
briefly, as celebrities.*

4   *Because the programme is carefully planned, the viewers are
    offered a snapshot of the celebrities as they would like to be seen
    and television makes that snapshot real.*

Through the Keyhole says as much about the real world as a 'What the
Butler Saw' peep-show at the end of a Victorian promenade. Yet it is
presented by the same man about whom the revered American journalist
Walter Cronkite once said, 'Whatever people think about him in
Britain, he was the epitome of the best of world TV'; the same man
whose collected interviews – some 10,000 of them – were bought up
by an Internet company as a 'resource for broadcasters and those
involved in education'; and the same man whose *Breakfast with Frost*
programme on BBC continues to command extraordinary loyalty from
real celebrities – prime ministers and potentates and those who need
television less than television needs them. Why do so many choose to
make their occasional public pronouncements on Frost's studio sofa?
His enemies say it's because they know they'll come to no harm from
his anodyne, cosy questioning. His friends and supporters, like the
BBC Chairman Gavyn Davies, dispute that: 'I believe that he gets
people to appear on BBC Television who wouldn't otherwise be keen
to do so – partly because they trust him, partly because they feel
comfortable. He gets people to relax, even senior politicians, and he
can be incisive without being aggressive.' Frost puts it like this: 'You
get a better interview if they like you, or if they trust you. There needs
to be some relationship between the two people.'

The fact is that David Frost counts many (even most) of his
distinguished breakfast-time interviewees, as well as many of the 'B'
or 'C' list celebrities' who open up their sock drawers to him, among
his huge circle of acquaintances and friends. The summer parties he
gives with his wife Carina (daughter of the late Duke of Norfolk, the
country's premier Catholic peer) are events with a social cachet to
match that of a Buckingham Palace Garden Party – only rather more
exclusive. Frost greets his guests with familiar bonhomie and that
total recall of their personal circumstances – a knack which has helped
to make him, in the judgement of the society magazine *Harpers and
Queen*, 'the best-connected man in Britain' and unquestionably the
country's leading networker. Even his critics have grudgingly come to

believe that he may really mean what he says – that, for him, it really is 'super to see' anyone who arrives at his door. John Fortune is reminded of annual trips to the zoo, where rare creatures are displayed for the delectation of the populace. 'Suddenly you turn round, and there's Margaret Thatcher,' he says.

This is not a one-way process, either. If somebody wants to give their project a celebrity imprimatur, they're likely to call on Frost. Want to persuade customers that Concorde is back in business after the Paris crash? Arrange a free flight for Sir David Frost and a handful of other notables. Want to boost tourist travel to South Africa? Offer a luxury holiday to Sir David Frost and his ilk. More ammunition here for the Frost sceptics, but he either doesn't notice or doesn't care. Gavyn Davies calls him 'a man without a mean gene in his body'. Most television people, he adds, are only too keen to talk about themselves – Frost is an aberration because he'd rather listen. In such circumstances – and faced with a target who apparently bears no grudges, refuses to gossip, gripe or bear his soul, and worst of all won't fight back – the critics tend to sigh, shrug and walk away. A recent profile in the *Independent on Sunday* records the writer's repeated efforts to goad the subject into an indiscretion and ends, 'I still don't know what David Frost thinks, other than that he's a lot cleverer than people have sometimes given him credit for. But he thinks something.'

Even when offered the opportunity to expound on themes close to his heart, Frost prefers to reveal as little as possible. In 2001 he was the guest on *Songs of Praise*, on the basis of his Methodist upbringing, his adherence to the tenets of Billy Graham and his readiness to have himself described as a believer. The interviewer, Sally Magnusson, wondered why he never spoke at any length about religion, which he had been quite prepared to criticise as a young man. 'Because it is a personal thing,' Frost replied. 'I think it could be mistaken for sanctimony.' That was that. Magnusson had no more luck when she asked about Frost's conversion from scourge to pillar of the Establishment. 'I'm still the same reformer,' he mutters uncomfortably and unconvincingly, before seeking sanctuary in a familiar anecdote about his wife.

David Frost himself remains irrepressibly, some might say infuriatingly, upbeat in the face of the carping, frequently quoting the cheery dictum that even a stopped clock is right twice a day. But another motto might be just as appropriate. In a recent CNN discussion he was reminiscing with Larry King and others about the Nixon interviews. He quoted a piece of advice Nixon gave White House staff in the course of a valedictory speech in 1974. 'Others may hate you,' the resigning President declared, 'but those who hate you don't win unless you hate them – and then you destroy yourself.' Nixon, who nurtured such a bitter animosity towards the press, must have had his fingers crossed behind his back. But Frost? He has indeed survived and thrived by looking on the bright side, viewing the world not as a place full of enemies and competitors, but as an inexhaustible source of material for the great maw of television. The result has been brilliantly successful for Frost himself, but in the process he has made a significant contribution to the blurring of the boundaries between good and bad, important and insignificant, real and unreal.

One can only imagine what fun the young David Frost might have had with the old man David Frost became.

EPILOGUE

*Celebrity is a mask that eats into the face. As soon as one is aware of being 'somebody' to be watched and listened to with extra interest, input ceases, and the performer goes blind and deaf in his over-animation. One can either see or be seen. (John Updike – Self-*Consciousness: Memoirs *1989)*

How to be seen, even at the lowest level of being 'noticed' or 'recognised', let alone of being respected or admired – is one of the great quandaries of our age. In a world dominated by categorisation and generalisation, (thanks in part to the idleness of much of the media) the protections against invisibility and isolation in society have been steadily stripped away.[138]

The Britain conjured up in my father's court sketches suffered from economic austerity, smog, vile working conditions (like Scargill's coal-screens), grinding poverty and the repression of individual endeavour (not to mention artificial cream). Although the quality of life has improved in many ways over the past half-century, a price has been paid.

In the disintegrating modern world far more of us than ever before have to endure family break-up, employment insecurity, social disorientation, rootlessness, or lack of respect and recognition – and sometimes a combination of these ills. My father, a divorced man who often had to rely on a freelance income, would at least have recognised those diseases. But since his death, other, more exotic, conditions have arrived to afflict the Queen's subjects. The dry-rot of unreality has

---

138 Everyone mentioned in a newspaper report has to be tagged according to their job, personal circumstances or crime: 'widow', 'farmer', 'evil pervert', 'mother-of-four', 'greengrocer' and so on. A name does not identify anyone sufficiently, except the famous.

caused their pensions to crumble. The shares they were exhorted to buy have withered or died. They are encouraged to borrow more and more against the notional value of a home they cannot sell. They are bombarded with mail from people they do not know, offering them services they do not want. When they try to complain they can only speak to recording machines or call-centres in Limerick and Bangalore. They win prizes in competitions which turn out to be lures to buy time-shares in unbuilt apartments in Marbella. They pour money into a Lottery they will never win.

For those seeking a quick way out in the fifties, it was not so straightforward to acquire celebrity unless it was 'ascribed' by an accident of birth. 'Attributed' (artificially created) celebrities were rare, because of the rudimentary state of the mass media. The only realistic route to fame and fortune was through achievements in some field of public endeavour – David Frost in front of the camera, Charles Saatchi at the copywriter's desk. The great mass of people got on with life as best they could, defining themselves by their relationships at home, in the community and at work, and through voluntary association in organisations like Churches, clubs, trade unions or political parties. A series of historical accidents meant that these structures were peculiarly solid in Britain, and when they started to crumble and collapse (in the sub-revolutionary atmosphere of the late Sixties and early Seventies) many of their adherents found themselves unable to escape the wreckage.

In a conversation with P. D. James, whose detective fiction is in some respects a throw-back to the pre-television age, she told me, 'We have lost the sense of belonging. When I was a child (in the 1930s) you had that as a bedrock of your life. You belonged to a nation, you knew what it stood for and who governed it. You belonged to a church – nearly everybody had some kind of religion. You belonged to a school, you belonged to your neighbourhood which might be quite poor, but it was supportive. In this terrifying world, you knew where you stood – and I think that's gone.'

She transfers this sense of disorientation into her novels. In *Devices and Desires* (1989), one of her characters sits in an old-fashioned country kitchen and wonders, 'Was it perhaps a memory of childhood … that made watching a woman cooking in her own kitchen so extraordinarily reassuring and satisfying? If so, modern children were being deprived of yet one more source of comfort in their increasingly disordered and frightening world.'

More melodramatically, in the prologue to his second novel, *Atomised*, the French writer Michel Houellebecq describes his hero living through 'a miserable and troubled age' (the latter half of the twentieth century): 'The country into which he was born was sliding slowly, ineluctably, into the ranks of the less developed countries; often haunted by misery, the men of his generation lived out their lonely, bitter lives. Feelings such as love, tenderness and human fellowship had, for the most part, disappeared; the relationships between his contemporaries were at best indifferent and more often cruel.' The language may be florid, but the concept of atomisation is recognisable in Britain today.

The insidious role of television has been to hasten the process of atomisation (by locking us into our own homes), while offering a spurious sense of a shared experience (because so many of us watch the same programmes). The wider danger arises because television creates its own alternative reality which is – by definition – filmic, telegenic and staged, but yet is still credited with an unmerited degree of authenticity. The hero of Martin Amis's 1984 novel *Money* says: 'Television is working on us. Film is. We're not sure how yet. We wait, and count the symptoms. There's a realism problem, we all know that. TV is real! Some people think. And where does that leave reality? Everyone must have, everyone demands their vivid personalities, their personal soap opera, street theatre, everyone must have some art in their lives ...'

That was an early warning of a great malaise. No wonder so many, especially the young, now look for a way out and are attracted by the instant celebrity on offer. But how ephemeral will fame seem to today's celebrities, for most of whom something easily earned will also turn out to be easily lost? Chris Rojek points out that celebrity culture is inflationary – it requires those involved to push constantly towards the extremes. Even the Catholic Church is not immune. By 1995 Pope John Paul II had canonised or beatified well over a thousand people, more than all his twentieth century predecessors put together.

Recent attempts in Britain to redress the balance have faltered, because they did not take account of the extent of social atomisation. In his early years in power, Tony Blair advanced the Big Tent theory of politics, the creation of a political space so warm and welcoming that all would feel at home. He found quite quickly that this was the opposite of what most people wanted, even his own friends and supporters. Everyone found something to quibble with: to paraphrase Groucho Marx, nobody wanted to belong to a club to which everyone could belong, just as they didn't want the same car that everyone else was driving. The Tent has gone the same way as the Dome, and Blair learned that you cannot so easily suppress the imperative of individual self-fulfilment.

The 'new' Labour Party has tested a range of other ideas to persuade individuals of their value within the wider group (i.e., 'new Labour').[139] One striking example was the notion of 'People's Peers', ordinary people who would be nominated to the House of Lords by ordinary members of the public. More than three thousand names were put forward, perhaps because of the rare opportunity to enjoy the magic of ascribed celebrity. Sadly, although the people themselves may have been real (or ordinary) the idea turned out to be an illusion. All the fifteen men and women chosen were proven members of the Establishment who would surely have been elevated to the peerage anyway.

The crisis of confidence in modern politics, characterised by disconnection and apathy, has been an evolutionary process, not a sudden event to be blamed on one or other of the political parties. Why do fewer people vote? Because their vote does not seem likely to make a real difference to what happens to them, or because, in an individualistic age, they do not accept the idea of a manifesto, a party creed covering every aspect of their lives. The fashion is for politics à la carte – an environmental interest here, an educational preference there: these are preoccupations that can be expressed far more gratifyingly by marching on Downing Street, than by campaigning for years to change its occupant. And often with more chance of victory for the cause you espouse. In the same way, trade unions have found it possible once again to rally support for militant action on carefully targeted issues, though it seems unlikely that any of the new generation of left-wing leaders will ever become as celebrated as Arthur Scargill.

---

139 These days, the correct word should probably not be tested, but 'trialled', one of very many examples of the abuse of nouns in modern politics and business: hence, 'to action', 'to task', 'to impact', 'to birth', 'to transition', 'to niche', 'to gift', 'to evidence' … and countless others which take the stuffing out of good, solid words and turn them into unconvincing verbs. In a similar vein, Matthew Parris has lamented the fact that, in modern British politics, 'the abstract noun is king'. 'Politicians strut around issuing empty threats and unlikely claims, making wild promises and spouting meaningless speeches, while the drains stink, the potholes in the road grow, and down at the market the ordinary peasantry carry on their daily commerce placing not a jot of credence in anything the politicians say. A modern Evelyn Waugh would not need to take his novel to Africa to write *Scoop*.'

Parliament, like royalty before it, had already succumbed to the irresistible lure of the cameras, and for similar reasons has been paying the price ever since. Televising the work of MPs and peers was supposed to open our eyes to the fine work going on at Westminster, thus increasing our affection and respect for the institution. Instead, it opened the eyes of viewers to all its shortcomings: the synthetic rows, the weary soundbites, the shocking emptiness of the chamber for most of the day. Unfortunately, most of the best things that happened there were not televisual at all – the closely argued speeches and detailed cross-questioning of ministers along the committee-corridors. No wonder younger generations, whose whole experience of politics came from brief clips on the news, were deterred.

Even war has not been immune from the general plague. The build-up to the bombing of Afghanistan in the autumn of 2001 drew television crews in droves to the rocky, barren deserts of central Asia. For a long time there was nothing to see at all, so that an endless succession of hapless reporters, choking in the dust, were reduced to 'pieces-to-camera' with anonymous grey mountains in the background. Inevitably, their pieces (wickedly parodied in *Private Eye*'s 'Going Live' column) often relied on information they'd been given a few minutes earlier by their teams back home in London or New York or Paris, because of the impossibility of discovering anything from laconic army spokesmen and untrustworthy warlords.

Then came a short period of intense, bloody and confusing activity which was hard for anyone to follow, let alone those on the ground in Afghanistan. In the third phase, after the collapse of the Taliban and the irksome disappearance not just of Osama bin-Laden but most of al-Qaeda too, Allied commanders were left staging what looked suspiciously like 'events' to satisfy television's insatiable demand for pictures. The most spectacular of these was the firework display produced when an 'al-Qaeda arms dump' was blown up, amid allegations that it had in fact been little more than a dumping-ground for the superannuated weapons of some friendly tribal chief.

The subjects of this book have each, in their different ways, been undoubted celebrities. They have thrived in the television age. Princess Margaret had celebrity thrust upon her, and enjoyed it to the full; Arthur Scargill should presumably have spurned the notion of a celebrity fanned by the capitalist media, but managed to exploit it ruthlessly; Charles Saatchi pretended to eschew celebrity, and still found imaginative and lucrative ways to enjoy its benefits; Delia Smith has wielded celebrity like a sword in pursuit of her vocation; and David Frost is celebrity made flesh. Only Elizabeth David found celebrity genuinely hard to bear, and even she could behave like a celebrity under duress. In each case, renown was real and substantial.

Their stories have much to tell us about the risks and rewards of the age of celebrity. And the prospects for a reversal of these trends seem meagre. As soon as a new series of *Big Brother* was proposed in the spring of 2002, 150,000 people expressed an interest in taking part. Seeking recognition in traditional, more long-winded, areas of activity still seems quaint by comparison. As a political reporter, I am drawn to the curious case of William Hague: he burst into public awareness with a precocious (and much-derided) conference speech in 1977. After this brief flirtation with instant celebrity, he buckled down to work his passage through the ranks of his chosen vocation, just like Arthur Scargill on the other side of the tracks. (It was the 1974 miners' strike that gave the teenaged Hague his passion for politics). In due course, Hague emerged as a youthful leader of his party. But he never managed to master television (as Scargill did so brilliantly), and finally television cast him down by emphasising relentlessly his youth, his droning voice and his bald pate. You can't do politics in the dark.

That was just one symptom of the celebrity-deficit that haunted the post-1997 Conservative Party who, being largely unrecognised by the media, found it hard to impinge on the public consciousness at election-time or in the years that followed. An extreme case of non-recognition involved a Labour Member of the European Parliament, Eryl McNally. After the 2000 European elections she became one of eight members of various parties representing six counties in Eastern England. This, she discovered, rendered her completely anonymous in the eyes of voters. 'No one has the foggiest idea who I am,' she declared, and announced that she would not stand again. Even a public election couldn't win her the recognition she, like all of us, craves.

One of the most interesting cases has been that of the monarchy. Princess Margaret would have been gratified by the huge public support for the Jubilee celebrations during 2002, if only as a reassurance that there was still a wellspring of respect for her sister in the country. The Buckingham Palace pop concert drew a million people to The Mall and the surrounding parks, (though inevitably it was television that enabled the rest of her subjects to share the experience of the main events, just as it had at the Coronation 49 years earlier.)

Did this active participation amount to a reprieve for the royal family? Much was made of the fact that all age-groups were represented in the crowds, suggesting that younger generations were making a positive statement about the monarchy. Appearances may prove to have been deceptive. The nostalgic instinct in Britain is strong, often irrationally strong, based on a folk-memory which has survived all the distractions that the modern world has thrown at it. What was on offer, half a century after the Queen's accession, were some spectacular public concerts and pageantry – with a strong emphasis on the involvement of television. Directly or indirectly, the Palace and its advisers (including many from the media, who were recognised in the next available Honours' List) realised that what people wanted was entertainment, a show with the Queen as the ultimate celebrity. In that sense, the entire proceedings can be seen as an act of national nostalgia akin to the last night of the Proms, (which also attracts a mixed audience, including many foreigners, revelling in an atmosphere which it may not fully understand).

The crucial difference was that the Golden Jubilee could not be repeated. Biology dictated that the next great royal occasion was more likely to be a death than another landmark anniversary. And when the Queen finally leaves the stage, the strength of the nostalgic affection that sustains the Monarchy will go with her. We shall then see what of substance is left behind, and what has been fatally corroded. The fall-out from the trial of Diana's garrulous butler, Paul Burrell, does not leave much cause for optimism.

It adds up to a puzzle which future generations – who do not have a mutual nostalgia bank on which to draw – will have to resolve. And they will do so in a world where television has dreamed up the ultimate reality show. In September 2002, a Rupert Murdoch channel in the United States announced its intention to audition for volunteers to become the People's Presidential candidate in 2004. After a lengthy process of elimination by viewers' vote, a winner would emerge – and would be invited to stand in the election itself. Murdoch's Sky Television network in Britain would surely not be far behind, and the shape of the future was clear. Perhaps the only way to restore confidence in public institutions is to hand them over, lock, stock and barrel, to the media moguls who will burnish them with make-up, place them under the studio lights, and make them real again.

ACKNOWLEDGEMENTS

I would like to thank all those who have spared time to help me with this book.

My thank-you list includes: Paul Bailey, Joan Bakewell, Stephen Bayley, Peter Bazalgette, Alistair Beaton, John Birt, Chris Booker, Consumers' Association, Matthew Collings, Michael Crick, Laura Cumming, Gavyn Davies, Ivan Fallon, John Fortune, Jonathan Freedland, Kim Howells MP, Angela Huth, Will Hutton, Armando Iannucci, Richard Ingrams, Tom Jaine, P.D. James, Antony Jay, Donald McIntyre, Reggie Nadelson, Jill Norman, Ian Rankin, Ron Rose, Paul Routledge, Ned Sherrin, Andrew Taylor, Emma Thompson, George Walden, Simon Walker, Paul Watson, Greg Wise, and several others who preferred to remain anonymous.

I am also grateful to all those from whose books, articles and broadcasts I have quoted – and credited, I hope, without too many omissions.

I have received great support and encouragement from Ion Trewin and his team at Weidenfeld & Nicolson, including Victoria Webb, and from David Miller at Rogers, Coleridge and White. Thanks also to Tom Clarke for his research, to Pete Clarke for his transcribing and to Ali Clarke for her transcribing and proof-reading. And of course to my much-loved wife, Barbara, who has inspired me to keep going with this project while enduring many trials of her own, on behalf of me, Benedict and Joel.

BIBLIOGRAPHY

GENERAL

Daniel Boorstin, *The Image*, Vintage, (1961) 1992
Bernard Levin, *The Pendulum Years*, Cape, 1970
Christopher Booker, *The Neophiliacs*, Collins, 1969
Christopher Booker, *The Seventies*, Allen Lane, 1980
Asa Briggs, *History of Broadcasting*, Vol. IV, OUP, 1995
Peter Clarke, *Hope and Glory (Britain 1900–1990)*, Penguin, 1996
Stephen Haseler, *The English Tribe*, Macmillan, 1996
Robert D. Putnam, *Bowling Alone*, Touchstone, 2000
Chris Rojek, *Celebrity*, Reaktion Books, 2001
Stephen Bayley, *General Knowledge*, Booth-Clibborn, 1986
George Walden, *Lucky George*, Penguin, 2000
Julian Barnes, *Something to Declare*, Picador, 2002
Martin Amis, *Money*, Penguin Classics, 2000

I   MARGARET

Marion Crawford, *The Little Princesses*, Cassell, London, Harcourt Brace
   & Co. New York, 1950
Frances Tower, *The Two Princesses*, National Union Sunday School
Godfrey Winn, *The Younger Sister*, Hutchinson, 1951
Willi Frischauer, *Margaret, Princess Without a Cause*, Michael Joseph,
   1977
Leonard Mosley and Robert Haswell, *The Royals*, Leslie Frewin, 1966
Robert Lacey, *Majesty*, Hutchinson, 1977
Peter Townsend, *Time and Chance*, Collins, 1978
Nigel Dempster, *A Life Unfulfilled*, Quartet, 1981
David Sinclair, *Snowdon, A Man for Our Times*, Proteus, 1982
Noel Botham, *The Untold Story*, Blake, 1995
Christopher Warwick, *A Life of Contrasts*, André Deutsch, 2000
Theo Aronson, *Princess Margaret*, Michael O'Mara, 2001
Ben Pimlott, *The Queen*, HarperCollins, 1996
Godfrey Winn, *The Infirm Glory*, Michael Joseph, 1967
Willie Hamilton, *My Queen and I*, Quartet, 1975

James Brough, *Margaret, Tragic Princess*, W. H. Allen, 1975

Trevor Hall, *The Royal Family Year*, Gallery Press, 1985

2 SAATCHI

Philip Kleinman, *The Saatchi & Saatchi Story*, Weidenfeld & Nicolson, 1987

Ivan Fallon, *The Brothers*, Hutchinson, 1988

Alison Fendley, *Saatchi & Saatchi*, Arcade, 1995

Kevin Goldman, *Conflicting Accounts*, Simon & Schuster, 1997

Rita Hatton and John A. Walker, *Supercollector*, Ellipsis, 2000

Matthew Collings, *Blimey*, 21 Publishing, 1997

Matthew Collings, *Art Crazy Nation*, 21 Publishing, 2001

Damien Hirst and Gordon Burn, *On the Way to Work*, Faber, 2001

Robert Hughes, *Nothing If Not Critical*, HarperCollins, 1991

Jeremy Tunstall, *The Advertising Man*, Chapman & Hall, 1964

John Pearson and Graham Turner, *The Persuasion Industry*, Eyre & Spottiswoode, 1965

David Butler and Dennis Kavanagh, *The British General Election 1979–1983*, Macmillan

Terry Nevitt, *Advertising in Britain*, Heinemann, 1982

David Reed, *The Popular Magazine*, The British Library, 1997

3 ELIZABETH AND DELIA

Elizabeth David, *A Book of Mediterranean Food*, John Lehmann, 1950

Elizabeth David, *An Omelette and a Glass of Wine*, Robert Hale, 1984

Lisa Chaney, *Elizabeth David*, Macmillan, 1998

Artemis Cooper, *Writing at the Kitchen Table*, HarperCollins, 1999

Delia Smith, *How to Cheat at Cooking*, Coronet, 1971

Delia Smith, *How to Cook: Book Three*, BBC Publishing, 2001

Alison Bowyer, *Delia Smith*, André Deutsch, 1999

Louis Golding and André Simon, *We Shall Eat and Drink Again*, Hutchinson, 1944

Michael Bateman, *Cooking People*, Leslie Frewin, 1966

Stephen Mennell, *All Manners of Food*, Blackwell, 1985

4 SCARGILL

Vic Allen, *The Militancy of British Miners*, The Moor Press, 1981

Paul Routledge, *Scargill*, HarperCollins, 1993

Michael Crick, *Scargill and the Miners*, Penguin, 1985

Martin Adeney and John Lloyd, *The Miners' Strike*, Routledge & Kegan Paul, 1986

Ian MacGregor, *The Enemies Within*, Collins, 1986

M. J. Parker, *Thatcherism and the Fall of Coal*, OUP, 2000

Ralph Darlington and Dave Lyddon, *Glorious Summer*, Bookmarks, 2001

John Mortimer, *In Character*, Penguin, 1984

Seumas Milne, *The Enemy Within*, Verso, 1994

5   FROST

David Frost, *From Congregations to Audiences*, HarperCollins, 1993

Willi Frischauer, *Will You Welcome Now David Frost*, Hawthorn Books, 1971

David Frost, *How to Live under Labour*, Heinemann, 1964

David Frost and Antony Jay, *To England with Love*, Hodder/Heinemann, 1967

David Frost, *Billy Graham Talks with David Frost*, Hodder & Stoughton, 1971

David Frost, *Frost on Nixon (I Gave Them a Sword)*, Macmillan, 1978

Patrick Marnham, *The Private Eye Story*, André Deutsch, 1982

Roger Wilmut, *From Fringe to Flying Circus*, Eyre Methuen, 1980

Humphrey Carpenter, *That Was Satire That Was*, Gollancz, 2000

Jack Tinker, *The Television Barons*, Quartet, 1980

Ned Sherrin, *A Small Thing Like an Earthquake*, Weidenfeld & Nicolson, 1983

George Brown, *In My Way*, Gollancz, 1970

Owen Chadwick, *Michael Ramsey, A Life*, Oxford, 1990

INDEX